The University of Michigan
Center for Chinese Studies

Michigan Monographs in Chinese Studies
Volume 58

Geographical Sources
of Ming-Qing History

by Timothy Brook

Ann Arbor

Center for Chinese Studies
The University of Michigan

1988

Library of Congress Cataloging in Publication Data

Brook, Timothy, 1951-
   Geographical sources of Ming-Qing history.

   (Michigan monographs in Chinese studies; v. 58)
   Bibliography: p. 73.
   Includes indexes.
   1. China—Gazeteers—Bibliography. 2. China—Description and
travel—Bibliography.   I. Title.   II. Series: Michigan monographs
in Chinese studies; no. 58.
Z3106.B76   1988   DS705   016.9151   87-15608
ISBN 0-89264-075-8
ISBN 0-89264-076-6 (pbk.)

Cover design by the author.

The cover shows a portion of the route section of the 1891 reprint of
Chaoshi congzai [Complete notes for going to market] (5.3.1), a
guidebook to the city of Peking. The right half of the front cover is
the closing section of the route from Peking to Guangzhou. The rest
is the route to Guizhou via Hubei.

Printed in the United States of America

Contents

PART I
ROUTE BOOKS

PART II
TOPOGRAPHICAL AND INSTITUTIONAL GAZETTEERS

Acknowledgments

In the course of compiling this research guide, I have received substantial assistance from numerous librarians and historians. In particular I wish to single out Mi Chü Wiens of the Asian Division of the Library of Congress for her enthusiastic interest in earlier work that led to this book, her assistance during my visits to the Library, and her generous help in correcting and verifying bibliographic details by mail. To her must go the credit for the idea of combining these bibliographies for publication. Hu Daojing, Joseph McDermott, and Bin Wong helped in pointing out overlooked sources and steering me to information that proved useful in understanding the historical emergence of route books and gazetteers. In addition, Timothy Cheek, Wolfram Eberhard, Takeshi Hamashita, Valerie Hansen, John Meskill, Peter Perdue, Elizabeth Perry, Diane Perushek, Harold Roth, Shen Jin, Frances Wood, and Chün-fang Yü kindly responded to inquiries about sources I could not personally consult. I wish to express special gratitude to the staffs of the Tōyō Bunka Kenkyūjo (Institute of Oriental Culture) at the University of Tokyo, the Tōyō Bunko, the Sonkeikaku Bunko, and the Japanese National Archives, all of whom in different ways made my research in Tokyo both pleasurable and rewarding. For their help in seeing the manuscript through to publication, I thank both Michelle Paul and Pamela Wilson of the Center for Chinese Studies. My deepest gratitude, finally, is reserved for Margaret Taylor, whose editorial scrutiny and personal support helped me through what turned out to be an unimaginably tedious project.

Sections of Part I appeared serially, though in a much different form, in Ch'ing-shih wen-t'i (vol. 4, pts. 5, 6, 8) under the title "Guides for Vexed Travelers: Route Books in the Ming and Qing." I am indebted to James Cole, editor of the issues in which they were published, for encouraging me to undertake the initial study and bearing with my submission of two supplements. Part II is an offshoot of research for my doctoral dissertation at Harvard University, for which Philip Kuhn served as my advisor. The bulk of the manuscript was written while I was enjoying the support of the Whiting Foundation and the Social Studies Program at Harvard

University; subsequent revisions were done while I was a Mactaggart Fellow at the University of Alberta. A travel grant from the Central Research Fund of the University of Alberta enabled me to consult the holdings of Columbia and Princeton, thereby bringing this project to completion. The direct and indirect support of all these bodies is gratefully acknowledged.

T. J. B.

Foreword

The purpose of this research guide is to introduce two genres of local-level sources for the study of China's social, economic, and cultural history in the Ming-Qing period (1368-1911): route books, which were practical handbooks for travelers in China; and topographical and institutional gazetteers, which were records of places such as mountains and monasteries. The bibliography of route books in Part I consists of 57 entries; the bibliography of topographical and institutional gazetteers in Part II, of 686 entries. Though both these genres blossomed under the impact of rising literacy and the expanding opportunities for travel, they otherwise bear no relationship to each other and are therefore explored separately in the introductions to the two parts.

A few words are necessary to explain the methods by which the material has been selected and organized. My basic principle has been to include only extant works, though occasional references are made to earlier, lost editions. Most of the books cited in these bibliographies are to be found in over a dozen libraries in Canada, England, Japan, and the United States; editions of certain works held in other libraries and other countries have been included where possible. These libraries are given in the List of Abbreviations immediately following this foreword.

There is no sense in which these bibliographies can claim to be exhaustive, especially since I have not personally investigated collections in China and Taiwan and have had to rely entirely on their published bibliographies, most of which are of rare editions only. A visit to the National Library in Peking would undoubtedly have turned up many works that I have not seen elsewhere. Still, this book is a beginning, and I think we can look forward to the appearance of more thematic bibliographies of this kind from Chinese scholars in the tradition of Xie Guozhen and Hong Huanchun. I have relied on the work of Hong and others to include numerous citations to works held in Chinese libraries, and I can only hope that these citations will lead both Chinese and non-Chinese historians on to discover works of a similar type that I have not been able to track down outside China.

The two bibliographies have been structured in different ways. The route books in Part I have been grouped into six generic sections based on the types of routes they document and ordered roughly according to the historical development of the books from simple to complex. The first four sections deal with routes designed and maintained by the state: (1) the national stage network, (2) provincial stage networks, (3) grain transport routes, and (4) imperial household routes. The last two sections group privately compiled works: (5) comprehensive route books, and (6) guides for specific routes. Within each section, subsections are indicated to highlight further distinctions by type of route or type of publication.

The gazetteers in Part II, on the other hand, have been grouped on the basis of the geographical location of the places they document. The prefectures, subprefectures, and counties of Ming China provide the basic units of organization here. These units are arranged according to the sequence given in *juan* 40 to 46 of the standard history of the dynasty, the *Ming shi*. Entries within counties are arranged alphabetically, and separate gazetteers of the same place are arranged chronologically even if they go by different names, resulting occasionally in a nonalphabetical sequencing of titles. For convenience of use, I have provided alphabetical indices of all authors and titles in both parts, as well as an alphabetical index of the prefectures, subprefectures, and counties by which the works in Part II have been arranged.

The individual entries have been composed according to the following guidelines:

(1) The title is usually given as it appears at the head of the book's table of contents or on the first page of the opening *juan*. Publishers frequently printed different or more elaborate titles and appended subtitles or other extra phrases on title pages. These are sometimes noted and included in parentheses. A translation of the title appears in square brackets on the next line of the entry. In translating the titles, I have made every effort to adhere to uniform conventions. *Zhi* is almost universally translated as "gazetteer," *lu* as "record," *ce* as "handbook," *huibian* as "compendium," etc. Individual translations may depart from these conventions when I have judged that a variant rendering might better convey the character or style of the work.

(2) The number of *juan* or chapters follows on the next line. The numbering usually reflects the author's own convention of numbering, in either his table of contents or his actual chapter divisions. Introductory matter is generally not counted as an additional *juan*

unless it contains substantially more than the usual prefatory material.

(3) The names of authors and editors appear on the same line directly after the number of *juan*. In the case of anonymous editions, the publisher is sometimes given here. It has not always been possible to distinguish real authorship from fictive authorship or honorary attribution, though every effort has been made to credit the works to the men chiefly responsible for compiling them. In the case of editors, the extent of their participation in the creation of works bearing their names is almost impossible to verify: whereas some editors were just that, helping to shape and revise a publication, others were actually sponsors, lending name and money rather than editorial effort to the works published partly in their names. Editors obviously of the latter type have been excluded. Personal dates are given for those for whom this information is readily accessible, preferably birth and death dates, otherwise dates of acquisition of *jinshi* (js.), *juren* (jr.), or *gongsheng* (gs.) degrees.

(4) The next line or lines list the various editions and reprints, mostly extant, of the work. Each line consists of a date of publication followed by the names of libraries where it is held. The date may be the one printed on the title page, for those books having a dated title page; usually, however, it is the date of the latest preface. When the date of compilation varies significantly from that date, some indication of this discrepancy is made. When no date is available, internal evidence has been used to estimate one; in the absence of such evidence, a reign title suffices. The library names which follow are given in shortened form. The full names are given in the List of Abbreviations. Dates appearing without locations after them signify nonextant first editions of works for which there are extant later editions or reprints. Books that have been reprinted in a collectanea are so indicated by the insertion of the collectanea title between the date and the word "edition" or "reprint"; the key for collectanea titles is also given in the List of Abbreviations. Modern reprints are indicated by date as well, with place of publication and publisher included in parentheses.

(5) Several other bibliographic studies have dealt with some of the works listed in these bibliographies, and these are noted, with the appropriate entry or page number, in the "bibliographic notice" line. Full citations for such works are given in the List of Abbreviations. Among them I should highlight in particular the studies by Wolfgang Franke and Endymion Wilkinson, which were extremely useful both in furnishing bibliographic data and in providing helpful models for

the format of the present work.

(6) The closing part of each entry is reserved for miscellaneous data about the book, the information it contains, and the place or places it chronicles. For the route books, the number of routes documented is given here. For some of the gazetteers bearing titles that do not clearly convey their subject matter, a note explains the title or identifies the gazetteer's subject more clearly.

With the exception of books held only in Chinese libraries, I have examined almost every work in these bibliographies in at least one edition. Still, the dedicated reader will soon note that such scrutiny has not guaranteed that authorship, date, and other such information have always been correctly transcribed. Errors and omissions are unavoidable in a project of this scope, which has been carried out by one amateur bibliographer in the course of other research and, with the exception of a travel grant from the Central Research Fund of the University of Alberta, without separate funding. I would be grateful therefore if readers would send me corrections and references to sources I have neglected, care of the Department of History of the University of Toronto.

List of Abbreviations

Libraries

Note: An asterisk indicates that the collection so marked has been searched extensively in the course of compiling the bibliographies. Of the holdings in the unmarked libraries, it has been possible to include only selected items.

Anhui	Anhui Provincial Museum, Hefei
Beida	Peking University (Beijing Daxue) Library
Beijing	Peking Library
BL	British Library, London*
Cambridge	Cambridge University Library
Chicago	University of Chicago Library
Columbia	Columbia University Library*
Dili	Nanjing Institute of Geography (Nanjing Dili Yanjiusuo)
EAHSL	East Asian History of Science Library, Cambridge, England*
Fu	Fu Sinian Library, Academia Sinica, Taiwan
Fudan	Fudan University Library, Shanghai
Gest	Gest Library, Princeton University*
Hangzhou	Hangzhou University Library
Harvard	Harvard-Yenching Library*
Hefei	Anhui Provincial Library, Hefei
Jiaxing	Jiaxing Municipal Library
Jimbun	Jimbun Kagaku Kenkyūjo, University of Kyoto*
Keji	Shanghai Science and Technology Library (Shanghai Keji Tushuguan)
Kexue	Chinese Academy of Social Sciences (Zhongguo Shehui Kexue Yuan), Peking

LC	Library of Congress, Washington (including microfilm copies of the Guoli Beiping Tushuguan collection, now in Taibei)*
Michigan	University of Michigan Library
Naikaku	Naikaku Bunko collection, National Archives (Kōbun Kōkan), Tokyo*
Nanda	Nanjing University Library
Nanjing	Nanjing Municipal Library
Palace	National Palace Museum, Taibei
Seikado	Seikado Library, Tokyo*
Shanghai	Shanghai Municipal Library
Shifan	Peking Normal University (Beijing Shifan Daxue) Library
SOAS	School of Oriental and African Studies, University of London*
Sonkeikaku	Sonkeikaku Library, Tokyo*
Suzhou	Suzhou Library
Taibei	National Library, Taibei (including the Guoli Beiping Tushuguan collection)
Tobunken	Tōyō Bunka Kenkyūjo, University of Tokyo (including the Niida and Ōki collections)*
Toronto	East Asian Library, University of Toronto*
Toyo	Tōyō Bunko, Tokyo*
UBC	Asian Library, University of British Columbia (including the Puban collection)*
Zhejiang	Zhejiang Provincial Library, Hangzhou

Collectanea

The collectanea that are listed in *Zhongguo congshu zonglu* [Union catalogue of Chinese collectanea] (Peking: Zhonghua Shuju, 1959-62) are indicated here by the identification numbers used in the locations chart toward the end of volume 1 (pp. 958-1133). To assist in locating these works I have included the names of some libraries outside China where copies may be found, though the listings are far from complete. Microfilm copies are indicated by an "(m)" appended to the library's name.

Anhui
Anhui congshu 安徽叢書
(1932-36; 1971 reprint). #455. Gest, Harvard,
Jimbun, LC, Tobunken, Toronto, UBC.

Anle
Anle yannian congshu 安樂延年叢書
(1895). #266.

Biexia
Biexia zhai congshu 另下齋叢書
(1837-47; 1856 and 1923-24 reprints). #126.
Columbia, Gest, Harvard, Jimbun, LC, Tobunken, Toronto.

Biji
Biji congbian 筆記叢編
(1969). Columbia, Gest, Harvard.

Bisan
Biji sanbian 筆記三編
(1970). Columbia, Gest, Jimbun, UBC.

Bisi
Biji sibian 筆記四編
(1971). Columbia, Gest, Toronto.

Biwu
Biji wubian 筆記五編
(1976). Gest, Toronto.

Chenfeng
Chenfeng lü congkan 晨風廬叢刊
(Republic). #1291. LC, Tobunken.

Chuanshan
Chuanshan yishu 船山遺書
(1842; 1865 and 1933 reprints). #682. Widely
available.

Congshu
Congshu jicheng 叢書集成
(1935-40). #402. Columbia(m), Gest, Harvard,
LC, Tobunken, Toronto, Toyo, UBC.

Daozang
Daozang xubian 道藏續編
(Republic). #2151. Gest, EAHSL, Harvard,
Toyo, UBC.

Gaochang
Gaochang miji jiaji 高昌秘笈甲集
(1927-28). #356. Gest, Harvard, Jimbun, Toyo.

Guanzhong
Guanzhong congshu 關中叢書
(1934-36; 1971 reprint). #434. Gest, Harvard,
Jimbun, LC, Toronto, UBC.

Guichi
Guichi xianzhe yishu 貴池先哲遺書
(1920; 1971 reprint). #458. Chicago, Gest,
Harvard, Jimbun, Toyo, UBC.

Guxue
Guxue huikan 古學彙刊
(1923; 1964 reprint). #299. Columbia, Gest,
Jimbun, LC, Tobunken, Toronto, Toyo, UBC.

Hanfen
Hanfen lou miji 涵芬樓秘笈
(1916-31; 1967 reprint). #351. Columbia, Gest,
Harvard, Jimbun, LC, Tobunken, Toyo.

Hanhai

Hanhai 函海
(Qianlong; 1809 and 1825 reprints; enlarged edition, 1881-82; 1968 reprint). #83, 84. Gest, Harvard, Jimbun, LC, Tobunken, Toronto, Toyo.

Hehai

Hehai congshu 河海叢書
(1969). Gest, Toronto.

Hengshan

Hengshan caotang congshu 橫山草堂叢書
(1910-19). #448. Jimbun, LC, Toyo.

Huaiyou

Huaiyou zazu 懷幽雜俎
(Guangxu). #270. Jimbun, Toyo.

Huangshan

Huangshan congkan 黃山叢刊
(1937). Harvard, LC.

Jiangsu

Jiangsu difang wenxian congshu 江蘇地方文獻叢書
(1985-).

Jiangzi

Jiang zi yishu 蔣子遺書
(Republic). #987.

Jiaoshi

Jiao shi congshu 焦氏叢書
(1808). #865. Harvard, Jimbun, Tobunken, Toronto, Toyo.

Jiaye

Jiaye tang congshu 嘉業堂叢書
(1913-26). #333. Gest, Jimbun, LC, Toronto, Toyo, UBC.

Jifu

Jifu hedao shuili congshu 畿輔河道水利叢書
(1824; 1970 reprint). #1688. Columbia, Gest, Harvard, Jimbun, LC, Tobunken, Toyo, UBC.

Jingchu

Jingchu xiushu zhiyao 荊楚修疏指要
(1839; 1872 reprint). #1691. Columbia, LC, Tobunken.

Jingkou

Jingkou sanshan zhi 京口三山志
(1904-05; 1974 reprint). #1684. Cambridge, Columbia, Gest, Harvard, Jimbun, LC, Toronto, Toyo, UBC.

Jingyuan

Jingyuan zhai congshu 景袁齋叢書
(Guangxu). #1135.

Jinling

Jinling congshu 金陵叢書
(1916). #438. Columbia, Gest, Harvard, Jimbun, LC, Toyo, UBC.

Jinsheng

Jinsheng yuzhen ji 金聲玉振集
(1550-61; 1959 reprint). #11. Columbia, Harvard, Jimbun, LC, Naikaku, Toyo.

Jude

Jude tang congshu 聚德堂叢書
(1929). #318. Harvard, Jimbun, LC, Toyo.

Kaijiang	*Wuzhong kaijiang shu* 吳中開江書 (1666). #1689.
Kuishan	*Zhang Kuishan sanzhong* 張簣山三種 (Kangxi). #688.
Lingnan	*Lingnan yishu* 嶺南遺書 (1831-63; 1968 partial reprint). #497. Gest, Jimbun, LC, Tobunken, Toronto, Toyo, UBC.
Lishan	*Lishan yuan quanji* 禮山園全集 (1689; Qianlong reprint). #723. LC.
Ouxiang	*Ouxiang lingshi* 藕香零拾 (1884; 1911 and 1968 reprints). #238. Gest, Harvard, Tobunken.
Qiaofan	*Qiaofan lou congshu* 峭帆樓叢書 (1917). Gest, Harvard, Jimbun, LC, Tobunken, Toyo, UBC.
Qijin	*Qijin zhai congshu* 奇晉齋叢書 (Qianlong; 1912 reprint). #76. Columbia, Gest, Jimbun, LC, Tobunken, Toronto, Toyo.
Rugao	*Rugao Mao shi congshu* 如皋冒氏叢書 (1903-23). #518. Jimbun, Toyo.
Shaoxing	*Shaoxing xianzhi ziliao* 紹興縣志資料 (1936-39).
Shenshi	*Shenshiji zhai congshu* 慎始基齋叢書 (1923). #347. Columbia, Gest, Harvard, Jim- bun, LC, Tobunken, Toyo.
Shewen	*Shewen zijiu* 涉聞梓舊 (1856; 1924 reprint). #127. Columbia, Gest, Jimbun, LC, Tobunken, Toronto, Toyo.
Shuili	*Zhongguo shuili yaoji congbian* 中國水利要籍叢編 (1971). Gest.
Shuofu	*Shuofu xu* 說郛續 (1646; 1964 reprint). #9. Gest, Jimbun, LC, Naikaku, Tobunken, Toyo.
Sida	*Sida mingshan zhi* 四大名山志 (1978). Gest.
Siku	*Siku quanshu* 四庫全書 (Qianlong; 1983-87 reprint). Beijing, EAHSL, Naikaku, Palace, Zhejiang.
Siming	*Siming congshu* 四明叢書 (1932-40; 1966 reprint). #471. Columbia, Gest, Harvard, Jimbun, LC, Tobunken, Toronto, Toyo.

Suoxu   *Xu Jinling suozhi*　續金陵瑣志
                (1918; 1970 ZC reprint). #1655.
Suozhi   *Jinling suozhi wuzhong*　金陵瑣志五種
                (1885-1908; 1970 ZC reprint). #1655.
Tanji   *Tanji congshu*　檀几叢書
                (1695). #58. Columbia, Harvard, Jimbun, LC (2
                copies), Naikaku, Toronto, Toyo.
Tianyuan   *Tianyuan zazhu*　田園雜著
                (1882). #1120. Harvard.
Tushu   *(Gujin) Tushu jicheng*　圖書集成
                (1725; 1936 reprint). Columbia, Gest, Harvard,
                LC, Tobunken, Toronto, Toyo (2 copies), UBC.
Wangchui   *Wangchui lou congshu*　望炊樓叢書
                (1924). #1661. Harvard, Jimbun, LC, Toyo.
Weishi   *Wei shi quanshu*　魏氏全書
                (1933). #1294.
Wenjing   *Wenjing tang congshu*　問經堂叢書
                (1801-1802; 1968 reprint). #97. Gest, Harvard,
                Jimbun, LC, Naikaku, Toyo.
Wenying   *Wenying lou yudi congshu*　問影樓輿地叢書
                (1908; 1967 reprint). #1630. Columbia, Gest,
                Harvard, Jimbun, LC, Tobunken, Toyo.
Wuxing   *Wuxing congshu*　吳興叢書
                (1922). #467. LC, Toyo, UBC.
WZ   *Wulin zhanggu congbian*　武林掌故叢編
                (1877-1900). #460. Widely available.
XF   *Xiaofanghu zhai yudi congchao*　小方壺齋輿地叢鈔
                (1891). #251. Widely available.
Xiangsu   *Xiangsu shanguan quanji*　香蘇山館全集
                (1843). #884. Jimbun, Nanda, Toyo.
Xiangyan   *Xiangyan congshu*　香豓叢書
                (1909-14; 1969 reprint). #2108. Gest, LC,
                Tobunken, Toronto, Toyo, UBC.
Xiaoshan   *Xiaoshan congshu*　蕭山叢書
                #474.
Xihe   *Xihe heji*　西河合集
                (Kangxi; 1770 and 1968 reprints). #693.
                Columbia, Gest, LC, Tobunken, Toronto, Toyo.
Xike   *Xike jushi quanji*　息柯居士全集
                (Guangxu). #1011. LC, Toyo.
Xiuben   *Xiuben tang congshu*　脩本堂叢書
                (1844). #906. LC.

Xuanlan *Xuanlan tang congshu chuji* 玄覽堂叢書初集
(1941). #406. Harvard, Jimbun, LC, Tobunken,
Toronto, Toyo, UBC.

Xuansan *Xuanlan tang congshu sanji* 玄覽堂叢書三集
(1948). #408. Tobunken, Toyo.

Xuanxu *Xuanlan tang congshu xuji* 玄覽堂叢書續集
(1947). #407. Columbia, Gest, Harvard, Jimbun, Tobunken, Toronto, Toyo.

Xuehai *Xuehai leibian* 學海類編
(1831; 1920 and 1967 reprints). #56. Gest, Jimbun, LC, Naikaku, Tobunken, Toyo, UBC.

Xunmin *Xunmin tang congshu* 遜敏堂叢書
(1851). #151. Jimbun, LC, Tobunken.

Yangzhou *Yangzhou congke* 揚州叢刻
(1934; 1970 reprint). #450. Gest, Harvard, Jimbun, LC, Tobunken, Toronto, Toyo, UBC.

Yanxia *Yanxia caotang yishu xuke* 煙霞草堂遺書續刻
(1923). #1106. Chicago, Columbia.

Yudi *Zhongguo yudi congshu* 中國輿地叢書
(1969). Gest, Harvard.

Yueya *Yueya tang congshu* 粵雅堂叢書
(1849-75). #150. Gest, Jimbun, LC, Tobunken,
Toronto, Toyo, UBC.

Yuezhong *Yuezhong wenxian jicun shu* 越中文獻輯存書
(1911). #473. Toyo.

Yunnan *Yunnan congshu* 雲南叢書
(1914-24). #501. Harvard, Jimbun, LC, Tobunken.

Yuyang *Wang Yuyang yishu* 王漁洋遺書
(Qianlong). #713. Naikaku, Seikado, Tobunken,
UBC.

Yuzhang *Yuzhang congshu* 豫章叢書
(1915-23; 1970 reprint). #494. Gest, Jimbun,
LC, Toyo, UBC.

ZC *Zhongguo fangzhi congshu* 中國方志叢書
(1967-83). Widely available.

ZF *Zhongguo fosi shizhi huikan* 中國佛寺史志彙刊
(1980). BL, Columbia, Gest, Harvard, Tobunken.

Zhenben *Siku quanshu zhenben* 四庫全書珍本
(1934; 1973 reprint). Columbia, Gest, Harvard,
Jimbun, LC, Tobunken, Toronto, Toyo, UBC.

Zhibuzu   *Zhibuzu zhai congshu* 知不足齋叢書
(Daoguang; 1921 and 1964 reprints). #80. Gest, Harvard, Jimbun, LC, Naikaku, Tobunken, Toronto, Toyo, UBC.

Zhugang   *Zhugang zhai jiuzhong* 竹岡齋九種
(1823). #889. Columbia, Harvard.

ZM   *Zhongguo mingshan shengji zhi congkan* 中國名山
勝跡志叢刊 (1971). BL, Columbia, Gest, Harvard, LC, Michigan, UBC.

References

Anhui   *Anhui dizhen shiliao jizhu* 安徽地震史料輯注
[Annotated historical materials concerning earthquakes in Anhui] (Hefei: Anhui Kexue Jishu Chubanshe, 1983).

Chen   Chen Qiaoyi 陳橋驛, *Shaoxing difang wenxian kaolu* 紹興地方文獻考錄 [Study of local documents concerning Shaoxing] (Hangzhou: Zhejiang Renmin Chubanshe, 1983).

DMB   L. Carrington Goodrich and Chaoying Fang, eds., *Dictionary of Ming Biography*, 2 vols. (New York: Columbia University Press, 1976).

ECCP   Arthur Hummel, ed., *Eminent Chinese of the Ch'ing Period*, 2 vols. (Washington: Government Printing Office, 1943).

EW   Endymion Wilkinson, "Chinese Merchant Manuals and Route Books," *Ch'ing-shih wen-t'i* 2:9 (January 1973), pp. 8-34.

Fanshu   Sun Dianqi 孫殿起, *Fanshu ouji* 販書偶記 [A bookseller's notes] (1936; repr. Shanghai: Guji Chubanshe, 1982).

Franke   Wolfgang Franke, *An Introduction to the Sources of Ming History* (Kuala Lumpur: University of Malaya Press, 1968).

HHC	Hong Huanchun 洪煥春, *Zhejiang wenxian congkao* 浙江文獻叢考 [Bibliographic studies of Zhejiang] (Hangzhou: Zhejiang Renmin Chubanshe, 1983).
Hong	Hong Huanchun, *Zhejiang difangzhi kaolu* 浙江地方志考錄 [Annotated bibliography of Zhejiang local gazetteers] (Peking: Kexue Chubanshe, 1962).
Huang	Huang Yuji 黃虞稷, *Qianqing tang shumu* 千頃堂書目 [Bibliographic catalogue of Qianqing Hall], in *Shiyuan congshu* 適園叢書 (1916).
JPM	Johannes Prip-Møller, *Chinese Buddhist Monasteries* (Copenhagen: Gads Forlag, 1937).
Morita	Morita Akira 森田明, "*Shōku henran* ni tsuite" 商賈便覽について [On *The easy-to-consult merchant manual*], *Fukuoka daigaku kenkyū jōhō*, no. 16 (1972), pp. 1-28.
Mizuno	Mizuno Masaaki 水野正明, "*Shinan gemban shishō ruiyō* ni tsuite" 新安原枚士商類要について [On *The original Xin'an edition of the encyclopedia for gentry and merchants*], *Tōhōgaku*, no. 60 (1980), pp. 96-117.
Niida	Niida Noboru 仁井田陞, *Chūgoku hōseishi kenkyū: dorei nōdo hō, kazoku sonraku hō* 中国法制史研究：奴隷農奴法, 家族村落法 [Studies in the history of Chinese law: slave and serf law, family and village law] (Tokyo: Tōkyō Daigaku Shuppankai, 1962), chs. 13, 14.
Nongcun	Fu Yiling 傅衣凌, *Ming-Qing nongcun shehui jingji* 明清農村社會經濟 [Rural socioeconomy of the Ming-Qing period] (Peking: Sanlian Shuju, 1961).
Ren	Ren Daobin 任道斌, *Fang Yizhi nianpu* 方以智年譜 [Chronological biography of Fang Yizhi] (Hefei: Anhui Jiaoyu Chubanshe, 1983).

Sakai   Sakai Tadao 酒井忠夫 "Mindai nichiyō ruisho to
                 shomin kyōiku" 明代日用類書と小民教育 [Ming
                 daily-use encyclopedias and the education of the
                 common people], in *Kinsei Chūgoku kyōikushi
                 kenkyū* 近世中国教育史研究   [Studies   in   the
                 history of Chinese education], ed. Hayashi
                 Tomoharu 林友春 (Tokyo: Kokudosha, 1958),
                 pp. 25-154.

Shanben   *Beijing tushuguan shanben shumu* 北京圖書館善
                 本書目 [Catalogue of rare books in the Peking
                 Library].

Sun   Sun Yirang 孫詒讓, *Wenzhou jingji zhi* 溫州經
                 籍志 [Bibliography of the writings of Wenzhou
                 natives] (1921), *juan* 12.

Wang   Wang Chongmin 王重民, *Zhongguo shanben shu
                 tiyao* 中國善本書提要 [Notes on Chinese rare
                 books] (Shanghai: Shanghai Guji Chubanshe,
                 1983).

Wu   Wu   Qingdi 吳慶坻, *Hangzhou   yiwen   zhi*
                 杭州藝文志 [Bibliography of the writings of
                 Hangzhou natives] (1908), *juan* 1.

Xiang   Xiang Yuanxun 項元勛, *Taizhou jingji zhi*
                 台州經籍志 [Bibliography of the writings of
                 Taizhou natives] (1915), *juan* 4.

ZFK   Hong Huanchun, *Zhejiang fangzhi kao* 浙江方
                 志考 [Notes on Zhejiang gazetteers] (Hangzhou:
                 Zhejiang Renmin Chubanshe, 1984).

Part I
Route Books

Introduction

A route book is a traveler's handbook of water and land routes. It differs from a map in relying on verbal description rather than visual representation, and hence its readership is literate. But the language of the route book is unsophisticated, and it was clearly designed not to be savored for its literary flavor but to be shoved dog-eared into travelers' satchels.

The standard format of a Chinese route book is to describe routes in terms of the places they traverse—such as towns, villages, and fords—and to give the distances between these places. This material is usually broken down into stages that could be covered in a day's journey. Some route books include additional information for travelers, such as the locations of inns and ferry schedules. Others go much further and incorporate advice for merchants and information relevant to commercial exchange. The route book thus naturally spawned the merchant manual within a few decades of its appearance. Since the focus of the present study is exclusively the route content of these books, the rich body of mercantile and other lore that many contain will be left out of this discussion.

The accompanying bibliography contains fifty-seven entries for route books, other popular works providing route information, such as almanacs, and a few route maps. With the exception of the last, most exist in published form. For a country as large as China, with as extended a network of communications as it had in the Ming-Qing period, fifty-seven is a surprisingly small number to have turned up, even granted that my search did not include Chinese collections. This survival rate is a reflection of the unprestigious character of the genre and its lack of appeal for book collectors. Though popular with printing houses and travelers, route books were not prized by bibliophiles and so descended quickly into oblivion. More await discovery in China, perhaps in lesser known local collections.[1]

Judging from the corpus of extant route books, they came into common use in the latter half of the sixteenth century, flourished in the seventeenth and eighteenth, and survived on through to the early twentieth, when they were superceded by modern guidebooks and train schedules. It is difficult to reconstruct their history prior to the

appearance in 1570 of the earliest extant route book, Huang Bian's
Yitong lucheng tuji [The comprehensive illustrated route book]
(5.1.1). The generic term *tuji* that Huang uses in his title hearkens
back to the local-gazetteer prototypes of the Sui and Tang dynasties,
known as *tuji* or *tujing*.[2] By the twelfth century, when the term *zhi*
or *tuzhi* had become the conventional designation for local gazetteers,
tuji and *tujing* were used to indicate more peripheral types of
geographical writing. These terms continued in use in the Ming, as is
attested in a short work by the Suzhou author Wang Zhideng
(1535-1612). Concerning his journey to Hangzhou in 1567, Wang
wrote, "As I did not know about the routes and distances for
traveling south, I went to a bookseller's and bought a *tujing*, which I
packed in my trunk."[3] Wang is probably using the term *tujing* to
mean a route book. If so, Wang's remark in 1567 is the earliest
mention of this genre that I have found in Ming sources. It is not
surprising that he found his *tujing* in Suzhou, since this was also the
place where Huang Bian's route book of 1570 was published.

In recounting in his preface how he came to produce *The comprehensive illustrated route book*, Huang mentions that he made use
of route maps:

> When I was living in Suzhou, I collected several route
> maps (*chengtu*) from merchants who traded in both
> capitals, all thirteen provinces, and the border
> regions. I examined them closely, compared their
> differences, then collated all the material. It took me
> twenty-seven years to work it into book form.

Huang's purpose in telling his reader this is to assure him that the
book is based on a large body of practical commercial experience
spanning all regions of China, though it reveals to us that the most
common guide available to merchants up until the sixteenth century
was the route map. It appears that no maps of land routes survive
from the Ming, but there are a few Qing copies in manuscript. The
route to be followed is marked with a solid or broken line. The
topography over which the line moves, however, is frequently
stylized in such a way that the route becomes visually a straight line,
reducing the meanderings of the actual route and imparting to it a
falsely linear character to make the map simpler and easier to
comprehend. Route maps also indicate distances between major
points along the routes. Whether the route maps in Huang's
possession were printed he does not say, though the few that survive

from the Qing come down to us only in handwritten copies. The route map was in use long before the sixteenth century. According to Aoyama Sadao, the earliest references to route maps are in 996 and 1006, in both cases to hand-copied maps of the grain-tribute route along the Grand Canal. Given the crucial importance of the canal in linking north and south China during the Northern Song dynasty, it is not surprising to learn that this route was provided with formal documentation. Aoyama has also determined that route maps of nautical courses and the overland postal system existed in the Song,[4] and these continued to be produced through the Ming and Qing. The oldest surviving route map, which exists only in an eighteenth-century copy, is a Ming-period map of the nautical route along the coast from Liaodong to the Pearl River delta outside Canton (6.1.1). The next oldest is a route map of the Grand Canal (3.1.1). Maps of water routes thus continued to be available to those who needed them, principally navigators, even at the time that Huang Bian was developing a more comprehensive format for route information.[5]

The transition from route map to route book seems to have occurred as part of the expansion of woodblock printing into a large-scale industry in the sixteenth century. Other factors were at work, as I shall suggest, but the publishing activity to which commercialization was giving new momentum in the latter part of that century made the production of printed guides for travelers feasible and, as the genre caught hold, lucrative. Nautical guides would have been much less in demand among the bookshop clientele of Suzhou, and accordingly such works never made the step from written to printed copies. But many of the residents of Suzhou and other major commercial centers in Jiangnan were inland travelers, whether for business or pleasure, and the growth of the bookselling business brought with it a trade in route books.

With *The comprehensive illustrated route book* of 1570, we are suddenly faced with a fully developed genre cut loose from its obscure antecedents.[6] The book begins with three maps: one of China's main river systems based on the Yuan-period atlas of Zhu Siben (1273-1337), which was first published in the 1550s by Luo Hongxian (1504-64); and two maps of the national courier networks of the Ming, reproduced here as Maps 1 and 2. Thereafter, the entire book is text. The 157 routes documented by Huang Bian are outlined by places at intervals of roughly fifty to eighty *li*, which was the standard staging distance between postal stations. The shortest routes name as few as ten places, the longest close to two hundred.

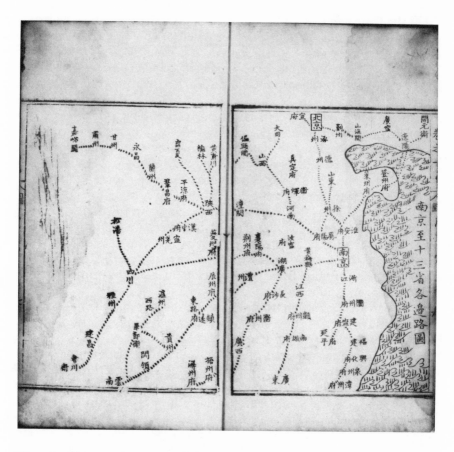

Map 1. The trunk routes of the early Ming courier system centering on Nanjing; from *Yitong lucheng tuji* [The comprehensive illustrated route book] (5.1.1) of 1570. This and the following illustrations are reproduced courtesy of the National Archives, Tokyo.

MMCS #58: GEOGRAPHICAL SOURCES OF MING-QING HISTORY
(paperbound edition)

NOTE FROM THE PUBLISHER:

A production error in our office resulted in Map 2 (page 7) being
placed upside down and the two sides of Illustration 2 (pages 56-
57) being transposed. We apologize for the inconvenience this may
cause to the reader.

Publications Office
Center for Chinese Studies
October 1988

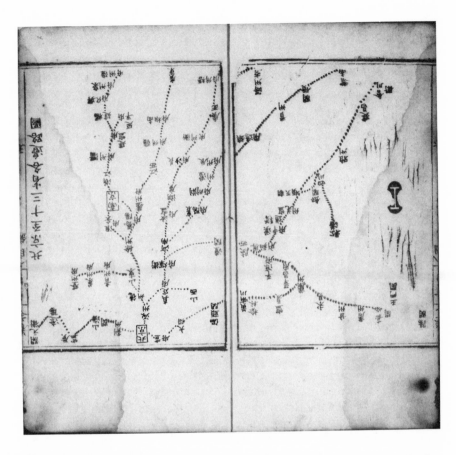

Map 2. The trunk routes of the later Ming courier system centering on Peking; from *The comprehensive illustrated route book* (5.1.1).

Besides place names and distances, the book provides other information, such as the location and administrative status of county seats, the gates by which towns are entered, difficult turnings in the road, the conditions of roads and waterways, alternative routes, and the occasional famous site or religious spot along the way.

Huang's book proved to be a popular work, judging from the number of other editions that were turned out. Shang Jun, a professional writer who was closely linked to the publishing business in northern Zhejiang, pirated it in 1617. In another edition, an unknown editor named Tao Chengqing added three extra routes and expanded its format to include census figures and information about local products in an upper panel on each page (5.1.2). This edition has one map, reproduced here as Map 3, showing the courier route network as it existed at that time. Tao's version was pirated in turn, though under Huang's name once again, in 1635. Presumably Huang's original book had earned him a sufficiently large reputation as an authority on commercial travel to induce that publisher to put the name of Huang Bian back on the cover, especially as he would have been safely dead by the 1630s.

There was in the Ming one other popularly available printed source to consult for information about routes, and that was the almanac or "encyclopedia of daily use," as it is often called (*leishu* or *quanshu*). An almanac was a compendium of all manner of material on subjects ranging from animal husbandry to popular deities, subjects that reflected the daily concerns of ordinary, though literate, people. In the late Ming, almanacs came to include a chapter on routes.[7] By 1597, and without exception subsequently, every almanac included routes in the upper panel of the second *juan*, entitled "Diyu men" [Primer on geography]. Being only half a chapter in a work whose size and price had to be kept within limits, the route section in an almanac was restricted to the official stage routes, usually in abridged form. In the accompanying bibliography, I have grouped the numerous extant editions of almanacs on the basis of the particular stage network chosen by the editors. Given the complex overlapping among the various editions within this much pirated genre, the route sections may serve as one means of determining the filiation of almanacs.[8]

The most commonly printed version is the basic stage network established by the Ming government in the fifteenth century: seven trunk routes originating in Peking and three in Nanjing. The places used to mark the routes tend to be seats of government, such as county towns, or government courier stations (*yi*). This trunk

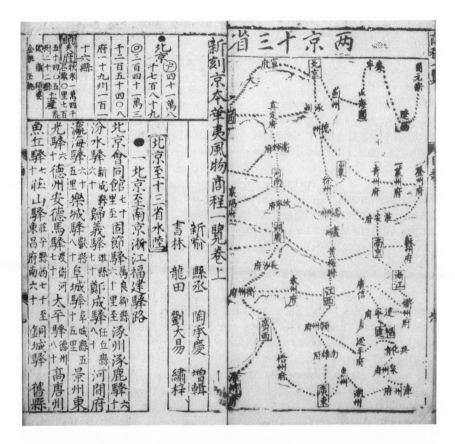

Map 3. The principal routes of the courier system at the turn of the seventeenth century; from *Shangcheng yilan* [Merchant routes at a glance] (5.1.2). The facing page gives the beginning of the first route, from Peking to Fuzhou via Nanjing and Hangzhou.

network appears in most versions of *Wanbao quanshu* [The treasury almanac] (1.2.1). Next most common is a more ramified stage network of forty-four routes, which is found in the most thorough and best produced of the late-Ming almanacs, *Wanyong zhengzong* [The correct source for a myriad practical uses] (1.2.6). This selection of routes begins with a set of seventeen stage routes linking the two national capitals to the provinces, which was the official set of routes established in the early Ming but later replaced by the system of ten trunk routes.[9] These seventeen are followed by another fifteen stage routes from the provincial capitals to their outlying counties. The route section of *The correct source* ends with an assortment of other routes: the Grand Canal, the Yangzi River, two southwestern routes, and eight routes in Fujian, Zhejiang, and Jiangxi. Other almanacs printed fifteen- and twenty-route versions (1.2.2, 1.2.4), in addition to abridgements of the forty-four route network (1.2.10, 1.2.11). While all these versions can be found in the almanacs of the late Ming, Qing almanacs (with only one exception (1.2.4), which gives the twenty-route version) print the simplest network of ten trunk routes from the two capitals. The tendency for later almanacs to adopt the most abbreviated network suggests that the route section may have been losing its importance for almanac readers. Was this because almanacs were being read by men of lower wealth and station, for whom knowledge of nationwide transportation networks was of no great importance? Or did the Qing traveler put away his almanac and turn more naturally to the route books then in circulation?

By the late seventeenth century, the original route book by Huang Bian had lost the preeminence it had enjoyed for a century in favor of *Shiwo zhouxing* [Traveling everywhere on my own] (5.1.3). Huang's edition died out, while *Traveling everywhere* was reprinted throughout the eighteenth century. We know that *Traveling everywhere* continued to be popular in the nineteenth century, for the editor of the route section of a Peking guidebook of 1864 (5.3.1) says that he relied on the 1774 edition to draw up his routes. The number of routes is roughly the same as in Huang's book: a basic set of 144, which is then augmented with routes in south and southeast China to 151 and 161 in two later editions.

Merchant manuals were the other main source for route information in the Qing. By comparison with route books, merchant manuals record a much wider set of route networks, with considerable variation from one edition to the next.[10] These manuals, published to provide merchants with practical information to help

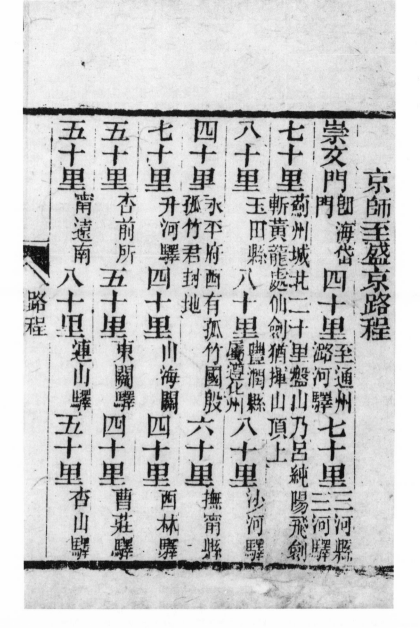

Illustration 1. First page of the route section of the 1891 reprint of *Chaoshi congzai* [Complete notes for going to market] (5.3.1), a guidebook to the city of Peking. This shows the route from Peking to Mukden.

them in conducting itinerant commercial transactions, developed
directly out of the route book in the early seventeenth century. The
development was a natural one, given the need that merchants had
for commercial information and the interest publishers might take in
expanding route books to include other material. The earliest extant
manual is *Shishang leiyao* [The encyclopedia for gentry and
merchants] (5.4.1), dated 1626. The better part of this book is
devoted to routes, though they are outlined in somewhat briefer
fashion here than in route books. The network consists of exactly one
hundred routes: fifty-three south of the Yangzi and forty-seven
north. This network is repeated in two later merchant manuals,
though by the time of *Shanggu bianlan* [The easy-to-consult
merchant manual] (5.4.4) of 1792, the route section has been
reduced to seventy-five routes, primarily at the expense of those in
north and central China.

There are, in addition to *Traveling everywhere on my own* and the
merchant manuals mentioned, more specialized types of route
publications from the Qing period. Some select one place and record
the routes running out from it: for example, a 1728 route book
(5.2.1) gives routes from the city of Guangzhou to places both within
and beyond Guangdong province; and the Peking guidebook *Dumen
jilüe* (5.3.1) outlines twenty routes leading from Peking to the
provinces. Others, such as *Wutai shan daolu quantu* [Complete map
of the roads on Wutai Mountain] (6.4.1), record routes within a
defined locality. Still others describe only one route, albeit in detail.
The bibliography includes two that, strictly speaking, fall outside the
category of route book but have been included because they document two routes in considerable detail. These are the route studies
compiled by the eminent Qing official Dong Xun (1807-92) of the
grain-tribute route from the Xiang River in Hunan to the northern
end of the Grand Canal in Peking (3.1.4, 3.2.1). In addition, there is
one route book that was compiled for a specialized audience: *Canxue
zhijin* [Knowing the fords on the way to knowledge] (5.5.1) was
published in 1827 for the use of Buddhist pilgrims. The only one of
its kind, *Knowing the fords* is remarkable also for being the earliest
extant route book to provide detailed information on routes in
Sichuan, Guizhou, and Yunnan provinces.

Most of the route books mentioned thus far were compiled and
printed by private individuals for commercial purposes. The Qing
government was also involved in the production of certain specialized
types of route books. The government first of all published
handbooks of the stage network within each province. The Ministry

of War, which was responsible for administering the postal system, ordered them compiled for every province in 1749. First published in 1751, they were revised subsequently and reissued in 1775, 1802, 1822, and again in the late 1880s. Copies were also published privately. There are extant nineteenth-century editions for Zhejiang, Hubei, Hunan, and Guangdong (2.1.1 to 2.2.1). A second type of government route book was that produced by the imperial household for those deputed to perform ritual duties connected with the imperial ancestors. These books document the routes from the Imperial City in Peking to the Eastern Tombs in Zunhua county and the Western Tombs in Yi county (4.2.1 to 4.2.3), and the route to Xingjing, the old Manchu capital in the northeast (4.1.1). Some of the books in this category of government publications, in addition to the usual information about routes and places, also included prescribed rates of travel, referred to as *xianxing*, "limits within which one could travel." This information is valuable for showing us what space meant in terms of time to travelers in the late imperial period. Its graphic depiction in a recent historical atlas shows that the empire in Qing times took between six and seven weeks to cross, which is the time it took a courier to get from Peking to the far southwest.[11]

For the historian, route books and almanacs are not the only sources for route information. The first place to look is county or prefectural gazetteers, which sometimes include route sections. Such sections might list the major routes within the county or prefecture;[12] some might distinguish between local roads and government courier routes;[13] and some might include a separate section for military routes.[14] On rare occasion a local gazetteer could give routes from its county seat to major cities throughout the country.[15] A second genre to consult for route information is studies concerning national defense and internal security. These can also include route sections, often of areas not adequately covered in commercial route books. Zheng Ruozeng in his *Chouhai tubian* [Illustrated compendium on naval defense] of 1562 provides maps showing the routes taken by Japanese and Chinese pirates to approach the southeast coast. Yan Ruyi in his *Miaofang beilan* [Complete conspectus of security against the Hmong] of 1820 lists land routes (*juan* 6) and water routes (*juan* 7) through western Hunan and northeastern Guizhou.

The significance of route books may be highlighted by considering briefly the route systems they record, the types of travelers for which they were published, and their importance to commercial circulation.

A centralized political state presupposes and requires a certain measure of territorial integration. The means of transportation, both routes and transportation technology, must be sufficiently well developed to permit the internal communication necessary to sustain central rule, both by providing ways to siphon tax revenues from local areas and by enabling adequate military supplies to be moved without delay. The Grand Canal was maintained and subsidized by the state for this kind of political purpose, though it also served as an enormous impetus for trade. Since the seventh century, the canal has been the most visible feature of China's route system, facilitating communication between the political centers in the north and the emerging economic heartland in the south. In the Ming dynasty, the canal was put back into operation under the Yongle emperor following an extensive project of cutting new channels and building new locks, which was completed in 1415.

If the Grand Canal was the backbone of China's state communication network since the Tang dynasty, the routes of the postal system made up the rest of the skeleton.[16] This system was reinstated in the first year of the Ming dynasty, and its network of routes remained relatively stable thereafter, though individual routes were occasionally modified.[17] Under the regulations that governed it, the system could be used only by those carrying a government pass, ordinarily issued only to men of appropriate rank traveling on official business.[18] By the late Ming, however, a much less restricted group of travelers felt empowered to make use of the postal system as they chose, and passes appear to have been handed out more freely.[19]

The postal system did not service solely bureaucratic travel and transport, for commercial goods moved along its routes, often in the hands of the transport corps that had been hired to move only requisitioned materials and tax payments for the state. As Hoshi Ayao has observed for the early Ming, merchants depended on the governmental transport system for the distribution of their goods.[20] Shiba Yoshinobu sees the late Song as an important turning point in the evolution of commercial transport networks because it was at this time, he argues, that an unofficial transport system distinct from the state system began to emerge. This system was "to some extent in competition with the official system, but also to some extent dependent for its existence upon it."[21] The overlap between the official and the unofficial systems was considerable, except perhaps in some areas of water transport where technological advances in the Song helped facilitate the operation of a nationwide market in certain commodities quite apart from the world of official water transport, as Mark Elvin has shown.[22] The data that Elvin presents regarding land transport, on the other hand, are limited entirely to the official system and do not demonstrate an independent system of roads. Indeed, the notion that an unofficial transport system should evolve in the direction of full independence from the official courier system is based on the assumption that administrative and economic networks were separating prior to the nineteenth century, an assumption that, as I have suggested elsewhere, is open to doubt.[23]

In the absence of a full-scale study of the actual routes recorded in the various route books included in this bibliography, it is difficult to draw conclusions about changes in the distribution and character of China's route network in the Ming-Qing period. It seems reasonable to hypothesize, at a minimum, that the state system used by government couriers formed the core of China's interregional route network in the early Ming, and that, as the volume of private commercial travel increased, the overall system of routes expanded.[24] The proliferation of route books in the Ming-Qing period reinforces the suspicion that not only were greater numbers of travelers in need of guides but the route network on which they were traveling was becoming more complex. As commerce expanded, more goods became commodities, and goods circulated in greater volume. The demand for route books reflected a need to know about a structure of routes that was constantly ramifying under the pressure of commercial use.

Such a hypothesis is supported by the essentially commercial character of these publications. Both the compilers and the readers, so far as we can determine, came from (or at least claimed) mercantile backgrounds. The first route-book compiler, Huang Bian, was a native of Xiuning county in the commercially vibrant Xin'an region southwest of Nanjing and had commercial experience working in Suzhou as an agent for his family's shipping business. He also traveled extensively with shipments for the business and in his preface recounts a journey that he, his father, and his brothers took from their home in Xiuning to Changsha (downriver from Xiangtan, the center of the Hunan rice trade), from Changsha via the Yangzi River to Yangzhou (near the Yangzi port for the Grand Canal), and from there by the Grand Canal north to Peking. Huang mentions that on their return journey back to Xiuning the Grand Canal was completely frozen to the bottom between Yanzhou in southern Shandong and Xuzhou across the border in South Zhili. This was probably the winter of 1567-68, when the weather in Shandong was

so abnormally cold that animals froze to death.[25] Another author,
Cheng Chunyu (5.4.1), came from one of the commercially successful
lineages of the Xin'an region and must have chalked up a similar
range of experience. Indeed, the publisher plays on the commercial
reputation of Cheng's hometown by advertising Cheng's manual as
being "the original Xin'an edition." The publisher was seeking to
appeal to a mercantile audience also through his choice of title,
Keshang yilan shuilu lucheng [Water and land routes at a glance for
traveling merchants]. Huang Bian had the same audience in mind,
for he says in his preface that he was prompted to publish the book
because of the difficulties he and his family had faced that winter on
the Grand Canal, when they were forced to abandon the waterways
and take overland roads, which proved extremely difficult to follow.
The book, he informs his reader, was meant as a service for other
merchants "who, like me, get lost on byways."

Were gentry and officials part of the route-book audience? Many
publishers included the expression *shishang* ("gentry and
merchants") in their titles, suggesting that they had both groups in
mind. One gets the same impression from the postface to Huang's
book:

> Should the gentry obtain this book, it will help them
> carry out the emperor's sagely commands. If mer-
> chants obtain it, it will inform them about the charac-
> teristics and problems of local areas.

A dual audience is also suggested by the author of the preface to
Traveling everywhere on my own, who pictures "officials and
merchants" (without route books, of course) "lugging their things
back and forth, vexed and asking the way." Such references may
indicate that both merchants and gentry were using these books,
though the likelier explanation is that they were intended to appeal
to the mercantile purchaser who had pretensions to status. I have
pointed out elsewhere that there was a tendency among people
involved in producing route books to assume studio names or
religious-sounding pseudonyms for themselves.[26] This was a convention among the lesser literati who were turning out popular works for
commercial publishers. Such men aspired to the gentility and
intellectual legitimacy of the elite gentry from whose circles they
were excluded. Those who produced route books wanted the patina of
high culture associated with the writings of the elite in order to
appeal to a public that was outside that realm. This is not to say

that the elite gentry were not buying route books, only that the main audience for them lay elsewhere.

The importance of route books to the circulation of goods, both in Ming-Qing China and in preindustrialized societies generally, should not be underestimated. When transportation relies on human and animal power and the unaided forces of wind and water, the movement of large volumes of goods is invariably cumbersome and slow. A few officials may travel about the country performing their duties, and a few traders may move valuable goods in limited amounts, making use of the transportation system that exists. As I have suggested, a state's transportation system can be crucial for its viability; however, the state may require only minimal efficiency from that system and may therefore make only a minimal investment in it. The stimulus for further development must come from trade.

When necessities circulate as commodities and significant numbers of people rely on the regular exchange of goods to survive, the cost at which goods can be transported in a preindustrialized society begins to matter. Under such conditions, transportation is pushed to become more efficient. Mark Elvin has proposed that improvements in transport and communications in the Song facilitated what he refers to as an economic revolution.[27] There were no great technical improvements in transportation in the Ming, so far as is presently known.[28] Yet it is clear that there was a significant shift, possibly of greater magnitude than the changes noted by Elvin for the Song, from limited commodity circulation and merchant travel in the fifteenth century to large-scale activity in the sixteenth. This shift is reflected, for example, in revisions of a county gazetteer from the rural area south of Suzhou. In 1488 the gazeteer notes with approval that the local people[29]

> do not travel great distances. Merchants grimace when they have to go more than a hundred *li* from home, leaving their families to stick to their home villages and carry on the farming. Only those sent out on official business travel great distances. Those who go off as merchants to other places, leaving their homes in search of profit, and letting the years pass by without ever returning, are looked on as faithless men.

In contrast, by 1548, the date when the next edition of the gazetteer was compiled, this passage has been dropped. Merchants were becoming involved more regularly in long-distance trade, and the stigma of that undertaking had faded with the growth of a nationwide commercial network.[30]

It is not surprising that the Ming apparently saw no obvious technological revolution of the sort Elvin has postulated for the Song, for this was a society in which traditional methods were already highly developed. Within that technology, transport was limited to short hauls, was not easily subject to coordination, and had probably reached limits in the amount of manpower and animal power that could be freed from agriculture.[31] The main obstacles to ease of transportation in this period were not so much technical as political and economic. Only the Chinese government had the power to keep the roads and canals in good repair, and it failed to do so. Even though the court might issue a regulation, as it did in 1439, requiring that "prefectural, subprefectural, and county officials maintain continual surveillance over bridges and roads, and repair them when necessary,"[32] the central government never mounted major projects for the constuction or maintenance of roads. The section on roads in the *Ming huiyao* [Digest of Ming statutes], in which the above regulation appears, lists only a handful of minor projects undertaken by regional or local officials. Ray Huang argues convincingly that the government's failure to commit funds to any transportation artery but the Grand Canal contributed to a general retarding of the economy in the Ming.[33] The decay of China's transportation system continued to be a problem into the nineteenth century, as European observers testify.[34] Clearly, political and economic conditions in Ming-Qing China were not what they were in seventeenth-century Europe, where, "although no spectacular transport innovations occurred, mundane investment in roads, canals, and coastal vessels achieved significant increases in the speed of passenger travel and reductions in the cost of freight carriage."[35]

Short of "mundane investment" on a grand scale, which was clearly not forthcoming even in the heady days of commercial expansion in the late Ming, the only feasible way to minimize the still enormous difficulties of transportation in China was to eliminate as many peripheral technical obstacles as possible, such as inefficient route location with regard to commercial resources, inadequate services for travelers, and ignorance of the best routes. These obstacles were, in fact, gradually being reduced, as a number of developments in the period suggest. First of all, the structure of existing routes came to be altered so as to facilitate access to commercially strategic areas. Second, beginning in the sixteenth century, such essential service facilities as inns, hotels, and charitable cemeteries for the itinerant[36] were being built more frequently, to accommodate merchants who traveled far from home. Finally, route books were being produced to provide the fullest possible information about routes. Prior to the period of increasing commercial activity and literacy in the late Ming, route information circulated only by private maps and word of mouth within the relatively closed networks of established mercantile families. As other families entered the world of itinerant commerce, the need for a published version of this information increased. (We find testimony to this need in a new and popular literary genre of the late Ming, the tales of lost merchants.[37])

The circulation of route books made the routes themselves more accessible, and herein lies the importance of route books to the development of commodity circulation during the Ming-Qing period. Books charting the best available routes should be thought of as counterparts in the commercial world of technological manuals, which as it happens were also being produced just at this time. Such manuals were published to provide information about the best available technology, thereby overcoming the various forms of inertia that stood in the way of the diffusion of technical knowledge. Better knowledge of superior agricultural technology meant improved productivity. So, too, a fuller knowledge of routes could increase the viability of commercial exchange by eliminating technical ignorance. Bureaucrats on assignment and gentry on the Grand Tour would of course benefit from the publication of route books: the laments of traveling officials in the early Ming about the difficulty of taking the postal roads attest to the need for better knowledge of the routes they traveled.[38] But these officials were not the ones restructuring routes, building facilities, or producing route books. This was the work of merchants and the effect of the expansion of the Chinese economy in the late Ming.

The route book should thus be seen not only as a repository of information about routes in Ming-Qing China, but also as an element in the gradual process of improving the technical conditions for commodity circulation from the sixteenth century forward. Their further study should be rewarding on both counts.

Notes

1. The prevalence of Japanese route books in local museums throughout Japan encourages me to hope that similar materials have been preserved at the local level in China. For example, in the small holding of written materials in Okuya, the village museum of Azuma, Nagano prefecture, which was on the old Nakasendō route, one can see displayed a copy of a pictorial route book entitled *Dōchū annaisho* [A guide to the Tōkaidō and Nakasendō routes], several other printed route books, and a few handwritten travel diaries. The Tōkaidō and Nakasendō were the two highways between Edo and Kyoto—one along the coast and the other through the mountains—under the direct control of the Tokugawa shogunate.

2. Aoyama Sadao, *Tō-Sō jidai no kōtsū to chishi chizu no kenkyū* [Studies of the transportation systems and the gazetteers and maps of the Tang and Song periods] (Tokyo: Yoshikawa Kōbunkan, 1963), pp. 456ff; Liu Guanglu and Hu Huiqiu, "Fangzhi fazhan shilüe" [A brief history of the development of local gazetteers], pt. 1, *Zhongguo difang shizhi*, 1982, no. 1, pp. 30-31. This usage continued very occasionally into the Ming-Qing period for county gazetteers, such as *Haiyan xian tujing* (1624), and for mountain gazetteers, such as *Huayue tujing* (1851). The author of the latter was intentionally seeking to imitate "the ancient style" of gazetteer compilation, which may explain his choice of title (see Wu's preface, 1a).

3. Wang Zhideng, *Keyue zhilüe* [Abridged record of traveling to the south] (1881 WZ ed.), 1a.

4. Aoyama, *Tō-Sō jidai*, pp. 546-48.

5. Pictorial representations of the coast and the Grand Canal, and also of the Yangzi and Yellow rivers, were also being published in Ming-Qing scholarly writings, such as Zhang Huang's *Tushu bian* [The illustrated compendium] (1613); however, these maps were made as components of security studies, not as guides for navigation. Maritime navigators relied instead on what were called compass manuals (*zhenjing*), in which routes were documented as a series of fixed places, such as islands or coastal markers, followed by compass bearings indicating direction between consecutive points. The Peking official Zhang Xie, in the course of compiling his *Dongxi yangkao* [Study of maritime countries to the east and the west] of 1617, relied on what he refers to as "old compass manuals" to write the section

on nautical routes, in which he preserves this format (*Dongxi yangkao* (Peking: Zhonghua Shuju, 1981), pp. 20, 171-85). A Fujian compass manual from the sixteenth century, and another from the early eighteenth, held in the Bodleian Library at Oxford, have been reprinted in Xiang Da, ed., *Liangzhong haidao zhenjing* [Two compass manuals of maritime routes] (Peking: Zhonghua Shuju, 1961). For a study of the former, see Tian Rukang, "*Duhai fangcheng*—Zhongguo diyiben keyin de shuilubu" [The first printed Chinese rutter— *Routes for crossing the ocean*], in *Explorations in the History of Science and Technology in China*, ed. Li Guohao et al. (Shanghai: Classics Publishing House, 1982), pp. 301-308.

6. The only precursor that comes to mind in the history of route documentation in China is the journey record (*chenglu* or *chengji*), which was a diary of a single journey. Some of these from the eleventh and twelfth centuries have been translated by Eduoard Chavannes in "Voyageurs Chinois chez les Khitan et les Joutchen" (2 pts.), *Journal Asiatique*, nos. 6, 8 (1897, 1898). The most detailed of these, in which the Song official Xu Kangzong recounts his official embassy to the Jurchen capital of Huining (in present-day Acheng county, Heilongjiang) in 1124, was reproduced by Gu Yanwu in his *Tianxia junguo libing shu* [Strengths and weaknesses of the various regions of the empire] (1662; repr. Shanghai: Shangwu Yinshuguan, 1936), 3:85a-91b. Route records abound in the Ming period. Wang Shizhen, for instance, wrote interesting records of his journeys in 1672 and 1695 by stage route to Sichuan (*Shudao yicheng ji* [Record of a journey by postal station along the Sichuan Road]; and *Qinshu yicheng ji* [Record of a journey by postal station through Shaanxi to Sichuan], both reprinted in XF).

7. Almanacs predating 1597, all from the Yuan period, do not include sections on routes; e.g., *Xinbian shiwen leiyao qizha qingqian* [Abridged encyclopedia and forms of correspondence as good as ready cash, newly revised] (1324; repr. Tokyo: Koten Kenkyūkai, 1963); *Xinkan zengxiu leibian shulin guangji* [Encyclopedic notes from all manner of books, enlarged and newly reprinted]; and the various editions of *Shilin guangji* [Extensive notes concerning all manner of affairs].

8. Chinese almanacs were not unique in including route sections. *The Farmer's Almanack*, first published in Boston in 1792 and annually thereafter, started including a section on stage routes in its second edition. This inclusion reflects the proliferation of stage lines in New

England during the last two decades of the eighteenth century. The stage lists continued to be included up until the 1845 edition, which was the edition in which the *Almanack* first printed a list of the towns served by the railroads and the distances covered. The 1830s were the turning point from horse-drawn transport to railroads in New England. The *Almanack* recognized this by dropping the old stage routes in subsequent editions. See George Kittredge, *The Old Farmer and his Almanack* (Cambridge, Mass.: Harvard University Press, 1920), pp. 286-304.

9. The early-Ming stage system is described in Hoshi Ayao, "Transportation in the Ming Period," *Acta Asiatica*, no. 38 (1980), p. 14.

10. Three Qing merchant manuals, including 5.4.4, are examined in Ju Qingyuan, "Qing kaiguan qianhou de sanbu shangren zhuzuo" [Three Qing merchant works from the time of the opening of the treaty ports], first published in 1937 and reprinted in *Zhongguo jindaishi luncong: shehui jingji* [Essays on modern Chinese history: socioeconomy], ed. Bao Zunpeng (Hong Kong: Zhengzhong Shuju, 1958), pp. 205-44.

11. Caroline Blunden and Mark Elvin, *Cultural Atlas of China* (New York: Facts on File, 1983), p. 94.

12. *Luoyang xianzhi* (1745; repr. 1924), 2.45a-47a; *Songjiang fuzhi* (1631), 2.18a-19a.

13. *Fugu xianzhi* (1783), *juan* 2.

14. *Songjiang fuzhi* (1631), 25.5b-14b.

15. *Yongqing xianzhi* (1779), 13.5a-7b.

16. The origins of the stage system are explored in Aoyama, *Tō-Sō jidai*, pp. 51ff. The most thorough study of the Ming system is Su Tongbing, *Mingdai yidi zhidu* [The Ming postal system] (Taibei: Zhongguo Congshu Bianshen Weiyuanhui, 1969). An overview of the Qing system may be found in Huang Caigeng, "Qingchao yichuan jianshu" [An outline of the postal relay system], *Qingshi yanjiu tongxun*, 1983, no. 2. Jin Feng has published three studies of Qing-period stage routes in Mongolia and Manchuria: see *Menggu shi lunwen xuanji* [Selected essays on Mongolian history], ed. Huhehaote shi Menggu yuwen lishi xuehui [Huhehot society for the study of Mongolian language and history], vol. 3 (Huhehot, 1983). The most detailed reconstruction of the routes of the state courier system in

any period is Yan Gengwang's ten-volume study, *Tangdai jiaotong tukao* [A study in maps of communications in the Tang dynasty] (Taibei: Zhongyang Yanjiuyuan Lishi Yuyan Yanjiuso, 1985-).

17. The Sichuan route was changed in the Shunzhi era, for example, though the old route was reinstated in 1684. See Wu Zhenyu, *Yangji zhai conglu* [Notes from Yangji Studio] (1896; repr. Peking: Beijing Guji Chubanshe, 1983), p. 320.

18. Traveling by post was a privilege that could sometimes be conferred on people without offical rank in recognition of their services. In the early decades of the Ming, a monk named Xinghui, who had been called to Nanjing in 1406 to assist in the editing of various imperially sponsored works including the *Tripitaka* of 1418 and the *Yongle Encyclopedia*, was given the right to travel by postal station when he retired to Ningbo, even though he had declined the state-conferred Buddhist title of Left Enlightener, which would have given him sufficient rank (*Yinxian zhi* (1788), 20.21b). The same honor was extended in 1647 to Qian Qianyi when he resigned from service to the Manchus and returned home under the disgrace of having served two dynasties (see Frederic Wakeman, "Romantics, Stoics, and Martyrs in Seventeenth-Century China," *Journal of Asian Studies* 43:4 (August 1984), p. 637). Arrogating the privilege of traveling by post without authorization, even by someone of rank, was a punishable offense. The Hongwu emperor in the 1370s reprimanded the Marquis of Henan, Lu Zhongheng—to whose son he had married his fifth daughter—for making personal use of the military courier system (see Edward Dreyer, *Early Ming China* (Stanford: Stanford University Press, 1982), p. 104).

19. The great traveler and geographer Xu Hongzu used the stage system in a private capacity when he was traveling in Guangxi in the 1630s, although this may have been necessary in areas where there were no other travel services. Concerning Xu's use of the stage system and his reliance on corveed transport labor, see Zhou Ningxia et al., "*Xu Xiake youji* yuanshi chaoben de faxian yu tantao" [The discovery of the original manuscript of *The diaries of Xu Xiake* and its assessment], *Zhonghua wenshi luncong*, no. 12 (1979), pp. 177-78.

20. Hoshi, "Transportation," p. 13.

21. Shiba Yoshinobu, *Commerce and Society in Sung China* (Ann Arbor: Center for Chinese Studies, Univ. of Michigan, 1970), p. 4.

22. Mark Elvin, *The Pattern of the Chinese Past* (Stanford: Stanford University Press, 1973), pp. 135-39.

23. Timothy Brook, "The Spatial Structure of Ming Local Administration," *Late Imperial China* 6:1 (June 1985), p. 45.

24. Hoshi has argued for recognizing the considerable impact of commerce on the expansion of the stage system itself, noting that "from the beginning of the sixteenth century onwards the primary concern in constructing new stage routes was their utility as commercial routes" ("Transportation," p. 29).

25. *Sishui xianzhi* (1662), 11.2b.

26. Timothy Brook, "Guides for Vexed Travelers: A Supplement," *Ch'ing-shih wen-t'i* 4:6 (December 1981), pp. 134-37.

27. Elvin, *The Pattern of the Chinese Past*, p. 131.

28. The common assertion that there were no improvements in transport technology in the Ming has yet to be proven. Recent work in transport technology in medieval England has reversed the accepted view that the expansion of the English economy in the twelfth and thirteenth centuries occurred without any technological improvements. Part of what underlay this expansion and the proliferation of markets in the mid-fourteenth century was a previously unnoticed shift from ox-hauling to horse-hauling. This switch was not accompanied by any documentable advances in technology, but it doubled the rate at which goods could circulate in local markets: a technical rather than technological revolution, which broke through a major bottleneck in the English economy. See John Langdon, "Horse-Hauling in Medieval England," *Past and Present*, no. 103 (May 1984), pp. 37-66. (For a discussion of horse- versus ox-hauling in China, see Joseph Needham, *Science and Civilisation in China* IV:2 (Cambridge: Cambridge University Press, 1965), pp. 312, 326.) There may be technical elements of similar impact in the Chinese case that historians of the Ming-Qing period have overlooked.

29. *Wujiang zhi* (1488), 5.26b. The subsequent edition, not published until 1561, is entitled *Wujiang xianzhi*.

30. Timothy Brook, "The Merchant Network in Sixteenth Century China," *Journal of the Economic and Social History of the Orient* 24:2 (May 1981), pp. 204-205.

31. Yuan-li Wu, *The Spatial Economy of Communist China* (New York: Praeger, 1967), p. 125.

32. Long Wenbin, ed., *Ming huiyao* (1887; repr. Peking: Zhonghua Shuju, 1956), vol. 2, p. 1455.

33. Ray Huang, *Taxation and Governmental Finance in Sixteenth-Century Ming China* (Cambridge: Cambridge University Press, 1974), pp. 317-18.

34. See, e.g., Evariste-Régis Huc, *A Journey through the Chinese Empire* (New York: Harper, 1855), vol. 1, p. 200, concerning the uneven maintenance of roads in Sichuan, and vol. 2, p. 281, concerning the poor state of repair of official roads in the Wuhan area.

35. Jan De Vries, *The Economy of Europe in an Age of Crisis, 1600-1750* (Cambridge: Cambridge University Press, 1976), p. 175.

36. Huang Liuhong in his administrative handbook of 1694, *Fuhui quanshu* (repr. 1893), 26.13b, argues that local magistrates should set up charitable cemeteries as a way of dealing specifically with the abandoned coffins of merchants who die away from home and have no one to oversee their burial. For an English translation, see *A Complete Book Concerning Happiness and Benevolence*, tr. Djang Chu (Tuscon: University of Arizona Press, 1984), p. 554.

37. See, e.g., Zhao Jishi, *Jiyuan ji suoji* [Reliance garden relies on what it relies on] (1695; repr. Taibei: Wenxing Shudian, 1965), vol. 2, p. 212. For other literary descriptions of the difficulties merchants encountered on the road, see Huang Renyu (Ray Huang), "Cong San yan kan wan Ming shangren" [Merchants in the late Ming as seen in *Three sets of tales*], *Xianggang zhongwen daxue Zhongguo wenhua yanjiusuo xuebao* 7:1 (1974), pp. 139-43.

38. E.g., Yao Guangxiao (1335-1418) complains in a poem that the post road from Nanjing up to the mouth of the Grand Canal was "bafflingly hard to follow" (*Wujiang xianzhi* (1561), 1.10b).

Bibliography

1. National Stage Networks

1.1. Stage Route Books

1.1.1. *Yizhan lucheng* 驛站路程
[Stage routes]
  1 *juan*, anonymous.
  1891 XF reprint.
  The 15 official courier routes from Peking to Jehol and the provincial capitals.

1.1.2. *Tianxia luchengtu* 天下路程途
[Routes of the empire]
  Pub. Hongwen Ge 宏文閣 (Peking).
  Qing. BL has an incomplete copy of 14 pages.
  20 overland routes; extremely abbreviated.

1.2. Stage Route Chapters in Almanacs

1.2.1. *Wanbao quanshu* 萬寶全書
[The treasury almanac]
  37 *juan*, attributed to Ai Nanying 艾南英 (1583-1646), pub. Chen Huaixuan 陳懷軒 (Jianyang, Fujian); preface signed Chen Jiru 陳繼儒 (1558-1639).
  1628. Tobunken.
  Variant editions:
  (1) undated, in 35 *juan*, pub. Wang Taiyuan 王泰源 (Jianyang); preface signed Chen Renxi 陳仁錫 (1579-1634; cf. B68, B108). Naikaku.
  (2) 1641, in 34 *juan*, entitled *Quanshu beikao* 全書備考 [The fully researched almanac], ed. Zheng Shangxuan 鄭尚玄 (Zuihua Jushi 醉花居士), pub. Renrui Tang 人瑞堂. Jimbun.

(3) undated, in 24 *juan*, re-entitled *Wanbao quanshu*, ed. Lushui Shanren 煁水山人, pub. Zuihua Ju 醉花居. Tobunken.

(4) 1747, in 30 *juan*, pub. Shuye Tang 書業堂 (Suzhou); dated preface signed Mao Huanwen 毛煥文 (cf. 1.2.4). Jimbun, Tobunken.

(5) 1806 reprint, with Mao's preface dated 1739. Tobunken.

(6) 1886 reprint, ed. Saoye Shanfang 埽葉山房. Tobunken.

Bibliographic notice: Niida 13-11, 13-12, 14-7; Sakai 10, 11, 13; EW 3.

The second *juan* gives the early-Ming stage network of 10 routes, 7 from Peking and 3 from Nanjing. It is extremely doubtful that either Ai Nanying or Chen Jiru, both eminent figures in the late-Ming literary world, had anything to do with this almanac; the publisher was simply capitalizing on their renown.

1.2.2. *Xuehai buqiuren* 學海不求人
[The reliable sea of learning]

22 *juan*, anonymous.

Wanli era. Tobunken (*juan* 10-17 missing).

1614 reprint, revised into 34 *juan*, under the title *Wanbao quanshu*, ed. Chonghuai 冲懷 (Guangzhou), pub. Xiong Duishan 熊對山 (Jianyang). Tobunken.

Bibliographic notice: Niida 13-10, 14-5; Sakai 14; EW 2.

15 routes: the 14 Ming stage routes linking Peking and the provincial capitals, and a river route from Guangdong via Jiangxi to Peking.

1.2.3. *Wanjin quanshu* 萬錦全書
[The tapestry almanac]

10 *juan*, anonymous.

Wanli era. Tobunken.

Bibliographic notice: Niida 14-1.

Same routes as 1.2.2.

1.2.4. *Wanbao quanshu* 萬寶全書
[The treasury almanac]

20 *juan*, pub. Jingyi Tang 經義堂 (Suzhou); preface signed Mao Huanwen (cf. 1.2.1), dated 1739.

1823. Tobunken.

20 stage routes from Peking to various parts of the empire.

This almanac has been derived from 1.2.1.

1.2.5. *Wuche bajin* 五車拔錦
[The voluminous tapestry]

    33 *juan*, ed. Xu Sanyou 徐三友, pub. Zheng Shikui 鄭世魁 (both of Jianyang); dated preface signed Yu Shengshu 余生書.

    1597. Tobunken.

    Bibliographic notice: Niida 13-5; Sakai 1.

    43 stage routes. The term *wuche* ("five carriages") is an allusion to the *Zhuang Zi*, in which the philosopher Hui Yuan was said to have traveled with five carriages full of books, deemed to represent all written knowledge (translated in Burton Watson, *Chuang Tzu* [New York: Columbia University Press, 1968], p. 374).

1.2.6. *Wanyong zhengzong* 萬用正宗
[The correct source for a myriad practical uses]

    43 *juan*, pub. Yu Xiangdou 余象斗 (Jianyang).

    1599. Tobunken (with notes by Niida Noboru dated 1955).

    Bibliographic notice: DMB 1612; EW 1; Niida 13-2; Sakai 7.

    44 routes. This is the best extant Ming almanac.

1.2.7. *Zhushu bolan* 諸書博覽
[The almanac for which all books have been consulted]

    37 *juan*, ed. Cheng Mingfu 承明甫, pub. Yang Qinzhai 楊欽齋 (Jianyang); colophon signed Yang Qinyang 楊欽陽.

    1604. Naikaku.

    1610 edition entitled *Wanshu yuanhai* 萬書淵海 [The complete library], ed. Guang Hanzi 廣寒子, pub. Yang Qinzhai. Sonkeikaku.

    Bibliographic notice: Niida 13-8; Sakai 4, 8.

    The 1604 edition has the same routes as 1.2.5, the 1610 edition the same routes as 1.2.6.

1.2.8 *Xuehai qunyu* 學海群玉
[Gems of wisdom in the sea of learning]

    23 *juan*, ed. Wu Weizi 武緯子, pub. Xiong Chongyu 熊冲宇 (both of Jianyang).

    1607. Tobunken.

    Bibliographic notice: Niida 13-3; Sakai 5.

    Same routes as 1.2.6.

1.2.9 *Jiyu quanshu* 積玉全書
[The gems-of-wisdom almanac]

> 32 *juan*, ed. Li Guangyu 李光裕 (Nanping), pub. Liu
> Xingwo 劉興我 (Jianyang); preface signed Sun Deguang
> 孫德光 .
> Chongzhen era. Tobunken.
> Bibliographic notice: Niida 14-4; Sakai 12.
> Same routes as 1.2.6.

1.2.10. *Wanyong zhengzong buqiuren quanbian* 萬用正宗不求人全編
[The reliable and correct source for a myriad practical uses, complete
edition]

> 35 *juan*, ed. Long Yangzi 龍陽子, pub. Yu Xiangdou (cf.
> 1.2.6).
> 1607, with preface dated 1609. Naikaku, Sonkeikaku,
> Tobunken.
> Bibliographic notice: Niida 13-7; Sakai 7.
> 36 routes; 8 of the last 11 routes of 1.2.6 have been cut in
> this condensed version of that almanac.

1.2.11. *Wanjuan xingluo* 萬卷星羅
[An almanac culled from volumes as numerous as the stars]

> 36 *juan*, ed. Xu Zengying 徐曾瀛, pub. Tian Lesheng
> 天樂生 .
> 1600. Tobunken (missing *juan* 1, 20, 21).
> Bibliographic notice: Niida 13-6; Sakai 3.
> 33 routes; routes #16 to #18 have been removed from those
> in 1.2.10.

1.3. Books of Stage Routes Centered on a Province

1.3.1. *Zhejiang zhi gesheng chengxian* 浙江至各省程限
[Routes and the times allotted to travel them from Zhejiang to other
provinces]

> 115 pages, anonymous.
> Tongzhi era. LC.
> The stage routes given are based on the handbooks
> imperially ordered in 1751 and 1775. Stage routes had
> ratings giving the amount of time a courier was permitted to
> take between one station and the next (cf. 2.1.1).

1.4. Master List of Stage Routes

1.4.1. *(Qinding) Fangyu lucheng kaolüe* 欽定方輿路程考略
[An abridged study by imperial order of all routes in the realm]
By Wang Shihong 汪士鈜, ed. Li Duo 李鐸.
Compiled 1707-1708, re-edited in the Qianlong era but never published. LC has a 3-fascicle fragment in manuscript giving stage routes in Shanxi province.

2. Provincial Stage Networks

2.1. Route Books Published by the Ministry of War

2.1.1. *Zhejiang dengchu chengzhan ce* 浙江等處程站冊
[Handbook of routes and stations in Zhejiang]
     1 *juan*, pub. Ministry of War.
     1751 (ordered compiled in 1749).
     1775 revised edition. Tobunken.
     21 routes: 16 in main text, 5 in supplement.

2.1.2. *Hubei sheng yizhan sizhi chengtu lishu xianxing shike qingce*
湖北省驛站四至程途里數限行時刻清冊
[Official handbook of the locations of stations, distances of routes, and times allotted for travel in Hubei province]
     4 *juan*, pub. Ministry of War.
     1802. Tobunken.
     42 routes within the province.

2.1.3. *E sheng yingzhi yichuan huibian* 鄂省營制驛傳彙編
[Compendium of military courier stations in Hubei province]
     4 *juan*, pub. Ministry of War.
     1889. Tobunken.
     32 routes in the third *juan*, as well as the internal route network of each county in the fourth. The first two *juan* give regulations regarding the operation of the system.

2.1.4. *E sheng manlü yingxun zhouxian yichuan quantu* 鄂省滿綠營汎
州縣驛傳全圖
[Subprefectural and county-level maps of the military relay network among the posts of the Manchu Army of the Green Standard in Hubei province]
     4 fascicles, pub. Ministry of War.
     Late 19th century. Tobunken.
     The first three fascicles provide detailed county-level route maps for Hubei; the fourth includes maps of the Army's pasture lands.

2.1.5. *Hunan sheng yizhan chengtu lishu xianxing gongwen shike ce*
湖南省驛站程途里數限行公文時刻册
[Handbook of the stations, routes, distances, and times allotted for
posts in Hunan province]
    1 *juan*, pub. Ministry of War.
    1802. Tobunken.
    47 routes. Identical in format to 2.1.2.

2.1.6. *Hunan jiangyu yichuan zongzuan* 湖南疆域驛傳總纂
[Compendium of courier stations within the borders of Hunan]
    11 juan, pub. Ministry of War.
    1822.
    1888 reprint by Qianjin Shanfang 慥硶山房; dated preface by
    Guo Songtao 郭嵩燾 (1818-91). Tobunken.
    48 routes, plus the internal route network of each county.

2.2. Privately Published Route Books

2.2.1. *Guangdong sheng geyi lishu* 廣東省各驛里數
[The distances between courier stations in Guangdong province]
    2 *juan*, anonymous.
    Qing. Jimbun.
    Stage routes between all counties in the province.

3. Grain Transport Routes

3.1. The Grand Canal

3.1.1. *You Juyong guan zhi Yangzhou fu hetu* 由居庸關至楊州府河圖
[Map of the river from Juyong Pass to Yangzhou prefecture]
    30 pages, anonymous.
    Qing manuscript. Tobunken.
    A route map indicating topographical landmarks and distances between major points along the way.

3.1.2. *Caohe tuzhi* 漕河圖志
[Illustrated gazetteer of the Grand Canal]
    8 *juan*, by Wang Qiong 王瓊.
    Hongzhi era. Sonkeikaku.
    More a gazetteer than a route book. For a list of other Ming works on the Grand Canal, see Huang 8.7a-8a.

3.1.3. *Yunhe tu zongshuo* 運河圖總說
[A general commentary on a map of the Grand Canal]
    Anonymous.
    Qing manuscript. LC.
    Includes a series of essays on the construction and maintenance of the Grand Canal.

3.1.4. *Jiangbei yuncheng* 江北運程
[The grain transport route north of the Yangzi River]
    41 *juan*, by Dong Xun 董恂 (1807-92; cf. 3.2.1), ed. Zhao Xihe 趙熙和, pub. Longwen Tang 龍文堂 (Peking).
    1867. Jimbun, Shifan.
    The opening *juan* is a route book of the Grand Canal; the following 40 furnish detailed commentary on the history of places along the way. Dong completed this work in 1860, four years after his appointment as circuit intendant in charge of waterways in southern Zhili.

3.2. The Xiang River Route

3.2.1. *Chucao jiangcheng* 楚漕江程

[The river route for the Hunan grain transport]

16 *juan*, by Dong Xun (cf. 3.1.4), pub. Longwen Zhai 龍文齋 .

1877. Harvard, LC (2 copies), Shifan.

The first *juan* is a route book, the latter 15 a detailed commentary. Dong completed this work in 1854, two years after his appointment as grain intendant of Hunan. Published in a uniform edition with 3.1.4.

4. Imperial Household Routes

4.1. Peking-Manchuria Route

4.1.1. *Donghua men dao Xingjing lucheng tu* 東華門到興京路程圖
[Map of the route from Donghua Gate to Xingjing]
  142 pages, anonymous.
  Qing manuscript. Toyo.
  Bibliographic notice: EW 18.
  A route map from the Imperial City in Peking to the former
  Manchu capital of 1605-1621 in Liaodong east of Mukden
  (Shenyang).

4.1.2 *Shengjing lucheng* 盛京路程
[The route to the Great Capital]
  2 fascicles, anonymous.
  Qing manuscript. Toronto.
  A small-format map of the same route charted in 4.1.1, both
  going and returning. The "great capital" is Mukden.

4.2. Routes to the Imperial Tombs

4.2.1. *Xiling xi lucheng* 西陵絀路程
[The route to the Western Tombs, in detail]
  Guangxu era.
  Variant manuscript copies:
   (1) 37 pages. Columbia.
   (2) 40 pages. Tobunken.
   (3) 46 pages. Tobunken.
  The route goes from the north gate of the Forbidden City to
  Yi county. All copies include the tomb of the Daoguang
  emperor (Mu Ling), who died in 1849, but not that of the
  Guangxu emperor (Chong Ling). Tobunken also has two
  route diaries of officials who traveled to the tombs. LC has a
  map of the route taken by the Jiaqing emperor in 1811,
  misfiled with 6.4.1.

4.2.2. *Dongling xi lucheng* 東陵細路程
[The route to the Eastern Tombs, in detail]
    Variant manuscript copies:
      (1) 33 pages; Tongzhi era. Tobunken.
      (2) 31 pages; Guangxu era. Columbia.
    The route goes from the east gate of the Imperial City to
Zunhua county. The Columbia copy includes the Tongzhi
emperor's tomb (Hui Ling), whereas the Tobunken copy does
not. Tobunken also has a colored map and two diaries of this
route.

4.2.3. *Dongdao tushuo bianlan* 東道圖說便覽
[Annotated and easy-to-use map of the route to the Eastern Tombs]
    By Provincial Administration Commissioner Yuchang 裕長.
    1880. Tobunken.
    The first fascicle is a map, the second a detailed description
of the route by stages.

5. Comprehensive Route Books

5.1. Universal Route Books

5.1.1. *Yitong lucheng tuji* 一統路程圖記
[The comprehensive illustrated route book]

> 8 *juan*, by Huang Bian 黃汴 (Xiuning), ed. Wu Xiu 吳岫 (Suzhou).
> 1570. Naikaku.
> 1617 edition under the title *Shuilu lucheng* 水陸路程 [Water and land routes], ed. Shang Jun 商濬 (Guiji) (cf. L35, L36). Sonkeikaku.
> Bibliographic notice: EW 4, 5.
> 158 routes, numbered as 144 in the table of contents (the last of these is missing from the 1570 edition). This is the earliest authoritative route book.

5.1.2. *Shangcheng yilan* 商程一覽
[Merchant routes at a glance]

> 2 *juan*, ed. Vice-Magistrate Tao Chengqing 陶承慶 (Xinyu), pub. Liu Dayi 劉大易 (Jianyang).
> Wanli era. Naikaku.
> 1635 edition under the title *Keshang yilan shuilu lucheng* 客商一覽水陸路程 [Water and land routes at a glance for traveling merchants], credited to Huang Bian, ed. Li Jinde 李晉德 . Yamaguchi University.
> Bibliographic notice: EW 6, Franke 8.2.7, Mizuno.
> The route network is the same as 5.1.1, with the addition of three new routes appended to route #94. Local products by county have been added in a panel at the top of each page.

5.1.3. *Shiwo zhouxing* 示我周行
[Traveling everywhere on my own]

> 3 *juan*, pub. Hehe Tang 鶴和堂 (Bixi, Anhui); dated preface signed Qingniu Daoren 青牛道人 (Bixi).
> 1694. Naikaku (part of third fascicle missing).
> Pirated reprint in 6 *juan*, dated 1694, pub. Qianyi Tang 謙益堂 . BL.
> 1774 edition, ed. Lai Shengyuan 賴盛遠 (Liancheng,

Fujian); pub. Linglan Tang 靈蘭堂 and Shancheng Tang
善成堂. Naikaku (2 copies).
1787 edition, ed. Hehe Tang, pub. Baoshan Tang 寶善堂.
LC.
Bibliographic notice: EW 7, 7d.
144 routes. The 1774 edition appears to have enjoyed the
widest circulation of any route book.

5.1.4. *Shiwo zhouxing* 示我周行
[Traveling everywhere on my own]
    6 *juan*, ed. Qiufangxin Zhai 求放心齋 (Suzhou); dated preface
signed Miaoyin Jushi 妙因居士 (Nanjing) (cf. 5.1.5).
1738, pub. Cuiyin Shanfang 翠隱山房. Toyo.
1738, pub. Yingde Tang 英德堂. BL, Tobunken.
Bibliographic notice: EW 7b.
145 routes (an extra route in Fujian has been added to those
in 5.1.3).
Qiufangxin Zhai was the original editor and publisher in
1742 of Pu Qilong 浦起龍, *Shitong tongshi* 史通通釋 [A comprehensive explication of *Generalities on historiography*].
Wilkinson has identified him as Chen Jin 陳勤 of Ningbo.

5.1.5. *Zhouxing beilan* 周行備覽
[Ready reference for traveling everywhere]
    3 *juan*, pub. Yisheng Tang 翼聖堂 (Hangzhou); dated preface
signed Miaoyin Jushi (cf. 5.1.4).
1738. Harvard.
Later revised edition, also dated 1738. Tobunken.
Bibliographic notice: EW 7a.
151 routes in the Harvard edition, 161 routes in the
Tobunken edition. Extra routes have been added to those in
5.1.3 for southern Guangdong, especially Qiongzhou
prefecture.

5.1.6. *Tianxia lucheng* 天下路程
[The routes of the empire]
    3 *juan*, ed. Chen Qiji 陳其楫 (Jian'an).
1741. Naikaku.
Bibliographic notice: EW 7a.
Reduces the number of routes to 130 by cutting and
combining routes in the third *juan*. The first *juan* provides
information for merchants.

5.2. Provincial Route Books

5.2.1. *Tianxia shuilu lucheng xinbian* 天下水陸路程新編
[Water and land routes of the empire, new edition]

    2 *juan*, ed. Xiao Yizhang 蕭奕璋 (Qingyang, Shaanxi), with additional material by Wang Qi 汪淇 (ca. 1600-ca. 1670) [Danyizi 澹漪子] (cf. 5.4.2) and Dai Shiqi 戴士奇 (cf. 5.4.3), both of Huizhou; pub. Pangui Tang 攀桂堂 (Guangzhou). 1728. BL.

Bibliographic notice: EW 8.

This is a route book for Guangdong province. The first *juan* gives sights of and routes from Peking, and 12 routes from Guangzhou (some via Nanchang); the second *juan* provides fiscal data for Guangdong counties (prepared by Dai Shiqi), plus 8 routes within the province. Advice for travelers has been added by Tan Yizi, dated 1728. The name of another publisher, Shiji Tang 師濟堂 of Peking, appears at the beginning of the second *juan*.

5.2.2. *Xinjiang daoli biao* 新疆道里表
[Chart of the roads and distances in Xinjiang]

    8 pp., included at the end of the first *juan* of *Xiyu suotan* 西域瑣談 [Desultory comments on the western regions] by Chunyuan 椿園.

1778 manuscript. Toronto.

This guide to Xinjiang routes, written while the author was in Kucha, begins with the route from Jiayuguan, the western terminus of the Great Wall, to Hami, and from there traces a network of routes spreading west: via Pichan to Turfan; from Turfan north to Urumchi and west via Kucha to Aksu; from Aksu south to Ush-Turfan, north to Ili, and west to Yarkand; from Yarkand west to Kashgar and south to Khotan; and from Hami north via Barkul and Urumchi to Ili. According to the distances given, these routes cover a total of 12,430 *li*. Xinjiang was incorporated into China as a military protectorate in 1757.

5.3. Guidebook Abridgements

5.3.1. *Dumen jilüe* 都門紀略
[Abridged notes on the capital]

    4 *juan*, by Yang Jingting 楊靜亭 (Tongzhou, Zhili); ed. Xu

Yongnian 徐永年 ; route section ed. Sun Gao 孫皋 (Tongcheng, Anhui); pub. Ronglu Tang 榮祿堂 (Peking).
1864. Tobunken.
1872, 1873, 1876, 1878, 1879 reprints. Harvard, Kyoto, Shifan, Tobunken.
1880 reprint. Tobunken.
1883, 1886, 1887, 1888, 1891 reprints under the title *Chaoshi congzai* 朝市叢載 [Complete notes for going to market], in 8 *juan*. Author's collection, Harvard, Shifan, Toronto, Toyo.
1907, 1909 reprints under original title. Harvard (3 copies), Shifan.
1971 reprint (Taibei: Wenhai Chubanshe). Harvard, Tobunken.
Bibliographic notice: EW 15.
20 routes from Peking, abridged from the 1774 edition of 5.1.3. In the 1870s editions the route to Jiangnan has been deleted; it is restored in subsequent editions.

5.4. Merchant Manuals

5.4.1. *Shishang leiyao* 士商類要
[The encyclopedia for gentry and merchants]
    4 *juan*, by Cheng Chunyu 程春宇 (Xin'an); preface signed Fang Yigui 方一桂 (She).
    1626. Sonkeikaku.
    Bibliographic notice: Mizuno.
    100 routes, 53 for routes south of the Yangzi in the first *juan* and 47 for routes north of the Yangzi in the second. The rest of the book is a manual for traveling merchants.

5.4.2. *Shishang yaolan* 士商要覽
[Essentials for gentry and merchants at a glance]
    3 *juan*, ed. Wang Qi [Danyizi] (cf. 5.2.1).
    Seventeenth century. Naikaku.
    Bibliographic notice: EW 10.
    Same routes as 5.4.1.

5.4.3. *Lucheng yaolan* 路程要覽
[Essentials of routes at a glance]
    2 *juan*, ed. Dai Shiqi (cf. 5.2.1); pub. Wanxuan Lou 萬選樓; preface signed Cui Tingzi 崔亭子.

Yongzheng era(?). Naikaku.
Bibliographic notice: EW 11.
Cui states in his preface that the route section of this book is
a copy of 5.4.2, with notes on local products appended. The
information for merchants has been dropped.

5.4.4. *Shanggu bianlan* 商賈便覽
[The easy-to-consult merchant manual]
      8 *juan*, by Wu Zhongfu 吳中孚.
      1792. Tobunken.
      Bibliographic notice: EW 12.
      75 routes, abridged from 5.1.5. Northern and Yangzi Valley
routes have been most heavily cut in favor of southern
routes. The route section of this manual has been reduced to
one *juan*.

5.5. Pilgrim Route Books

5.5.1. *Canxue zhijin* 參學知津
[Knowing the fords on the way to knowledge]
      2 *juan*, by Xiancheng Ruhai 顯承如海, former abbot of
Kaihua Monastery 開化寺, ed. Yirun Yuanhong 儀潤源洪 of
Zhenji Monastery 眞寂寺 (both of Hangzhou).
      First published 1827.
      1876 reprint, with list of publication contributors. Harvard.
      56 routes, many with alternate routes given. Based on the
pilgrimage experience of the author. The introductory section
(6b-10a) includes "The Ten Essentials of Pilgrimage," which
has been paraphrased in Reginald Johnston, *Buddhist China*
(London: John Murray, 1913), pp. 158-67. Johnston's source
was a Fuzhou reprint of this guide entitled *Chao sida
mingshan luyin* 朝四大名山路引 [Guide for traveling to the
four famous mountains]. Yuanhong has appended a
place-name directory (*diyu mingmu* 地輿名目) at the end of
the book.

6. Guides for Specific Routes

6.1. Maritime Routes

6.1.1. Untitled, reprinted in *Gu hanghai tu kaoshi* 古航海圖考釋
[Study of old nautical maps]
> 69 pages, anonymous.
> 18th-century copy of a Ming original.
> 1980 reprint (Peking: Haiyang Chubanshe), with notes and an introductory essay by Zhang Xun 章巽 .
> Map of coastal route from Bohai Gulf to the mouth of the Pearl River, with route indicated sometimes by a navigation line (*chuanlu* 船路) and sometimes by written description.

6.2. Land Routes

6.2.1. *Tongjing dadao* 通京大道
[The great road to the capital]
> 87 pages, by Ma Chongxuan 馬崇塘; pub. Shanquan Tang 善全堂.
> 1870. Toyo.
> Bibliographic notice: EW 17.
> The route from the provincial capital of Yunnan to Peking.

6.2.2. *Zi Hankou zhi Xi'an lucheng* 自漢口至西安路程
[The route from Hankou to Xi'an]
> 7 pages, anonymous.
> Late Qing. Jimbun.
> Bibliographic notice: EW 19.
> Four routes: the main one, western and eastern ones, and a river route.

6.2.3. *Ru Dian lucheng kao* 入滇路程考.
[Notes on the land route to Yunnan]
> 1 *juan*, by Shi Fan 師範 (cf. 6.2.5, 6.3.4).
> Qing.
> 1891 XF edition.

6.2.4. *Ru Zang chengzhan* 入藏程站
[The route and stations for going to Tibet]
 1 *juan*, by Sheng Shengzu 盛繩祖.
 1891 ZF reprint.
 The route in eight stages from Chengdu, Sichuan, to Nielamu
 on the present-day border with Nepal.

6.2.5. *Ru Mian lucheng* 入緬路程
[The route to Burma]
 1 *juan*, by Shi Fan (cf. 6.2.3, 6.3.4).
 Qing.
 1891 XF reprint.

6.3. River Routes

6.3.1. *Jiangcheng Shu dao xianshi shu* 江程蜀道現勢書
[Handbook of the current conditions of the Yangzi route from
Sichuan]
 1 volume, by Fu Chongju 傅崇榘 (Chengdu).
 1904. Harvard.
 The route by water from Chengdu to Kobe, Japan, via
 Shanghai, plus a land route from Yichang to Chengdu.

6.3.2. *Xiajiang tukao* 峽江圖考
[An annotated map of the upper Yangzi]
 2 fascicles, by Jiang Guozhang 江國璋.
 1889. Gest, LC.
 1969 Yudi reprint of 1906 edition (with J17 and 6.3.3).
 Route outlines are given at the beginning and end of each
 fascicle for the route from Yichang, Hubei, to Chongqing,
 Sichuan; the rest is a sequence of pictures of the route.

6.3.3. *Xing Chuan biyao* 行川必要
[The essentials of traveling to Sichuan]
 50 pages, anonymous.
 1969 Yudi reprint of 1906 edition (with J17 and 6.3.2).
 Depicts the same route as 6.3.2. Sites along the shore are
 given without reference to distance. Includes advice for
 navigators at certain difficult points along the route.

6.3.4. *Ru Dian jianglu kao* 入滇江路考
[Notes on the Yangzi River route to Yunnan]
    1 *juan*, by Shi Fan (cf. 6.2.3, 6.2.5).
    Qing.
    1891 XF edition.

6.4. Local Routes

6.4.1. *Wutai shan daolu quantu* 五臺山道路全圖
[Complete map of the roads on Wutai Mountain]
    25 pages, anonymous.
    Qing. LC.
    A route map of the roads on this Buddhist mountain in
    Shanxi, giving distances.

Part II
Topographical and Institutional Gazetteers

Introduction

Local gazetteers are chronicles of the history, present conditions, and noted people of local areas, arranged by topic. Best known to historians are those compiled for administrative units, from the canton (*xiang*) and county (*xian*) up to the provincial level and finally the country as a whole.[1] But there are many other types of local gazetteer in the Chinese historiographical tradition. Most of these may be categorized, in the absence of any other convention, as topographical or institutional gazetteers. Rather than chronicling units in the state administrative structure, these gazetteers take as their subjects places—both topographical features and individual institutions—whose territorial definition is "natural" rather than administrative. At the topographical end of this category are the gazetteers of mountains, caves, and rivers; at the institutional end, the gazetteers of monasteries, temples, academies, and other institutions of that sort. Between these poles lie the ambiguous types, such as the dozen or so gazetteers of Hangzhou's scenic West Lake which generally record almost nothing about the lake, but concentrate on both the topography and institutions of the surrounding hills.

The generic term for gazetteer in Chinese is *zhi*. With a few exceptions, this is the term used in the titles of the works in this bibliography. *Shanzhi* are mountain gazetteers, though a gazetteer bearing the name of a mountain is sometimes a Buddhist monastic gazetteer posing under the monastery's mountain alias. True mountain gazetteers are the most common type of topographical or institutional gazetteer and make up roughly one third of the entries in the bibliography. Only slightly less numerous are *sizhi*, the gazetteers of Buddhist monasteries. Next in importance are the gazetteers of nondenominational religious institutions, such as *cizhi* (gazetteers of shrines), *miaozhi* (of temples), and *muzhi* (of tombs); combined, they account for roughly a tenth of the entries. Less common, in decreasing order, are *shuyuan zhi* (gazetteers of academies), *hezhi* (of rivers), *huzhi* (of lakes), *guanzhi* (of Daoist monasteries), *gezhi* (of pavilions), *yuanzhi* (of gardens), *dizhi* and *weizhi* (of dikes and embankments), *qiaozhi* (of bridges), *quzhi* (of

49

canals), *yanjing zhi* (of salt wells), and various other individual types of gazetteers.[2]

Falling into the cracks between recognized genres, this host of major and minor gazetteer types has suffered almost complete neglect by historians of China.[3] Even in their own day, these records were considered of only limited importance. A gazetteer of a nationally prominent site, such as Shandong's venerated Tai Shan, could attract a broad readership and, more significantly, the patronage needed to pay for publication. For a site whose renown was primarily local, however, the printing of a gazetteer was an exceptional event. The unpublished records of local institutions, of which only a handful are cited in the present bibliography, probably outnumbered published gazetteers, but few may ever be retrieved from obscurity.

Though not as numerous as the gazetteers of administrative units, of which close to six thousand are extant today, topographical and institutional gazetteers are nonetheless sufficiently common to have generated this bibliography of 686 entries. This number, it should be noted, excludes subsequent reprints of earlier editions; when pre-1960 reprint editions are included, the total is well over 900 (see Table 1). Even this number does not represent a complete count, for one can readily find cited in essays, local gazetteers, and bibliographies from the period titles of topographical and institutional gazetteers no longer extant.[4] Most of these lost works were consumed by the ravages of bookworms, fire, wars, and time. Fuzhou's Changqing Monastery, for example, had a Ming gazetteer whose blocks were destroyed in the fighting during the Ming-Qing transition; by the end of the eighteenth century, the surviving copies were wormeaten and incomplete.[5] The greatest single despoiler of the printing blocks of monastic gazetteers was the Taiping Rebellion, for which monastic institutions were often a target of anti-idolatrous attacks. The blocks of the gazetteers of many Hangzhou monasteries went up in flames along with the monasteries when the Taiping forces captured Hangzhou in 1861, though many monasteries were able to cut new blocks on the basis of surviving copies once peace had been restored.[6]

Incomplete though the sample in this bibliography may be, the spatial distribution of its entries by province suggests a clear pattern. Zhejiang and Jiangsu together account for close to half the extant gazetteers and are individually of a magnitude well beyond any other province. Next to them rank Jiangxi, Guangdong, and Anhui, each claiming between five and seven percent; beneath these,

Table 1. The Production of Institutional and Topographical
Gazetteers, 1400-1959[7]

twenty-year period	extant editions	lost editions	total
Ming dynasty			
1400-19	1	2	3
1420-39	0	0	0
1440-59	0	2	2
1460-79	0	5	5
1480-99	1	0	1
1500-19	4	6	10
1520-39	11	1	12
1540-59	9	6	15
1560-79	13	8	21
1580-99	26	10	36
1600-19	45	16	61
1620-39	33	22	55
Qing dynasty			
1640-59	15	14	29
1660-79	28	9	37
1680-99	66	14	80
1700-19	30	20	50
1720-39	23	8	31
1740-59	43	8	51
1760-79	33	10	43
1780-99	22	8	30
1800-19	43	9	52
1820-39	43	7	50
1840-59	30	11	41
1860-79	77	5	82
1880-99	135	6	141
1900-19	62	5	67
Republican era			
1920-39	124	2	126
1940-59	12	0	12
totals	**929**	**214**	**1,143**

in order of decreasing magnitude, are the gazetteers of Fujian, Shandong, Hunan, Hebei, Hubei, Sichuan, Henan, Shaanxi, Yunnan, and Shanxi, plus a handful from Guangxi and Guizhou. The concentration of this sample of topographical and institutional gazetteers in Jiangnan is similar to the pattern of distribution of lineage genealogies, for Taga Akigorō has found that Jiangsu and Zhejiang together account for two-thirds of the total number of extant genealogies.[8] The tendency for both genres to be centered on the two main provinces of the Jiangnan region is not adequately explained with reference to population there, since in the eighteenth century this area could claim only about twenty percent of China's population. Clearly more significant was the high development of gentry culture in this part of the country. It was, as I shall show, mainly the gentry who produced genealogies and gazetteers, who patronized the building and maintenance of the institutions highlighted in these works, and who personally savored the scenery of the places about which the gazetteers were written.

Like county gazetteers, topographical and institutional gazetteers are works that belong to the Ming-Qing period. They have antecedents from the Song, which is when the term *zhi* comes into use for identifying gazetteers generally, though it is not until the sixteenth century that topographical and institutional gazetteers become common. The editor of a Daoist monastic gazetteer from Hangzhou says that the earliest monastic gazetteers from that region date from the Southern Song,[9] when the court's presence in that city (as of 1127) stimulated interest in the culture and cultural institutions of the region. The earliest surviving edition of a monastic gazetteer is a six-*juan* gazetteer of a Daoist monastery in a peripheral Hangzhou county, completed in 1305 with subsequent addenda by a Daoist abbot in the following decade.[10] In the sixteenth century, as Table 1 shows, the production of topographical and institutional gazetteers becomes regular, increasing steadily through the Jiajing and Wanli eras, and rising markedly during the opening decades of the seventeenth century. A second peak of greater magnitude is reached at the end of that century. Smaller rises occur during the middle of the eighteenth century and again at the beginning of the nineteenth, though the most striking peak comes in the closing decades of that century.

The irregularity of the temporal distribution shown in Table 1 is significant in the light of what we know of the social history of the Ming-Qing period. The first surge in gazetteer production in the Wanli era may be linked to the expansion of gentry society at the local level at that time, and more particularly to the increasing involvement of degree-holders in local institutions. As the ranks of the gentry expanded and men of status chose to remain in their local areas rather than seek in the capital for bureaucratic appointment, the gentry became more involved in the affairs of their local areas and more concerned with elevating the prestige of their home townships or counties. In the case of monastic gazetteers, the surge in their production must be linked to the growing interest in Buddhism among the gentry from the mid-sixteenth century forward.[11] The vitality of the academy movement, even after the state's attempts to interfere with academies in the latter part of the sixteenth century, similarly may account for the production of academy gazetteers at this time. The renewed interest in all types of gazetteers toward the end of the seventeenth century coincides with the reestablishment of social order following the consolidation of rule by the Manchus. Although intellectuals in the latter part of the seventeenth century insisted that a sharp line be drawn between their interests and styles and those of the late-Ming thinkers, the resurgence of gazetteer production attests to the strong cultural continuity spanning the Ming-Qing transition. Least ambiguous is the tide of gazetteer publishing that began in the late 1860s and the 1870s and was in full flood in the 1880s, for this was a time when traditionally minded intellectuals, especially in Jiangnan but also throughout the Yangzi region as a whole, sought to reconstruct their social world after its devastation in the Taiping Rebellion. Gazetteers, and the institutions and places they chronicled, were restored to their familiar places in post-Taiping culture.

Although an antiquarian interest encouraged considerable reprinting of many topographical and institutional gazetteers in the twentieth century, the enthusiasm for compiling new works in this genre declined. The dynamic Buddhist conservatives, Yinguang (1861-1940) of the Pure Land sect and Xuyun (1840-1959) of the Chan sect, attempted a minor revival by editing and sponsoring several monastic gazetteers in the 1930s and 1940s (E4, H20, I21, L59, O23).[12] By this time, however, Buddhist monasteries were not sufficiently powerful, nor sufficiently critical to the lives of the local elite, to warrant a widespread renewal of gazetteer publishing on their behalf. Even less so were other traditional institutions. There has been in the 1980s a renewed interest in producing county gazetteers, and this interest has also led to the publication of a few new topographical and institutional gazetteers (eg., C6, H7, N29). The mildly archaic tone of these recent editions suggests that the genre will remain antiquarian.

Both in style and organizational format, topographical and institutional gazetteers are much like county gazetteers. Their shared sense of how to categorize subject matter and organize it for presentation is apparent when one looks over their tables of contents. A popular early-eighteenth-century gazetteer of the Lu Mountains in northern Jiangxi (I9), for instance, is organized according to the following headings: astrological location, geography, sacrificial rituals, biographies, local products, miscellany, unusual occurrences, and literary writings. The 1607 gazetteer of the monasteries on Putuo Island just off the Zhejiang coast from Ningbo (M49) is divided into chapters on imperial writings, topography, buildings, biographies, local products, literary writings, historical notes, and poetry. A Fuzhou monastic gazetteer of 1761 (N2) is arranged slightly differently: famous sights, buildings, ancient sites, biographies, land and taxation, epigraphy, prose, poetry, and a closing section of miscellany. The only material one would expect to find in a county gazetteer that is missing in these examples is administrative records: the financial regulations of the county government, lists of degreeholders, and records of local officials. Otherwise, topographical and institutional gazetteers look much like their county gazetteer counterparts.

One even finds the same prefaces by officials and other local men of reputation, the same explanatory notes (*fanli*), the same illustrations: diagrammatic maps (see Illustration 2), pictures of noteworthy landscapes, and drawings and floor plans of buildings. The similarities between the two types of local gazetteer spawned a certain self-righteousness among the more conservative compilers of county gazetteers, who elevated their work above topographical and institutional gazetteers, insisting that county gazetteers "are different from the illustrated gazetteers of famous mountains: the latter just describe landscapes, whereas the former put together and arrange literary writings."[13] Such a distinction was quite unfairly drawn, since mountain gazetteers are major compendia of "literary writings" and in almost every other way replicate the structure, concerns, and even the ideological posture of county gazetteers.[14] Many authors in fact compiled both types and saw no difference between the two undertakings.[15]

One might not expect this similarity in the case of monastic gazetteers. Despite the religious association of their name, however, monastic gazetteers were basically secular in nature. Aside from biographies of monks and devoted laymen, texts dealing with specifically religious matters are rarely included. This is because monastic gazetteers, though intended in part to be reading matter for the faithful, were not devotional publications. The information they might contain about the area where the monastery was located ranged widely, from reports on local customs to reprints of land contracts, but these after all were secular matters with which a monastery's managerial personnel had to concern themselves. Some monastic gazetteers are no more than collections of literary scribblings about scenic spots, yet even publications of this type can incorporate material useful for reconstructing the history of local areas.

Topographical and institutional gazetteers were written, according to an author writing in 1874, by three types of men: local literati, officials who had returned home after retiring from bureaucratic service, and local magistrates;[16] in other words, the gentry at all levels. Their education and sense of history qualified them for the task; indeed, some interpreted their qualifications as generating a duty in this regard. Thus the sons of a would-be compiler of a gazetteer for a Daoist mountain in Sichuan urged him to the task by saying: "That the documentation is incomplete is the fault of warring soldiers. To preserve what shreds remain is the responsibility of the Confucian scholar."[17] Although producing a mountain gazetteer was generally considered a less onerous project that compiling a county gazetteer, this was not always the case. Lu Tinggan, an early-eighteenth-century native of Huangyan county, Zhejiang, fervently hoped to produce a new edition of the county gazetteer, which had last been published in 1699. Unable to raise the support he needed for such a project, he settled instead on the plan of compiling a gazetteer of the county's Weiyu Mountain. As it turned out, however, the scope of the latter work was more than he had anticipated (it went to ten *juan*), and he could not afford to bring his completed manuscript to publication.[18]

Gentry authorship was not only a function of the gentry's particular educational skills. It also grew within a cultural milieu that placed a high aesthetic value on the appreciation of beautiful scenery and historical sites. This appreciation is constantly echoed in the writings of the Ming gentry, who were keen to go on group outings to admire the landscape, travel locally and beyond to view famous sites and the remnants of earlier ages, and build studios and private gardens in picturesque spots. This quest for eminent sites in the late Ming was animated by a veneration of refuge and retreat. What the gentry sought were places set apart from the bustle of everyday life,

Illustration 2. A diagrammatic map of the Lamaist mountain Wutai Shan, from the prefatory matter to *Qingliang shanzhi* (1596, 19th-century reprint) [E2]. The paths mark the way to the five

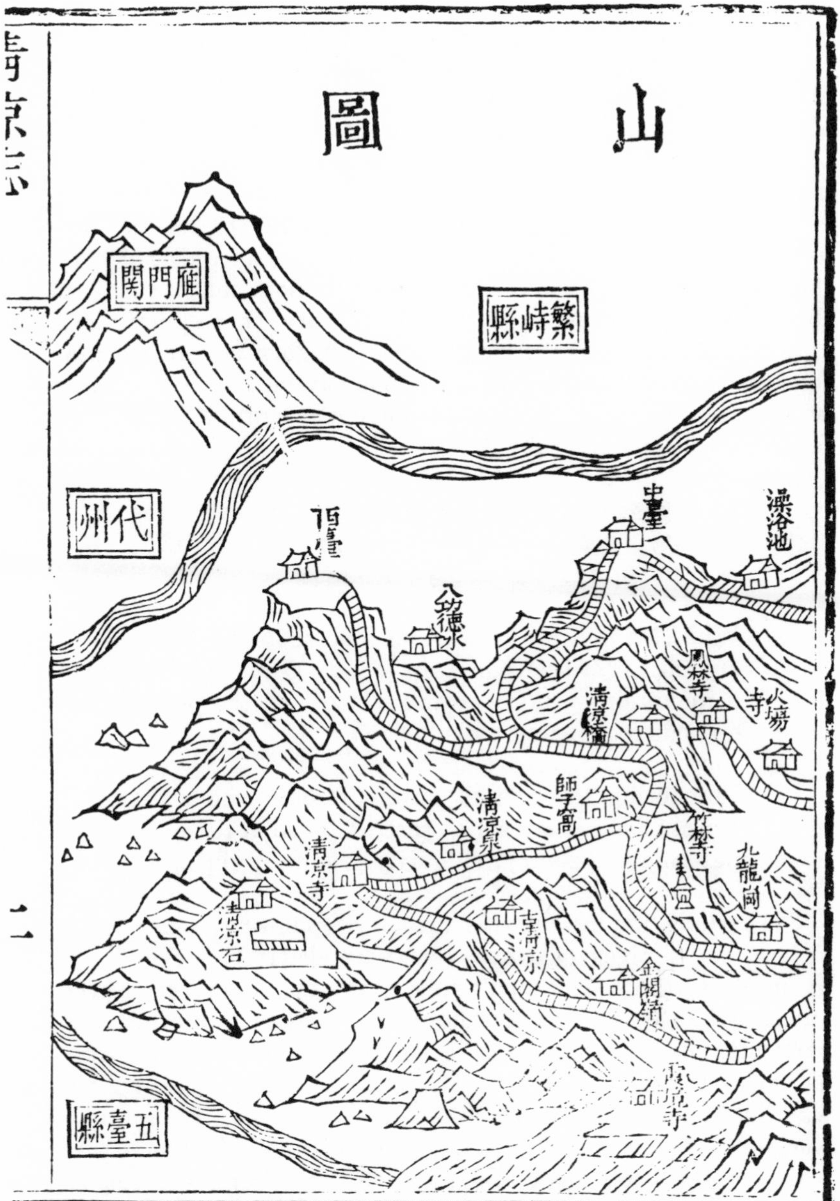

"terraces" (*tai*) for which the mountain is named. The south terrace (*Nantai*) has been placed by the artist in the foreground, the other four, along the visual horizon. The boxed names indicate walled administrative towns.

places that could be symbols to them of their ideal of separation from
all that corrupted moral perfection—including, of course,
bureaucratic factionalism and class conflict. The image of the
mountain was most heavily laden with this type of meaning, for
which reason a respected Buddhist abbot would come to be addressed
as "mountain monk" (shanseng), or the head of an academy given
the title "mountain elder" (shanzhang). In both cases, the symbol of
the mountain served explicitly to identify these men and their
institutions with the convention of separation from mundane
concerns. The aphorisms of the religiously inclined Hong Yingming,
writing at the turn of the seventeenth century, echo with the
resonance of the mountain ideal:[19]

> The gentleman of the mountain forest lives in
> poverty, yet he is absorbed in his avocation of
> retirement and has plenty for himself.
>
> While living in fine mansions, one should not be with-
> out the air of the mountain forest. While dwelling by
> a mountain spring, one must hold onto the principles
> embodied in sacred halls.
>
> Wandering through mountain forests and streams,
> wordly desires are set at rest. At ease in the realm of
> painting and poetry, vulgarity gradually slips away.

As Hong implies in this last line, painting and poetry were
artistic correlatives of what gentry intellectuals hoped to find in
mountain settings. Not surprisingly, art and reality reinforced each
other, and one finds a great volume of poems and paintings depicting
particular places in the Ming. Such depictions amount to what may
be called topographical art. The passion behind topographical art
was this concern for finding analogues of the pure realm in the real
world, or at least distilling the real world into forms that resonated
with the reclusion ideal and shut out the social sources of their
anxiety. James Cahill, in his study of Ming painting, has observed
this relationship between place and ideal in the course of noting a
shift in styles of painting between the middle and late Ming:[20]

> If we say of Soochow school painting of the middle
> Ming that the people in it seem to be inhabiting works
> of art, we imply that they have in reality arranged

their lives and their environments so as to be surrounded by the aesthetic order and security that a work of art can afford—or so, at least, their paintings and poems suggest. Late Ming people can be said also to inhabit works of art, . . . but the relationship and the effect are dramatically different: they typically appear more like people who have taken refuge in the realm of art from a world in which they have no secure place, and who find that the realm of art does not receive them comfortably either. They look out at us as if compelled by some need to assert their existence as individuals, to communicate some sense of their situation.

Hong's expression about "escaping vulgarity" is a sign of the growing insecurity plaguing gentry intellectuals in the late Ming; hence, the retreat to the mountains, both in art and in real life.

A recurring convention in Ming-Qing topographical art is the *jing*, or "prospect." A prospect is an established and well-defined view onto a known landscape, not a view that the artist selects or defines himself. Being conventional, it provides precise terms, both visual and emotive, within which a landscape might be translated into painting or poetry, while leaving the artist a narrow range of freedom in which to express himself through limited variations. A place with any pretensions to physical beauty or cultural refinement came to have associated with it a set of these prospects, usually eight or ten, often more, occasionally as many as a hundred and eight. A poet writing about a scenic place would use these prospects as the subjects for a poem cycle, as the noted traveler Xu Hongzu (1586-1641) did when he wrote on "the ten prospects of Jizu Mountain" in Yunnan.[21] Similarly, when a painter wanted to portray a famous landscape in terms that would immediately declare its identity, he would paint an album of its prospects. The best-known examples of this genre are *Twelve Prospects of Tiger Hill* by Shen Zhou (1427-1509) and *Eight Prospects of Huang Shan* by Shitao Daoji (1642-1708).[22] As much as possible in these works, the artist himself does not intrude, though he may arrange the required elements of the prospects in individual ways; nor does he depict people, except as anonymous viewers directing our attention to certain portions of the landscape. The goal in such paintings is to impart a sense of both the uniqueness and enduring stability of the place itself. More significantly, however, at the hands of artists like

Zhang Hong (1577-after 1652), topographical painting aimed at
faithfully representing the physical world, albeit according to certain
prospects, rather than reducing places to visual stereotypes.[23] The
particularity of place was becoming important, perhaps for the first
time in China. Gazetteers, I would suggest, also embodied this sense
of the particularity of place.

An indication that topographical art and gazetteers were the
products of a single cultural environment in the latter half of the
Ming is the involvement of the same individuals in both activities. To
mention two examples, Shen Zhou's patron, Wu Kuan (1434-1504),
was not only an enthusiastic admirer of topographical art but also an
editor of the great Suzhou prefectural gazetteer of 1506 (*Gusu zhi*);
and Xu Hongzu compiled a gazetteer (Q14) of the mountain on which
he composed his poem cycle. The overlapping of two endeavors is
perhaps most nicely illustrated in the case of the scholar Chen Jiru
(1558-1639), a friend and critic of the greatest Jiangnan landscape
artists of the late Ming: Chen not only contributed a preface to the
1614 gazetteer of Helin Monastery, east of Nanjing (B113), but also
within the year wrote a colophon on a painting of one of the
monastery's cloisters by the naturalistic landscapist Zhao Zuo (ca.
1570-after 1633).[24] Gentry intellectuals could thus be involved in
both the artistic and the historical recording of the places that were
important to them. Indeed, when an editor tells his readers that a
certain gazetteer was being brought back into print "so that
gentlemen who delight in the marvelous might renew their senses
and refresh their hearts,"[25] one might almost think that he was
referring to a handscroll of a mountain landscape or a volume of
verse. Pictures and verses, in fact, are often major components of
topographical and institutional gazetteers. But the gazetteer was
ultimately the more reliable objective record, as we are told in no
uncertain terms in a preface to a 1671 work on Hangzhou's West
Lake: "Some of the breath-taking landscapes of the realm have been
immortalized in poetry, and some in art, . . . but I maintain that no
one who has ever seen West Lake can hope to make a painting or a
poem that truly depicts it."[26]

The enhanced sense of place in the late imperial period found its
subjective expression most frequently as pride in one's native area.
Local pride is most frequently cited as the inspiration to undertake
the compilation of a topographical or institutional gazetteer, and it
also played a role in stimulating the support and cooperation from
the rest of the local gentry that was usually needed to see a gazetteer
into print. But other motives for producing a gazetteer could also be

invoked. Gazetteer authors occasionally expressed a concern with establishing a historical record through which the character of the times in which they lived might be reflected. A sixteenth-century author observes in this vein that, by recounting the fortunes of a Suzhou monastery, he was recording not just details to delight tourists but important testimony concerning the state of the realm, since a monastery cannot flourish except during times of good government.[27] Finally, there were the practical motives, especially in the case of gazetteers of institutions subject to dismemberment and decay: encouraging interest in restoration work, securing a land endowment to provide the institution with regular income, or creating a lasting testimonial to contributions already made.

This range of motivations from the cultural and general to the practical and specific was sufficiently compelling to draw men of national reputation into compiling topographical and institutional gazetteers. While home in Fuzhou observing mourning for his father in 1608, Xie Zhaozhe (1567-1624) compiled a monastic gazetteer from notes left by the deceased uncle of a friend (N1), in the following year produced a gazetteer of Tailao Mountain in the adjacent subprefecture to the north (N33), and in 1611 compiled a gazetteer of a monastery in an outlying county (N11). (He also published in 1614 a gazetteer on the northern section of the Grand Canal [D26].) In addition to being an acceptable pastime during the enforced period of mourning for the death of a parent, putting together a gazetteer could be a pleasant distraction from other duties. Chen Renxi (1579-1634) in 1611 prepared for publication a revised edition of a famous gazetteer of five monasteries east of Nanjing as a diversion while studying for his *jinshi* examinations (B108). (Chen also wrote a mountain gazetteer (B68), which was published posthumously in 1638.) For most compilers, there were strong personal associations with the places they wrote about. This was certainly true for the three most eminent scholars of the seventeenth century, Huang Zongxi (1610-95), Wang Fuzhi (1619-92), and Gu Yanwu (1613-82), all of whom wrote topographical gazetteers at mid-century. Huang's (M30) was of the mountains that rose above his ancestral home in Shaoxing; Wang's (K12) was of the mountain to which he had fled for safety during the rebel insurgency in southern Hunan in the winter of 1643-44; and Gu's (A16) was of the area of the Ming imperial tombs, which he visited almost annually after the fall of the Ming and which were to him powerful symbols of the greatness of the dynasty to which he had chosen to remain loyal.

Although men of this stature compiled gazetteers, most authors were otherwise undistinguished members of the local gentry. There were, however, a few professional writers in their midst. One is Hu Fengdan (1823-90) who became involved in the professional publishing business after a career as a circuit intendant. Hu produced two gazetteers in 1874 for a mountain and a monastery in Hubei province (J1, J4), one in 1877 for a mountain in Hunan (K11), and three in the same year for famous sites in Huaian, Yangzhou, and Shaoxing (B29, B40, M18). He also published in 1877 two tomb gazetteers, one of the tomb of the Tang imperial concubine Yang Guifei in Shanxi (G8, compiled in 1876), and the other of a Han imperial consort's tomb in Shanxi (E15). Hu was not a native of any of these places but hailed from Jinhua prefecture in Zhejiang, for which he would later compile an anthology of writings. His only connection to them was having lived near some of them at various times during his career. In 1874, for instance, he was in Hubei working for Chongwen Shuju, a private publishing business in Wuhan; shortly thereafter he was in northern Zhejiang, where he established his own business, Tuibu Zhai Shuju.[28] Hu was thus a professional editor rather than an interested individual tied to a particular locale or institution. Although he was exceptional among compilers in this genre, he was part of the trend toward professionalization among county-gazetteer editors in the nineteenth century.

Despite their obvious prominence, the gentry were not the only authors of gazetteers. In the case of monastic gazetteers, and other types as well, Buddhist monks—both eminent monks like Zhuhong (1535-1615) and the local clergy—became actively involved. From the bibliography, I would estimate that Buddhist monks compiled or edited at least one in three Buddhist monastic gazetteers. Monks were also involved in the production of gazetteers of the mountains on which their monasteries stood and of other neighboring institutions, such as shrines and bridges. The most active ecclesiastic compiler was Bichu Guangbin, also known by his Buddhist title of Master Xinhai, the abbot of a cloister affiliated to a major monastery in the western part of Hangzhou prefecture. During the 1630s and 1640s, he compiled four gazetteers for monasteries in the prefecture, including his own. [29] The extent of clerical participation in this form of literary creation requires that we question the present assumption that Buddhist monks had no significant place in the elite culture of the late-imperial period. In addition to authoring and editing gazetteers, the Ming-Qing ecclesiastic establishment was also active in the physical and financial aspects of publishing and printing them.

The larger monasteries and temples operated their own printing shops; they also had the considerable storage space needed to keep the bulky woodblocks. Besides producing and selling their own gazetteers, some religious institutions cut, stored, and printed from the blocks of other types of gazetteer.[30] In most of these cases, ecclesiastic personnel not only printed the gazetteers but also funded their production.

The task of compiling and publishing a gazetteer was a large one, sometimes taking as long as a decade. As the author of a preface to an eighteenth-century Hangzhou monastic gazetteer put it, "Building a monastery is certainly difficult, but producing a gazetteer is even tougher."[31] The first major difficulty was finding adequate sources. Tracking them down usually required the close cooperation of local people, and many compilers began their work by traveling around the local area to purchase useful books, consult the private libraries of local gentrymen and monks, and talk to long-time residents of the area.[32] If an author were compiling a gazetteer for a monastery, he would work closely with its residents (who may have engaged him in this task), though one gentry writer complained that monks could be woefully ignorant of events in even the more recent past.[33] Once the information had been collected, there was the further, and usually more serious, difficulty of paying for the blocks to be cut. The funds could be raised by subscription from the local gentry, who were often rewarded for their generosity by having their names listed in the book they were funding. Only a very few gazetteers, generally of places popular with tourists, were produced by printing houses for commercial distribution (e.g., L95, L96, L98).

The evident difficulties of finding sources and funding did not prevent a large number of gazetteers from being published or circulating widely. We know that print runs could go into the hundreds, a considerable number in this period.[34] The catalogues of institutional and private libraries list gazetteers,[35] and they are mentioned with some frequency in contemporary writings. A county magistrate in Henan in 1660 says that topographical gazetteers were his favorite type of casual reading, "transporting me as though I were there myself seeing it with my own eyes."[36] The Buddhist master Zhuhong records that he was given a copy of a gazetteer of Wuyi Shan, the famous Daoist mountains in Fujian, to read while he was ill sometime in the latter half of the Wanli era.[37] Gentry artist Dong Qichang (1555-1636) mentions in a short essay that he had read a gazetteer of Tai Mountain in Shandong, probably the 1587 edition entitled *Dai shi* (D8) by Zha Zhilong (js. 1559).[38] Wang Fuzhi,

writing in southern Hunan, cites a Wuxi academy gazetteer in one of
his essays.[39] The correspondence of an abbot of a major monastery
east of Peking testifies that the gazetteer of his monastery, which he
published in 1693, had circulated among higher officials in Peking.[40]
A visitor to Putuo Island in 1840 says he bought a copy of the
island's gazetteer at one of the small shops adjacent to the main
monastery;[41] given the volume of tourist traffic to Putuo, many must
have been purchased and taken home. We know that the gazetteer of
Guangdong's Qingyun Monastery circulated widely within that province, for the author of a preface in the 1717 edition argues that it
was the gazetteer rather than the place itself that drew visitors.[42]
And in what reads more like an advertisement than a foreword, the
author of a preface to a mid-nineteenth-century gazetteer of a
mountain in southern Shanxi assures the reader that many who
have wanted to climb this particular mountain have been content to
satisfy this desire by reading the gazetteer, and that "true
bibliophiles" are sure to value this edition highly.[43] Certain editions
clearly did become popular, for a casual reference in the preface of
Hu Fengdan's mountain gazetteer of 1874 to seven Ming monastic
and mountain gazetteers suggests that he expected an educated
reader to be familiar with all of them.[44]

Topographical and institutional gazetteers can be of considerable
use for the historical study of late-imperial society, economy,
biography, and institutions. First of all, they preserve texts that are
not available elsewhere and would otherwise be lost. For example,
an essay by the artist Wen Zhengming (1470-1559) on the
restoration in the late 1540s of a Buddhist chapel in Suzhou laments
the decline of Suzhou monasteries; the essay has been preserved in a
1696 pavilion gazetteer from Suzhou (B72) but does not appear in
Wen's own essay collection. While texts in these gazetteers can often
be found in other publications as well, their inclusion in a gazetteer
can be used to adduce textual or biographical information that could
not otherwise be ascertained. For example, a preface by Gu Yanwu
to the gazetteer of Lao Mountain in eastern Shandong (D29) is
undated both in the gazetteer and in Gu's collected works. Gu
sojourned in Shandong at several different times between the 1650s
and the 1670s, so it is impossible to date the text on its own. We
know, however, that the gazetteer was published in the Shunzhi
reign, which allows us to date the preface to the period between 1657
and 1659, the only time during the Shunzhi era when Gu is known to
have been in the region.[45] This finding helps date the gazetteer and

provides one more datum concerning the life and work of a major figure in Qing history. A biographer who has put this type of source to good use is Ren Daobin, whose 1983 biography of Fang Yizhi (1611-71) relies heavily on monastic gazetteers. Besides a Nanjing mountain gazetteer (B16), Ren cites a monastic gazetteer from Nanjing (B10), two from Anhui (C5, C13), and one from Jiangxi that Fang himself edited (I39).[46]

In other areas, John Meskill has used academy gazetteers in his research on academies,[47] and Edouard Chavannes, Reginald Johnston, and Wolfram Eberhard have made selective use of monastic gazetteers in their studies of religious institutions.[48] In the realm of economic history, Fu Yiling has found in a temple gazetteer from central Fujian (N26) useful material concerning the terms under which land was rented in eighteenth-century Fujian, as well as the rates tenants paid for their land.[49] And three editions of the monastic gazetteer of the Wutai Mountains have provided valuable information for a study of soil use and deforestation in the border region between Hebei and Shanxi.[50]

The area of research for which these gazetteers should be most useful of all is the history of local society and, in particular, of the gentry. Let me hint briefly at this potential by referring to a monastic gazetteer from Tongcheng county, Anhui, entitled *Fushan zhi* [Gazetteer of Fu Mountain] (C5). This gazetteer includes an essay by Zhang Ying (1638-1708) concerning the land endowment of Tongcheng's Huayan Monastery. The essay was written in 1683 to commemorate the enlargement of the monastery's landholdings under Abbot Shanzu through the contributions of local gentry patrons. Shanzu first went to Huayan Monastery in 1670 under orders from Fang Yizhi to compile this gazetteer. Fang himself had been invited to come as abbot in 1668 but had declined on account of ill health. After Shanzu died, it was none other than Zhang Ying who was responsible for writing the formal invitation that the Tongcheng county gentry sent to the monk who succeeded to the abbotship at the turn of the eighteenth century.[51] Zhang Ying is best known to students of Chinese history as the leading character in Hilary Beattie's *Land and Lineage in China* (1979), though Beattie does not mention his extensive relationship with this monastery. Taking note of Zhang's activities as a leading patron of a Buddhist monastery might have led Beattie to make an even broader analysis of the relationship between his and other elite lineages in Tongcheng, by examining, for instance, who shared the Zhang lineage's interest in Huayan Monastery and who did not. A recognition of Zhang Ying's position as a patron of the monastery might also have enriched her otherwise excellent sense of the economic strategies pursued by his lineage.

In such ways as this, historians versed in the histories and elites of particular regions should be able to find in topographical and institutional gazetteers valuable data for their work. The bibliography that follows has been arranged by county in order to facilitate this kind of locality-focused research.

Notes

1. Gazetteers of this sort have long been valued for the study of local society in China, and their accessibility has been maximized by the publication of several excellent bibliographies. The most complete is *Chūgoku chihōshi sōgō mokuroku* [Union catalogue of Chinese local gazetteers] (Tokyo: Kokuritsu Kokkai Toshokan Koshoshibu, 1969). Also useful are the two catalogues by Zhu Shijia (Chu Shih-chia), *Catalog of Chinese Local Histories in the Library of Congress* (Washington: Library of Congress, 1942) and *Zhongguo difangzhi zonglu* [Union catalogue of Chinese local gazetteers] (Shanghai, 1958). For local gazetteers just of the Ming period, see Franke, pp. 233-36, 242-309, and Yamane Yukio and Hosono Kōji, *(Zōhō) Nihon genzon Mindai chihōshi mokuroku* [Catalogue of Ming local gazetteers in Japan, revised and enlarged] (Tokyo: Tōyō Bunko, 1971). There are also separate bibliographies of the gazetteers of individual provinces, of which the finest are by Hong Huanchun (see Hong, HHC, and ZFK in the List of Abbreviations).

2. The reader should be aware of the types of geographical-historical writings that have been excluded from this bibliography: (1) Topographical records that lie outside the gazetteer category, such as Wang Mengjuan's anecdotal collection about the famous tea-producing region just outside Hangzhou, *Longjing jianwen lu* [A record of things I have seen and heard about Longjing] (1762); or the "famous sights" (*mingsheng*) compendia that became so popular in the late Ming, notably Yang Erzeng, *Hainei qiguan* [Marvelous sights within the empire] (1610), and He Tang, *Mingshan shenggai ji* [Record of the sights at famous mountains] (1634). (2) Chorographical gazetteers (monographs on local history with particular reference to surviving physical remains), such as Li Lian's study of Kaifeng in the Song, *Bianjing yiji zhi* [Gazetteer of historical sites of the capital on the Bian River] (1545). (3) Most "tomb records" (*mulu*), which are almost exclusively records of the deceased's accomplishments rather than gazetteers of the topography or temple at his resting place. (4) Gazetteers of government offices and ministries (most of which date from the later part of the Ming) which have already been fully documented by Franke (6.2.1-6.2.10, 6.5.5-6.5.9, 6.5.12-6.5.13). (5) Urban surveys, such as Liu Tong, *Dijing jingwu lüe* [Abridged record of the sights of the imperial capital] (1635), one of many of Peking; or Dong Fu, *Erlou jilüe* [Abridged record of the city of two towers] (1720), of Xuancheng,

Anhui. (6) Although this bibliography does include gazetteers of rivers and canals, it excludes—with a few exceptions—gazetteers specifically addressing the problems of water resources and water control (*shuili zhi*), which are differently structured and properly deserve a separate and detailed study of their own.

3. The fullest, though still brief, notice they have received is from Liu Guanglu, whose guide for the preparation of contemporary gazetteers, *Zhongguo fangzhixue gaiyao* [An outline for the study of Chinese gazetteers] (Peking: Zhongguo Zhanlan Chubanshe, 1983), pp. 5-6, places them in the general category of "specialized gazetteers" (*zhuanzhi*).

4. E.g., the Yin county gazetteer of 1788 cites gazetteers for Yanqing Monastery (*Yanqing sizhi*) and Shouchang Monastery (*Shouchang sizhi*), two of the major Buddhist monasteries within the city of Ningbo (*Yinxian zhi* (1788), 25.1b, 3b); neither is extant. Gazetteers yet to be recovered appear in more recent sources as well. Shimizu Taiji, in an essay first published in 1924, mentions a *Minglan sizhi* [Gazetteer of Minglan Monastery] for which I have been unable to locate an extant copy (see his *Mindai tochi seido shi kenkyū* [Studies in the history of the land system of the Ming dynasty] (Tokyo: Daian, 1968), p. 208).

5. *Changqing sizhi* (1800) [N4], *fanli*, 1a.

6. E.g., *Jingci sizhi* (1888) [L75] Yu's preface, 1b; *Xi tianmu zushan zhi* (1876) [L99], Lu's preface, 1a.

7. This table has been constructed on the basis of dated editions mentioned in the bibliography. Reprints as well as original editions are enumerated in these statistics; "lost editions" include only those that can be conclusively identified and dated from editions in the bibliography.

8. Taga Akigorō, *Sōfu no kenkyū* [Studies of lineage genealogies] (Tokyo: Tōyō Bunko, 1960), p. 63.

9. *Jingu dongzhi* (1877) [L76], Zhu's preface (1807), 1a.

10. Deng Mu, *Dongxiao tuzhi* [Illustrated gazetteer of Dongxiao Monastery], reprinted in Zhibuzu, Congshu, and elsewhere. The expression *tuzhi* was a conventional Song designation for local gazetteers; this particular gazetteer may never have been illustrated, despite my translation.

11. Timothy Brook, "Gentry Dominance of Chinese Society: Monasteries and Lineages in the Structuring of Local Society, 1500-1700" (Ph.D. diss., Harvard University, 1984), ch. 3.

12. Concerning Yinguang and Xuyun, see Holmes Welch, *The Buddhist Revival in China* (Cambridge, Mass.: Harvard University Press, 1968), p. 71.

13. *Daming xianzhi* (1790), *fanli*, 2a.

14. As one mountain-gazetteer compiler insisted, he was following the ideological standards set by the state for county gazetteers by "refusing to record privately built shrines and licentious forms of worship" (*Wushi shanzhi* (1842) [N6], *fanli*, 1a).

15. Among authors of topographical and institutional gazetteers, Wang Huanru (B65) compiled the Wu county gazetteer of 1642; Piao Yinzhi (J9) was the chief compiler of the 1669 gazetteer of Dangyang county, Hubei; Wen Xingdao (M39) compiled a gazetteer of Yin county, Ningbo, in 1686; Hang Shijun (L33, L85) assisted in the compilation of the 1736 Zhejiang provincial gazetteer; Ruan Yuan (B32, B105, L87, M1, M67) headed the Yunnan provincial gazetteer project of 1835, in which Li Cheng (Q3) also participated; Ye Changchi (B52) was an associate editor of the 1882 Suzhou prefectural gazetteer; Xie Zhaozhe (N1, N11, N33) edited the Fuzhou prefectural gazetteer of 1613; Zhang Xuecheng (cf. A5) has a host of local-gazetteer credits to his name.

16. *Huanghu shanzhi* (1874) [J1], Zhang's preface, 1a.

17. *Qingcheng shanzhi* (1982) [H9], p. 1.

18. *Huangyan xianzhi* (1858), 26.24b.

19. Hong Yingming, *Caigen tan* [Vegetable-root discourses] (repr. Shanghai: Zhengxin Chubanshe, 1940), pp. 4, 33, 43.

20. James Cahill, *The Compelling Image: Nature and Style in Seventeenth-Century Chinese Painting* (Cambridge, Mass.: Harvard University Press, 1982), p. 124.

21. Xu Hongzu, *Xu Xiake youji* [The travel diaries of Xu Xiake] (Shanghai: Shanghai Guji Chubanshe, 1980), pp. 1151-55.

22. James Cahill, *Parting at the Shore: Chinese Painting of the Early and Middle Ming Dynasty, 1368–1580* (Tokyo: Weatherhill, 1978), p. 91; idem., *The Compelling Image*, p. 200.

23. James Cahill, *The Compelling Image*, pp. 9-13.

24. James Cahill, *The Distant Mountains: Chinese Painting of the Late Ming Dynasty, 1570-1644* (Tokyo: Weatherhill, 1982), p. 80, pl. 29.

25. *Fangguang yanzhi* (1885) [N12], Lin's preface.

26. *Xihu mengxun* (1984) [L39], Qi's preface, p. 326.

27. *Dengwei sheng'en sizhi* (1644) [B51], Lu's preface (1536), 1b.

28. *Huanghu shanzhi* (1874) [J1], Zhang's preface, 3a; Chen, p. 163.

29. Guangbin compiled *Shang tianzhu jiangsi zhi* (1646) [L28], *Xi tianmu zushan zhi* (1638) [L99], both of which are extant, *Tianlong sizhi*, and *Jingshan zhi*. The latter two are cited in Hong, pp. 391, 399.

30. The blocks of the gazetteer of a long embankment along the Pearl River estuary in southern Guangdong (O6) were stored in the temple to the river god erected as part of the embankment project recorded by the gazetteer. The blocks of two editions of canton gazetteers from Wuxi (*Meili zhi* [Gazetteer of Meili Canton], 1820s reprint of 1724 edition; and *Taibo meili zhi* [Gazetteer of Taibo and Meili Cantons], 1897) were stored at the Daoist Taibo Temple.

31. *Li'an sizhi* (1878) [L15], Hang's preface (1760), 4a.

32. The compiler of the Guangzhou mountain gazetteer *Luofu shanzhi huibian* (1717) [O31] mentions in his preface (3a) that he tried to find books in the local bookshops. The compiler of *Lushan jishi* (1561) [I6], the gazetteer of the famous Lu Mountains in northern Jiangxi, says in his preface that he visited local private libraries in search of sources.

33. *Tiantong sizhi* (1633) [M38], Zhang's preface, 2b.

34. E.g., the print run of the 1894 reprint edition of the gazetteer of Tiantai Mountain was three hundred copies (*Tiantai shan fangwai zhi* (M65), *mulu*, 6b).

35. E.g., the 1613 gazetteer of a Shaanxi academy includes an academy gazetteer, *Zhengxue shuyuan zhi*, in the list of the holdings of its library (*Guanzhong shuyuan zhi* (1613) [G3], 8.2a). In the catalogue of his family's library, Huang Yuji lists 5 mountain and temple gazetteers from the Yuan period and 312 monastic, temple, and mountain gazetteers from the Ming (Huang, 8.14a-39b).

36. *Xiangyan lüeji* (ca. 1746) [F16], Zheng's preface (1660), 1a.

37. Zhuhong, "Zhuchuang suibi" [Jottings under a bamboo window], in his *Yunqi fahui* [Collected writings on the dharma by the master of Yunqi] (1897), 24.40b. Zhuhong could be referring to any one of three Ming editions of the Wuyi gazetteer (N17-N19).

38. Dong Qichang, *Huachan shi suibi* [Jottings from the Room Where I Paint Chan] (1720), 3.9b.

39. Wang Fuzhi, *Saoshou wen*, 2a, in Chuanshan, referring to *Xishan shuyuan zhi*. The relevant passage is translated in Ian McMorran, "Wang Fu-chih and the Neo-Confucian Tradition," in *The Unfolding of Neo-Confucianism*, ed. W. T. de Bary (New York: Columbia University Press, 1975), p. 428.

40. *Panshan zhi buyi* (1696) [A18], 1.11a.

41. Zheng Guanglu, *Yiban lu zashu* [Miscellaneous notes appended to *Yiban lu*] (1845), 3.45b. This "gazetteer" could, however, have been as insubstantial as M54.

42. *Dinghu shanzhi* (1717) [O19], Chen's preface (1717), 1b.

43. *Huayue tujing* (1851) [G14], Wu's preface, 1a-b.

44. *Huanghu shanzhi* (1874) [J1], Zhang's preface, 3a.

45. Willard Peterson, "The Life of Ku Yen-wu (1612-1682)," *Harvard Journal of Asiatic Studies*, vol. 29 (1969), p. 202. Gu's preface can be found in his *Rizhi lu* [Record of daily knowledge] (Shanghai: Shangwu Yinshuguan, 1934), 10.74-75; and in *Gu Tinglin shiwen ji* [Collected prose and poetry of Gu Yanwu] (Peking: Xinhua Shuju, 1983), pp. 38-39.

46. Ren, pp. 257, 292-93.

47. In the bibliography of *Academies in Ming China: A Historical Essay* (Tucson: University of Arizona Press, 1982), pp. 192-96, Meskill includes six academy gazetteers.

48. Eduoard Chavannes, *Le T'ai Chan: Essai de Monographie d'un Culte Chinois* (Paris: Ernest Leroux, 1910), uses three gazetteers of Tai Shan (D9, D12, D13) in his study of the Tai Shan cult. Reginald Johnston, *Buddhist China* (London: Murray, 1913), ch. 12, recounts the history of the sacred island of Putuo from one of its gazetteers (M50 or a later edition) and quotes a particularly vivid passage about

Dutch desecration of the island in 1665 (pp. 344-46). Wolfram Eberhard used material from a gazetteer of Hua Mountain (G13) in his collaboration with Hedda Morrison, *Hua Shan* (Hong Kong: Vetch and Lee, 1974). He also cites a 32-*juan* mountain gazetteer by Bi Yuan, which I have been unable to locate despite Professor Eberhard's help; Bi Yuan's general gazetteer of sites in Shaanxi (G1) is probably the work in question.

49. Nongcun, pp. 47-50, 160-67.

50. W. C. Lowdermilk and Dean Wilkes, *History of the Soil Use in the Wu T'ai Shan Area* (Peking: North China Branch of the Royal Asiatic Society, 1938), using E2 in its 1701 and 1755 editions and E3. I am grateful to Nick Menzies for making a copy of this monograph available to me.

51. *Fushan zhi* (1873) [C5], 4.22a-23a, 6.39b.

Bibliography

A. North Zhili

A1. *Hebei sheng shuyuan zhi chugao* 河北省書院志初稿
[Provisional draft gazetteer of academies in Hebei province]
    1 *juan*, by Wang Lanyin 王蘭蔭 .
    1936. Tobunken.

A2. *Zhili hequ zhi* 直隸河渠志
[Gazetteer of the rivers and canals of Zhili]
    1 *juan*, by Chen Yi 陳儀 (js. 1715).
    1824 Jifu edition.

Shuntian

A3. *Tonghui hezhi* 通惠河志
[Gazetteer of the Tonghui River]
    2 *juan*, by Wu Zhong 吳仲 .
    1558.
    1941 Xuanlan reprint; 1970 reprint (Taibei: Zhengzhong Shuju).
    Bibliographic notice: Franke 8.2.4.
This river supports the system of canals linking the Peking water supply to the Grand Canal. This work is more a collection of memorials than a gazetteer.

A4. *Yongding hezhi* 永定河志
[Gazetteer of the Yongding River]
    12 *juan*, by Chen Wangzong 陳王宗 .
    Qing manuscript. Beijing.

73

A5. *Yongding hezhi* 永定河志
[Gazetteer of the Yongding River]
      32 *juan*, by Li Fengheng 李逢亨.
      1815. Columbia, Jimbun, LC (2 copies), Tobunken.
      1971 Shuili reprint.
      An earlier edition was compiled by Zhang Xuecheng 章學誠
      (1738-1801) in 1783-84.

A6. *Yongding he xuzhi* 永定河續志
[Supplementary gazetteer of the Yongding River]
      16 *juan*, by Jiang Tinggao 蔣廷皐.
      1882. Columbia, Jimbun, LC (2 copies).
      1971 Shuili reprint.

Shuntian: Daxing

A7. *Erzhong ci jilüe* 二忠祠紀略
[Abridged record of the shrine to the two loyal men]
      1 *juan*, by Huang Zantang 黃贊湯.
      1869.
      1933 reprint of 1904 edition. Tobunken.
      This shrine was the guildhall in Peking for merchants from
      Ji'an prefecture, Jiangxi. An earlier edition was destroyed in
      1868 when the building burned down. Preceded by an edition
      of 1649 entitled *Ji'an erzhong ci jishi.*

A8. *Yueci jilüe* 越祠紀略
[Abridged record of Shaoxing Shrine]
      1 *juan*, by Ding Caisan 丁采三 and Ma Jisheng 馬吉生.
      1920. Kyoto, Tobunken.
      A shrine for Shaoxing merchants, attached to their
      association (Zheshao Huiguan 浙紹會館) in Peking.

Shuntian: Wanping

A9. *Baiyun guanzhi* 白雲觀志
[Gazetteer of Baiyun Monastery]
      7 *juan*, by Koyanagi Shikita 小柳司氣太.

1934 (Tokyo: Tōhō Bunka Gakuin). Columbia, Tobunken. Compiled by a Japanese scholar writing in classical Chinese. Baiyun Guan [White Cloud Monastery] was the main Daoist institution in Peking. *Juan* 5 and 6 are devoted to Dongyue Miao 東嶽廟 across the city within the jurisdiction of Daxing county.

A10. *Hongci guangji si xinzhi* 弘慈廣濟寺新志
[New gazetteer of Hongci Guangji Monastery]
    3 *juan*, by Abbot Bieshi Zhanyou 別室湛祐.
    1684. Shifan, Toyo.
    1704 edition with additions, ed. Prior Rancong 然叢.
    Harvard, Jimbun, LC.

A11. *Tanzhe shanzhi* 潭柘山志
[Gazetteer of Tanzhe Mountain]
    2 *juan*, by Shenmude 神穆德
    1739. Harvard, Shifan, Toyo.
    The gazetteer of the Buddhist monastery Xiuyun Si 岫雲寺.

A12. *Tanzhe shan xiuyun sizhi* 潭柘山岫雲寺志
[Gazetteer of Xiuyun Monastery on Tanzhe Mountain]
    2 *juan*, by monk Yian 義庵.
    1883. Jimbun, LC, Toronto, Toyo.
    A supplemented edition of A11.

A13. *Xishan zhilüe* 西山志略
[Abridged gazetteer of the Western Hills]
    6 *juan*, by Lu Xinyuan 陸心源 (1834-94).
    1924 reprint of Qing edition. Toyo.
    Printed together with *Kuangshan bishu lu* 匡山避暑錄
    [Record of the summer retreat at Kuang Mountain].

Shuntian: Zhuozhou: Fangshan

A14. *Shangfang shanzhi* 上方山志
[Gazetteer of Shangfang Mountain]

5 *juan*, by monk Ziru Dawen 自如達聞.
1764. Harvard, LC.
1845 reprint. Jimbun.
1877 reprint. LC, Toyo.
1892 reprint. Shifan.
The gazetteer of Tushita Monastery (Doushuai Si 兜率寺),
famous for its stone inscriptions of Buddhist writings.

A15. *Shangfang shanzhi* 上方山志
[Gazetteer of Shangfang Mountain]
10 *juan*, by monk Puru 溥儒.
1927. LC.
1933 edition. Jimbun.
1948 edition under the title *Baidai shanzhi* 白帶山志. Shifan.

Shuntian: Changping

A16. *Changping shanshui ji* 昌平山水記
[Topographical record of Changping subprefecture]
1 *juan*, by Gu Yanwu 顧炎武 (1613-82; cf. D29).
Reprinted in the various collections of Gu's works.
1962 reprint with his *Jingdong kaogu lu* 京東考古錄
[Study of historical remnants east of the capital] (Peking:
Beijing Chubanshe); 1980 reprint (Peking: Beijing Guji
Chubanshe).
A descriptive account of the thirteen Ming tombs north of
Peking, written out of Ming-loyalist sentiment.

Shuntian: Jizhou

A17. *Panshan zhi* 盤山志
[Gazetteer of Pan Mountain]
10 *juan*, by Abbot Zhipu 智朴 (cf. A18).
1694. Beijing, LC (2 copies), Palace, Shifan.
1696, published together with A18. Harvard, Naikaku,
UBC.
1872 reprint. Jimbun, SOAS, Tobunken, Toyo.
The blocks were cut in 1693 and a draft version circulated
before publication in 1696. Pan Shan was the major

Buddhist mountain of Zhili province, the site of many monasteries.

A18. *Panshan zhi buyi* 盤山志補遺
[Addenda to the gazetteer of Pan Mountain]
    4 *juan*, by Abbot Zhipu (cf. A17), ed. Wang Shizhen 王士禎 (1634-1711; cf. D3, K24).
    1696, published together with A17. Harvard, Naikaku, UBC.
    1872 reprint. Jimbun, SOAS, Tobunken, Toyo.

A19. *Panshan zhi* 盤山志
[Gazetteer of Pan Mountain]
    16 *juan*, ed. Jiang Pu 蔣溥 (js. 1730).
    1755. Columbia, Gest, Harvard, Jimbun, LC, Naikaku, Palace (2 copies), Seikado, Toyo.
    An imperially authorized expansion of A17.

A20. *Shuo pan* 說盤
[On Pan Mountain]
    3 *juan*, by Zhou Songnian 周崧年.
    1915. Jimbun, LC, Seikado, Shifan.
    The latest date in this gazetteer is 1754 (3.39b).

Shuntian: Jizhou: Zunhua

A21. *Changrui shan wannian tongzhi* 昌瑞山萬年統志
[Comprehensive gazetteer of the imperial tombs at Changrui Mountain]
    16 *juan*, by Bulantai 布蘭泰, ed. Ying Lian 英廉 (1707-83).
    1741. Toyo.
    1883 manuscript. LC.
    Undated manuscript. Shifan.
    Bibliographic notice: Wang 204.
    The gazetteer of the Qing imperial tombs east of Peking.

Daming: Kaizhou

A22. *Puyang heshang ji* 濮陽河上記
[Record of the Puyang River]
    4 *bian*, by Xu Shiguang 徐世光.
    1915. Columbia.
    Primarily an account of the work done following the flooding
of the Puyang River in 1913.

Guangping: Qinghe

A23. *Huang yun hekou gujin tushuo* 黃運河口古今圖說
[Illustrated study of the point where the Yellow River meets the
Grand Canal in ancient and modern times]
    1 *juan*, by Linqing 麟慶.
    1840. Columbia.
    A series of ten detailed maps with commentary showing the
progressive development of channels, embankments, and
locks in the Jiajing era, 1672, 1676, 1695, 1765, 1776,
1785, 1808, 1827, and 1828. Writings by several officials
are appended.

Yongping: Funing: Shanhai wei

A24. *Shanhai guanzhi* 山海關志
[Gazetteer of Shanhai Gate]
    8 *juan*, by Zhan Rong 詹榮 (js. 1526).
    1535. Fu has a manuscript copy, Taibei has a
photo-reproduced copy.
    Shanhai Gate, the eastern terminus of the Great Wall, was
the point of crossing between northeast China and the
Liaoxi-Liaodong frontier region.

Yongping: Changli

A25. *Jieshi congtan* 碣石叢談
[Notes on the Jieshi Mountains]
    10 *juan*, by Guo Yingchong 郭應寵.
    1610 reprint of 1592 edition. Naikaku.

Miscellaneous historical notes on Yongping prefecture and Changping and Jizhou subprefectures.

Yongping: Luanzhou: Leting

A26. *Leting xian xinjian zundao shuyuan lu* 樂亭縣新建尊道書院錄 [Record of the newly built Zundao Academy of Leting county]
  1 *juan,* by Chen Yipei 陳以培.
  1876. Tobunken.

B. South Zhili: Jiangsu

Yingtian

B1. *Jinling fancha zhi* 金陵梵刹志
[Gazetteer of Buddhist monasteries in Nanjing]
> 53 *juan*, by Director of the Bureau of Sacrifice Ge Yinliang
> 葛寅亮 (js. 1601; cf. N18).
> 1607. Taibei, Toyo.
> 1627 reprint. Naikaku.
> 1936 reprint (Nanjing). Harvard, Jimbun, LC, Shifan,
> Tobunken.
> 1976 Biwu reprint; 1980 ZF reprint.
> Bibliographic notice: Franke 8.5.4.
> A comprehensive gazetteer of all Buddhist monasteries in the
> Nanjing region, compiled within the Ministry of Rites and
> published by the Central Buddhist Registry in Nanjing.

B2. *Jinling xuanguan zhi* 金陵玄觀志
[Gazetteer of Daoist monasteries in Nanjing]
> 13 *juan*, anonymous.
> Late Wanli era.
> 1937 reprint. Columbia, Gest(m), Jimbun, LC, Shifan.
> Bibliographic notice: Franke 8.5.3.
> Identical in format to B1. As the Bureau of Sacrifices in
> 1603 undertook an investigation of Chaotian Gong, the
> leading Daoist monastery in the city (*Jinling fancha zhi*,
> 50.1b), this work may have been produced by the bureau at
> that time.

Yingtian: Shangyuan

B3. *Houhu zhi* 後湖志
[Gazetteer of Back Lake]
> 1 *juan*, by Wang Zuoyu 王作楫, ed. Qian Fuzhen 錢福臻.
> 1910. Columbia.
> A Wanli-era work of the same name is not a gazetteer at all

but a compendium of Yellow Register (*huangce*) statistics, the registers being housed in a government archive by this lake; hence it has not been included.

B4. *Jingxue zhi* 京學志
[Gazetteer of the prefectural school in the (southern) capital]
  8 *juan*, by Jiao Hong 焦竑 (1541-1620; cf. B21).
  1603. Taibei.
  1965 reprint (Taibei: Guofeng Chubanshe).
  Bibliographic notice: Franke 6.7.5.

B5. *Linggu chanlin zhi* 靈谷禪林志
[Gazetteer of Linggu Chan Monastery]
  15 *juan*, by Xie Yuanfu 謝元福.
  1887 reprint of Daoguang edition, with insertions to 1891.
  Harvard, LC, Toyo.

B6. *Ming xiaoling zhi* 明孝陵志
[Gazetteer of the tomb of the Filial Emperor of the Ming]
  1 *juan*, by Wang Huanbiao 王焕鑣.
  1934. Columbia, Gest, Jimbun, LC, Shifan, Tobunken, Toyo.
  The gazetteer of the tomb of the founding emperor, Zhu Yuanzhang 朱元璋 (1328-98).

B7. *Moqiu huzhi* 莫愁湖志
[Gazetteer of Moqiu Lake]
  6 *juan*, by Ma Shitu 馬士圖.
  1815.
  1882 reprint. Columbia, Harvard, Jimbun, LC, Shifan, UBC.
  1933 edition (Nanjing: Hanwen Shudian). Gest.
  1983 ZC reprint of 1882 edition.

B8. *Nanyong zhi* 南雍志
[Gazetteer of the Southern Academy]
  24 *juan*, by Huang Zuo 黃佐 (1490-1566; cf. O27).
  1543, revised 1626 as *Nanyong xuzhi* (18 *juan*).
  1931 reprint of 1626 edition. UBC.

1976 reprints (Taibei:Weiwen Tushu Gongsi). Toronto,UBC.
Bibliographic notice: Franke 6.7.2.
An earlier gazetteer was published in 1458 by Wu Jie   吳節.

B9. *Qixia xiaozhi* 棲霞小志
[Short record of Qixia Monastery]
    1 *juan*, by Sheng Shitai 盛時泰 (cf. B19).
    1884 Ouxiang edition.
    Written about 1578. Huang, 8.33b, also credits Sheng with a
    one-*juan* monastic gazetteer entitled *Qize sizhi* 祈澤寺志.

B10. *Sheshan zhi* 攝山志
[Gazetteer of She Mountain]
    8 *juan*, by Chen Yi 陳毅.
    1790. Harvard, Jimbun, LC, Naikaku, Seikado, Shifan,
    Tobunken.
    She Mountain was the site of Qixia Monastery. Previous
    edition of 1693 by monk Chuyun 楚雲. Ren, p. 293, cites a
    Tongzhi-era edition.

B11. *Qixia xinzhi* 棲霞新志
[New gazetteer of Qixia Monastery]
    By Chen Bangxian 陳邦賢.
    1934 (preface 1930). Gest, Jimbun, Harvard (2 copies), LC,
    Toyo.
    1971 ZM reprint.

B12. *Qixia shanzhi* 棲霞山志
[Gazetteer of Qixia Mountain]
    By Zhu Jiexuan 朱潔軒.
    1962 (Hong Kong: Luyu Yuan). Columbia, Gest, Harvard,
    Toronto, UBC.
    A modern monastic gazetteer written in exile.

B13. *Xuanwu huzhi* 玄武湖志
[Gazetteer of Xuanwu Lake]
    8 *juan*, by Xia Renhu 夏仁虎.

1932. Harvard, Shifan, Toyo.
1970 Bisan reprint.

Yingtian: Jiangning

B14. *Boshan zhi* 盎山志
[Gazetteer of Bo Mountain]
    8 *juan*, by Gu Yun　顧雲.
1883. Columbia, Harvard, Jimbun, LC, Shifan, Toyo.
Bo Mountain was a gentry resort area.

B15. *Shicheng shanzhi* 石城山志
[Gazetteer of Shicheng Mountain]
    1 *juan*, by Chen Yifu　陳詒紱.
1918 Suoxu edition.
1955 reprint (Beijing: Wenxue Guji Kanxingshe). LC.
1970 ZC reprint.
Derived from B14.

B16. *Fenglu xiaozhi* 鳳麓小志
[Short gazetteer of the area around Fenghuang Terrace]
    4 *juan*, by Chen Zuolin　陳作霖.
1900 Suozhi edition.
Fenghuang Tai　鳳凰臺　was in the southwest corner of
Nanjing.

B17. *Jinling da baoen sita zhi* 金陵大報恩寺塔志
[Gazetteer of Nanjing's Great Baoen Monastery and Pagoda]
    10 *juan*, by Zhang Huiyi　張惠衣.
1937. Gest, Harvard, Jimbun, LC, Toyo.
1980 ZF reprint.

B18. *Longjiang chuanchang zhi* 龍江船廠志
[Gazetteer of the Longjiang Shipyard]
    8 *juan*, by Li Zhaoxiang　李昭祥　(js. 1547).
1553.
1947 Xuanxu reprint.

Bibliographic notice: Franke 6.5.10.
Li Zhaoxiang was appointed the executive director of the state shipyard in 1551.

B19. *Niushou shanzhi* 牛首山志
[Gazetteer of Niushou Mountain]
    2 *juan*, by Sheng Shitai (cf. B9).
    1579, with one-*juan* appendix dated 1592. LC(m), Taibei.
    1980 ZF reprint.
    The bulk of the gazetteer was composed in 1554-55. The monastery here received the title Hongjue Si 弘覺寺 in 1436.

B20. *Suiyuan tu* 隨園圖
[Pictures of Sui Garden]
    By Yuan Qi 袁起.
    1867. Columbia.
    Primarily a literary collection.

B21. *Xianhua yanzhi* 獻花巖志
[Gazetteer of Xianhua Grotto]
    2 *juan*, by Chen Yi 陳沂 (1469-1538).
    1603. Columbia(m), Gest(m), LC(m), Taibei.
    1980 ZF reprint.
    In his preface, Jiao Hong (1541-1620; cf. B4) says that Chen compiled this gazetteer in the Jiajing era. Chen is also coeditor of the 1534 prefectural gazetteer of Nanjing, *Nanji zhi* (Franke 8.5.2).

Yingtian: Jurong

B22. *Baohua shanzhi* 寶華山志
[Gazetteer of Baohua Mountain]
    15 *juan*, by Liu Mingfang 劉名芳 (cf. B43, B120).
    1784. Harvard, Jimbun, LC, Toyo.
    Guangxu-era reprint. Shifan, SOAS.
    1980 ZF reprint.
    The gazetteer of Huiju Monastery 慧居寺. Previous edition

1690. JPM, p. 229, mentions a 1930 edition with minor emendations.

B23. *Chishan huzhi* 赤山湖志
[Gazetteer of Chishan Lake]
    6 *juan*, by Shang Zhaoshan 尙兆山.
    1916 Jinling edition.
    Detailed account of the topography and fiscal status of the region around the lake.

B24. *Maoshan zhi* 茅山志
[Gazetteer of Mao Mountain]
    15 *juan*, by Liu Dabin 劉大彬.
    1328. Beijing.
    Yongle-era reprint. Beijing, Gest(m), LC(m), Taibei.
    1550 reprint, with supplementary *juan* appended to *juan* 13 and 15 by Wang Yongnian 汪永年. Gest(m), Naikaku (2 copies), Sonkeikaku, Taibei(m).
    Mao Shan was the sight of a major Daoist monastery. There is a 33-*juan* edition in Daozang, vols. 153-54.

B25. *Maoshan zhi* 茅山志
[Gazetteer of Mao Mountain]
    13 *juan*, by Da Changuang 笪蟾光.
    1669. Columbia, Jimbun.
    1877 reprint. Shifan.
    1894 reprint. Toyo.
    1898 reprint. Harvard, LC.
    1971 ZM reprint of the 1898 edition.

Yingtian: Jiangpu

B26. *Pukou tangquan xiaozhi* 浦口湯泉小志
[Short gazetteer of the Pukou hot springs]
    2 volumes, by Gong Xinming 龔心銘.
    1927. Harvard.
    The captions to the photographs and the analytical table are in both Chinese and English. The hot springs are located

about 20 km. northwest of Nanjing.

Huaian

B27. *Huaijun wenqu zhi* 淮郡文渠志
[Gazetteer of Wen Canal in Huaian prefecture]
　　2 *juan*, by He Qijie 何其傑.
　　Guangxu-era Jingyuan edition.

Huaian: Shanyang

B28. *Bochi shanzhi* 鉢池山志
[Gazetteer of Bochi Mountain]
　　6 *juan*, by Mao Guangsheng 冒廣生 (b. 1873).
　　1920 Rugao edition.
　　Compiled about 1912; the gazetteer of Jinghui Chan
　　Monastery 景會禪寺.

Huaian: Qinghe

B29. *Piaomu cizhi* 漂母祠志
[Gazetteer of Piaomu Shrine]
　　7 *juan*, by Hu Fengdan 胡鳳丹 (1823-90; cf. B40, E15, G8,
　　J1, J4, K11, M18).
　　1877. Tobunken, Toyo (2 copies).

Huaian: Haizhou

B30. *Yuntai shanzhi* 雲臺山志
[Gazetteer of Yuntai Mountain]
　　8 *juan*, by Cui Yingjie 崔應階 (d. ca. 1780).
　　1772. Jimbun, Shifan.
　　1978 ZC reprint with B31; 1983 ZC reprint.
　　1978 reprint (Taibei: Wenxing Chubanshe). Columbia, Gest,
　　LC.

B31. *Yuntai xinzhi* 雲臺新志
[New gazetteer of Yuntai Mountain]
    18 *juan*, by Xu Qiaolin 許喬林.
    1937. Harvard, Shifan, SOAS, Toyo.
    1978 ZC reprint with B30.
    1978 reprint (Taibei: Wenxing Chubanshe). Columbia, Gest, LC.

Yangzhou

B32. *Yangzhou shuidao ji* 楊州水道記
[Record of the water courses of Yangzhou]
    4 *juan*, by Liu Wenqi 劉文淇 (1749-1840).
    1845 (completed 1838). Columbia.
    1872 reprint. UBC.
    Preface by Ruan Yuan 阮元 (1764-1849; cf. B105, L87, M1, M67) dated 1837.

Yangzhou: Jiangdu

B33. *(Yangzhou) Beihu xiaozhi* 北湖小志
[Short gazetteer of North Lake]
    6 *juan*, by Jiao Xun 焦循.
    1808 Jiaoshi edition; 1983 ZC reprint.

B34. *Yangzhou beihu xuzhi* 楊州北湖續志
[Supplementary gazetteer of Yangzhou's North Lake]
    6 *juan*, by Ruan Xian 阮先.
    Daoguang era.
    1934 Yangzhou edition.

B35. *Pingshan lansheng zhi* 平山攬勝志
[Sightseeing gazetteer of Pingshan Hall]
    10 *juan*, by Wang Yinggeng 汪應庚.
    1742. LC.
    This is a gazetteer not only of the Buddhist monastery Pingshan Hall but of the other monasteries, pavilions, and

temples around Baozhang Lake 保障湖 just outside the city of Yangzhou.

B36. *Pingshan tang xiaozhi* 平山堂小志
[Short gazetteer of Pingshan Hall]
　　12 *juan*, by Cheng Mengxing 程夢星.
　　1752. Naikaku, LC, Toyo.

B37. *Pingshan tang tuzhi* 平山堂圖志
[Illustrated gazetteer of Pingshan Hall]
　　10 *juan*, by Salt Commissioner Zhao Zhibi 趙之壁.
　　1765. Harvard, LC, Shifan, Toyo, UBC.
　　1843 Japanese reprint. Columbia, Gest, Harvard, Naikaku
　　(2 copies), Toyo.
　　1883 reprint. Columbia, Harvard, LC.
　　1895 reprint. Jimbun, Shifan.
　　1971 ZM reprint; 1980 ZF reprint; 1983 ZC reprint.

B38. *Tianning situ* 天寧寺圖
[Pictures of Tianning Monastery]
　　Anonymous.
　　Manuscript, after 1783. Toyo.
　　A folio of pictures and brief notices of Tianning and other
　　monasteries and gardens around Yangzhou.

B39. *Yangzhou xiuyuan zhi* 楊州休園志
[Gazetteer of Xiu Garden in Yangzhou]
　　By Zheng Qinggu 鄭慶估 (b. 1737).
　　1773. Taibei, Toyo.

Yangzhou: Gaoyou zhou

B40. *Loujin cizhi* 露筋祠志
[Gazetteer of Loujin Shrine]
　　5 *juan*, by Hu Fengdan (cf. B29, E15, G8, J1, J4, K11,
　　M18).
　　1877. Jimbun.

Yangzhou: Taizhou: Rugao

B41. *Wang shi liangyuan tuyong* 汪氏兩園圖詠
[Illustrated poetical writings on Master Wang's two gardens]
    By Wang Chengyong 汪承鑪.
    1813. Columbia.
    Wen Garden 文園 was built by the author's
    great-great-grandfather, Lüjing Garden 綠淨園 by his
    father. Mostly poetry.

Yangzhou: Tongzhou

B42. *Lang wushan zhi* 狼五山志
[Gazetteer of the five peaks of Lang Mountain]
    4 *juan*, by Wang Yangde 王揚德.
    1616.
    1936 reprint. Jimbun, LC, Shifan, Toyo.
    The five peaks were the site of several temples to the god of
    war, Guan Di, and the goddess of mercy, Guanyin.

B43. *Nan Tongzhou wushan quanzhi* 南通州五山全志
[Complete gazetteer of the five peaks in southern Tongzhou]
    20 *juan*, by Liu Mingfang (cf. B22, B120).
    1751. Columbia, Harvard, Jimbun, Shifan, Toyo.
    Liu also wrote an abridged version, *Wushan zhilüe*, collected
    in XF (4).

Suzhou

B44. *Zhenze bian* 震澤編
[Anthology of writings on Zhenze]
    8 *juan*, by Cai Sheng 蔡昇, ed. Wang Ao 王鏊
    (1450-1524).
    1505. Columbia(m), Gest(m), Jimbun(m), LC (2 copies),
    Naikaku.
    Bibiliographic notice: Wang 211.
    1617 reprint. Beijing.
    Zhenze, a river flowing into Lake Tai, is used as a literary

name for that lake. Cai's original edition was written in the early Ming. Beijing holds another Ming edition of this work.

B45. *Juqu zhi* 具區志
[Gazetteer of Juqu]
    16 *juan*, by Weng Shu   翁澍.
    1689. LC, Shifan.
    Juqu is a literary name for the Lake Tai region.

B46. *Taihu zhilüe* 太湖志略
[Abridged gazetteer of Lake Tai]
    4 *juan*, by Cheng Siyue   程思樂.
    1799. Harvard.

B47. *Taihu beikao* 太湖備考
[Complete study of Lake Tai]
    16 *juan*, by Jin Youli   金友理.
    1750. Columbia, Gest, LC (3 copies), Tobunken.
    1970 ZC reprint.

B48. *Taihu beikao xubian* 太湖備考續編
[Complete study of Lake Tai, continued]
    4 *juan*, by Zheng Yanshao   鄭言紹.
    1903. Columbia, Harvard.

B49. *Taihu quanzhi* 太湖泉志
[Gazetteer of the springs of Lake Tai]
    1 *juan*, by Pan Zhiheng   潘之恒.
    1646 Shuofu edition.
    Shanben lists another work by Pan under the title *Huang hai*
    [The Yellow Sea].

B50. *Wujiang shuikao zengji* 吳江水考增輯
[Expanded edition of the *Study of the rivers of Wujiang*]
    5 *juan* plus 2-*juan* appendix, ed. Huang Xiangxi   黃象曦.

1894. Columbia.
Based on a Ming work, *Wujiang shuikao*, by Shen Qi 沈啟,
published in 1726. A broad survey of Yangzi Delta rivers
within and beyond Wujiang county's borders; includes
schematic maps of the Wusong, Lou, and Baiyuan rivers.

Suzhou: Wu

B51. *Dengwei sheng'en sizhi* 鄧尉聖恩寺志
[Gazetteer of Sheng'en Monastery on Dengwei Mountain]
    18 *juan*, by Zhou Yongnian 周永年 (1582-1674; cf. B76).
    1644. Naikaku, UBC.
    1930 reprint of 1644 edition, with additional material to
early Qianlong. Harvard, Jimbun, LC (2 copies), Shifan,
Toyo.
    1980 ZF reprint.
    Previous gazetteer of 1536 compiled by Shen Runqing
沈潤卿.

B52. *Hanshan sizhi* 寒山寺志
[Gazetteer of Hanshan Monastery]
    3 *juan*, by Ye Changchi 葉昌熾 (1848-1917).
    1911. Harvard.
    1922 reprint. Harvard, Jimbun, LC, Toyo.
    1980 ZF reprint; 1986 Jiangsu reprint.

B53. *Hengshan zhilüe* 橫山志略
[Abridged gazetteer of Heng Mountain]
    6 *juan*, by Gu Jiayu 顧嘉譽.
    1748. Beijing.
    18th-century manuscript. Columbia(m), Gest(m), LC(m),
Taibei.

B54. *Kaiyuan sizhi* 開元寺志
[Gazetteer of Kaiyuan Monastery]
    By Pan Zengyi 潘曾沂 (1792-1853).
    1922. Harvard, Jimbun, LC, Shifan, Toyo.

B55. *Wuzhong lingyan shanzhi* 吳中靈巖山志
[Gazetteer of Lingyan Mountain in Suzhou]
    8 *juan*, by Huang Xiyuan 黃習遠.
    Wanli era. Beijing (2 copies).

B56. *Lingyan jilüe* 靈巖紀略
[Abridged record of Lingyan Mountain]
    2 *juan*, by monk Shuzhi 殊致.
    Early Qing. Beijing.
    1971 ZM reprint; 1980 ZF reprint.
    Shifan has a copy of either B56 or B57.

B57. *Lingyan zhilüe* 靈巖志略
[Abridged gazetteer of Lingyan Monastery]
    1 *juan*, by Wang Hao 王鎬.
    1756. Beijing.
    1971 ZM reprint; 1980 ZF reprint.

B58. *Lingyan shanzhi* 靈巖山志
[Gazetteer of Lingyan Mountain]
    By Yu Youqing 兪友清.
    1935. Gest.
    A traditional gazetteer produced in a modern format.

B59. *Loujiang zhi* 婁江志
[Gazetteer of the Lou River]
    2 *juan*, by Gu Shilian 顧士璉 (cf. B60).
    1666 Kaijiang edition.

B60. *Xin liuhe zhi* 新劉河志
[Gazetteer of the new Liu River]
    2 *juan*, by Gu Shilian (cf. B59).
    1666 Kaijiang edition.
    Liuhe is a newer name for Loujiang.

B61. *Shihu zhilüe* 石湖志略
[Abridged gazetteer of Stone Lake]
    2 *juan*, by Lu Xiang 盧襄.
Jiajing era. Beijing.
Qing manuscript copy, with notes by Gu Yuan (cf. L52).

B62. *Shangfang shan shihu* 上方山石湖
[Stone Lake at Shangfang Mountain]
    1 *fascicle*, anonymous.
Qing manuscript. Shifan.

B63. *Shizi lin jisheng ji* 獅子林紀勝集
[Anthology on the sights of Lion Grove]
    2 *juan*, by Abbot Daoxun 道恂.
Composed ca. 1374.
1857 reprint, with B61. LC.
Lion Grove is the name of a garden by which Bodhi
Zhengzong Monastery 菩提正宗寺, which Daoxun founded
in 1342, came to be known.

B64. *Shizi lin jisheng xuji* 獅子林紀勝續集
[Supplementary anthology on the sights of Lion Grove]
    3 *juan*, by Xu Lifang 徐立方.
1857, published with B63. LC.

B65. *Suzhou fuxue zhi* 蘇州府學志
[Gazetteer of the prefectural school of Suzhou]
    18 *juan*, by Liu Minyue 劉民悅 (jr. 1619), Liu Yilin
劉一霖, and Wang Huanru 王煥如.
1624, with additional material to 1641. Naikaku.
Bibliographic notice: Franke 6.7.7.

B66. *Wumu yuan xiaozhi* 五畝園小志
[Short gazetteer of Five-Mu Garden]

4 *juan*, by Xie Jiafu 謝家福 and Ling Si 淩泗.
1890. Columbia, LC, Shifan.
1924 Wangchui edition.

B67. *Yangshan zhi* 陽山志
[Gazetteer of Yang Mountain]
   3 *juan*, by Yue Dai 岳岱.
   1530. Gest (manuscript), Gest(m), LC, Taibei.
   1632 edition, ed. Chen Rucheng 陳汝成. Beijing.
   1693 reprint. Beijing.
   1857 Qiaofan edition.
   Bibliographic notice: Wang 207.

B68. *Yaofeng shanzhi* 堯峰山志
[Gazetteer of Yaofeng Mountain]
   6 *juan*, by Chen Renxi (cf. 1.2.1, B108), ed. posthumously by
   Zhang Feng 張封.
   1638. Gest(m), Taibei.
   1980 ZF reprint.
   Yaofeng Mountain was the site of Shousheng Monastery
   壽聖寺.

B69. *Zhide zhi* 至德志
[Gazetteer of Zhide Temple]
   10 *juan*, by Wu Dingke 吳鼎科.
   1766. LC.
   1876 reprint. Toyo.
   1886 reprint. Toyo.
   Zhide Miao was a state-recognized shrine of a lineage
   surnamed Wu.

Suzhou: Changzhou

B70. *Baoen sizhi* 報恩寺志
[Gazetteer of Baoen Monastery]
   Anonymous.
   Undated. Jimbun.

B71. *(Suzhou fu) Baoen sizhi* 蘇州府報恩寺志
[Gazetteer of Baoen Monastery in Suzhou prefecture]
    2 *juan*, by Abbot Rizhong Minxi 日種敏曦.
    1920. LC.
    1932 edition, ed. Han Qingyun 韓慶雲. Harvard.
    The first *juan*, by Minxi, includes materials dated
    1899-1901. The second *juan* of the LC edition is a collection
    of fund-raising documents dated 1920. The Harvard edition
    includes materials to 1932. A fund-raising appeal dated
    1921 has been inserted in front of the first *juan* of the LC
    edition.

B72. *Canglang xiaozhi* 滄浪小志
[Short gazetteer of Canglang Pavilion]
    2 *juan*, by Song Luo 宋犖 (1634-1713).
    1696. Columbia, LC, Toyo.
    1884 reprint. Gest, LC, Shifan.
    Canglang was a pavilion built in the Song just outside the
    south wall of Suzhou by Su Shunqin 蘇舜欽. The gazetteer
    also contains material pertaining to nearby institutions such
    as Nanchan Jiyun Monastery 南禪集雲寺 and Dayun
    Chapel 大雲庵.

B73. *Canglang ting xinzhi* 滄浪亭新志
[New gazetteer of Canglang Pavilion]
    8 *juan*, by Jiang Hancheng 蔣瀚澄.
    1929. Columbia, Jimbun, Shifan.

B74. *Huqiu shanzhi* 虎丘山志
[Gazetteer of Huqiu Mountain]
    1 *juan*, by Wang Bin 王賓, 3 *juan* added by monk Rumao
    茹昂.
    1486. Beijing, Cambridge, Columbia(m), Gest(m), LC(m),
    Taibei.
    Wang first compiled this gazetteer in the Hongwu era. His

great-grandfather Wang Wu 王玖 compiled Huqiu's first gazetteer in the Yuan.

B75. *Huqiu shanzhi* 虎丘山志
[Gazetteer of Huqiu Mountain]
    5 *juan*, by Wen Zhaozhi 文肇祉 (1519-87).
    1578. LC.
    Bibliographic notice: Wang 206.

B76. *Huqiu shanzhi* 虎丘山志
[Gazetteer of Huqiu Mountain]
    10 *juan*, by Gu Mei 顧湄 .
    1676. Beijing, Shifan.
    1702 reprint. Harvard, LC, Toyo.
    Previous gazetteer from the late Ming by Zhou Yongnian (cf. B51).

B77. *Huqiu shanzhi* 虎邱山志
[Gazetteer of Huqiu Mountain]
    24 *juan*, by Gu Yilu 顧詒祿.
    1767. Columbia, Jimbun, LC, Naikaku.

B78. *Hufu zhi* 虎阜志
[Gazetteer of Huqiu Mountain]
    10 *juan*, by Lu Zhaoyu 陸肇域.
    1792. Gest, LC, Seikado, Shifan, Toyo.

B79. *Huqiu shan xiaozhi* 虎丘山小志
[Short gazetteer of Huqiu Mountain]
    By Lu Xuanqing 陸璇卿.
    1925 (Suzhou: Xinsu Shuju). BL, Gest, LC.

B80. *Huqiu xinzhi* 虎邱新志
[New gazetteer of Huqiu Mountain]
    By Huang Houcheng 黃厚誠.
    1935. Columbia, LC.

B81. *Suting xiaozhi* 蘇亭小志
[Short gazetteer of the Su Shi Pavilion]
    10 *juan*, by Li Yanzhang 李彥章.
    1838. Harvard, LC.
    The gazetteer of a garden associated with Su Shi 蘇軾
    (1037-1101) at Dinghui Chan Monastery 定慧禪寺.

B82. *Zhutang sizhi* 竹堂寺志
[Gazetteer of Zhutang Monastery]
    4 *juan*, by monk Zhenjian 眞鑑.
    1917. Jimbun.
    The four *juan* of this edition represent four separate works: a
    gazetteer of Zhutang Monastery (preface 1888), a gazetteer
    of an affiliated chapel, Jingfu An 景福庵, and supplements
    for both.

Suzhou: Kunshan

B83. *Yushan mingsheng ji* 玉山名勝集
[Collection on famous sights at Yu Mountain]
    4 *juan*, by Gu Ying 顧瑛.
    Ca. 1369. LC(m), Taibei.
    1597 reprint. Naikaku (missing first *juan*), Harvard(m),
    LC(m), Taibei.
    Primarily poetry.

Suzhou: Changshu

B84. *Changshu xian ruxue zhi* 常熟縣儒學志
[Gazetteer of the Confucian school of Changshu county]
    8 *juan*, by Yan Nan 嚴枏.
    1610. Naikaku.

B85. *Poshan xingfu zhi* 破山興福志
[Gazetteer of Xingfu Monastery on Po Mountain]
    4 *juan*, by Cheng Jiasui 程嘉燧.
    1642, with material to 1643. Gest(m), LC(m), Taibei.
    1919 reprint. Jimbun, LC, Toyo.

B86. *Weimo sizhi* 維摩寺志
[Gazetteer of Vimalakirti Monastery]
    2 *juan*, by Qu Rugan 屈如榦.
    1922. Shifan.

B87. *Yushan canghai sizhi* 虞山藏海寺志
[Gazetteer of Canghai Monastery on Yu Mountain]
    2 *juan*, by monk Kongjian 空見, ed. Ding Yin 丁蔭.
    1920. Shifan.

B88. *Yushan shuyuan zhi* 虞山書院志
[Gazetteer of Yushan Academy]
    10 *juan*, by Zhang Nai 張鼐.
    Ca. 1606. Beijing.
    Originally called Wenxue Shuyuan 文學書院, this academy
was renamed by Magistrate Geng Ju 耿橘 in 1606 when it
alone of all the academies in Changshu county was permitted
to survive imperial proscription. Geng sponsored the
publication of the gazetteer in commemoration. In the same
year he also published *Changshu xian shuili quanshu*
常熟縣水利全書 [Complete handbook of water resources in
Changshu county].

Songjiang

B89. *Jiangsu haitang xinzhi* 江蘇海塘新志
[New gazetteer of the Jiangsu sea wall]
    8 *juan*, by Li Qingyun 李慶雲, ed. Jiang Shiche 蔣師轍.
    1890. Columbia, LC.

Songjiang: Huating

B90. *Huating haitang jilüe* 華亭海塘紀略
[Abridged record of the sea wall in Huating county]
    By Cao Jiaju 曹家駒.
    Kangxi era. Beijing.

Songjiang: Qingxi

B91. *Kongzhai zhi* 孔宅志
[Gazetteer of the Kong residence]
    10 *juan*, by Sun Hong 孫鉉.
    1722. Columbia, LC.
The gazetteer of an academy that served as a Jiangnan residence for descendants of Confucius. Previous editions of 1609 and 1681.

B92. *Kongzhai zhi* 孔宅志
[Gazetteer of the Kong residence]
    8 *juan*, by Kong Yuqi 孔毓圻 (fl. 18th century).
    1831 reprint, pub. Fang Zufan 方祖範. Tobunken.

Changzhou: Wujin

B93. *Furong hu xiudi lu* 芙蓉湖修隄錄
[Record of the embankment built around Furong Lake]
    8 *juan*, by De Yuan 德元.
    1908. LC.
Based on 1889 edition; previous edition in 1846. Furong Lake is actually the name of a large polder.

B94. *Gaoshan zhi* 高山志
[Gazetteer of Gao Mountain]
    5 *juan*, ed. Magistrate Yun Yingyi 惲應翼.
    1608, with additions to 1616.
    1877 edition with B95. LC, Toyo.
    1937 reprint. Shifan.
Yun edited this from an earlier Ming edition by Gu Shideng 顧世登. The mountain lies at the intersection of Wujin, Wuxi, Jiangyin, and Yixing counties.

B95. *Gaoshan xuzhi* 高山續志
[Supplementary gazetteer of Gao Mountain]
    1 *juan*, by Wu Yong 吳鏞 (preface dated 1849).
    1877 edition with B94. Toyo (misdated in catalogue to 1937).

B96. *(Wujin) Tianning sizhi* 武進天寧寺志
[Gazetteer of Tianning Monastery in Wujin county]
　　11 *juan*, by Pu Yicheng 濮一乘.
　　1947.
　　1973 reprint (Taibei: Zhonghua Dadian Bianyinhui).
　　Harvard.

B97. *Wanshou ting chongjian jishi* 萬壽亭重建紀事
[Record of the reconstruction of Wanshou Pavilion]
　　1 *juan*, anonymous.
　　1910. LC.
　　A collection of texts from 1777 to 1910.

Changzhou: Wuxi

B98. *Donglin shuyuan zhi* 東林書院志
[Gazetteer of Donglin Academy]
　　4 *juan*, by Yan Jue 嚴瑴, supplemented by Pan Weiyu
　　樊維域.
　　Kangxi era. Taibei.

B99. *Donglin shuyuan zhi* 東林書院志
[Gazetteer of Donglin Academy]
　　22 *juan*, by Diao Chengzu 刁承祖 (js. 1715), ed. Gao
　　Tingzhen 高廷珍.
　　1733. Taibei.
　　1881 reprint. Jimbun, LC, Nanda, Shifan, Toyo.

B100. *Huishan gujin kao* 惠山古今考
[Notes on the history of Hui Mountain]
　　14 *juan*, by Tan Xiu 談脩.
　　1599. LC.
　　Bibliographic notice: Wang 207.

B101. *Huishan ji* 慧山記
[Record of Hui Mountain]

4 *juan*, by monk Yuanxian 圖顯, ed. Minister of Rites Shao
Bao 邵寶 (1460-1527).
1510.
1868 edition with B102. Columbia, Harvard (2 copies), LC,
Seikado, Shifan, Tobunken, Toyo, UBC.
1884 reprint with B102. LC.
The gazetteer of Huishan Chan Monastery 慧山禪寺.

B102. *Huishan xubian* 慧山續編
[Supplementary record of Hui Mountain]
    4 *juan*, by Shao Hanchu 邵涵初.
    1855.
    1868 edition with B101. Columbia, Harvard (2 copies), LC,
    Seikado, Shifan, Tobunken, Toyo.
    1884 reprint with B101. LC.

B103. *Rencao anzhi* 忍草庵志
[Gazetteer of Rencao Chapel]
    4 *juan*, by Liu Jizeng 劉繼增.
    1887. Shifan.

B104. *Xishan jingwu lüe* 錫山景物略
[Synopsis of the sights of Xi Mountain]
    10 *juan*, by Wang Yongji 王永積.
    1898. Shifan, Toyo.

B105. *Zhucha xiaozhi* 竹垞小志
[Short gazetteer of Zhucha Garden]
    5 *juan*, by Ruan Yuan (cf. B32, L87, M1, M67), ed. Yang
    Pan 楊蟠.
    Guangxu-era Jingyuan edition; 1971 Bisi reprint of undated
    Qing edition.
    The garden, belonging to Zhu Xichang 朱錫鬯, was built in
    1669. The gazetteer is principally a collection of literary
    works.

Zhenjiang: Dantu, Danyang, Jintan

B106. *Jingkou sanshan zhi* 京口三山志
[Gazetteer of the three mountains at the approach to Nanjing]
    10 *juan*, by Zhang Lai 張萊 (js. 1514).
    1512. Naikaku.
    1911 Hengshan edition.
    Joint gazetteer of Jin Shan, Jiao Shan, and Ganlu monasteries.

B107. *Jingkou sanshan zhi* 京口三山志
[Gazetteer of the three mountains at the approach to Nanjing]
    12 *juan*, by Xu Guocheng 許國城.
    1600. Gest(m), LC(m), Sonkeikaku, Taibei.
    1980 ZF reprint.
    An expansion of the 1512 edition, including one-*juan*
    gazetteers of Luquan Monastery 鹿泉寺 and Helin Monas-
    tery 鶴林寺, both compiled by Gao Yifu 高一福 in 1599.

B108. *Jingkou sanshan zhi* 京口三山志
[Gazetteer of the three mountains at the approach to Nanjing]
    20 *juan*, edited by Chen Renxi (cf. 1.2.1, B68).
    1612. Gest(m), LC, Taibei.
    Bibliographic notice: Wang 206.

B109. *Jingkou shanshui zhi* 京口山水志
[Gazetteer of the mountains and rivers at the approach to Nanjing]
    19 *juan*, by Yang Qi 楊棨.
    1844. Columbia.
    1847 reprint. Jimbun, Shifan, Toyo, UBC.
    Guangxu-era reprint. LC.
    ZC reprint.
    For an abbreviated but thorough list of places in the region,
    see Qi Juancao 祁寯藻, *Jingkou shanshui kao* 京口山水考
    (Qing manuscript in Taibei, microfilm in Gest).

Zhenjiang: Dantu

B110. *Baojin shuyuan zhi* 寶晉書院志
[Gazetteer of Baojin Academy]
    11 *juan*, by Zhao Youchen 趙佑宸.
    1880. Jimbun, LC, Nanda. Tobunken, Toyo.
    Based on a 1763 edition by Gui Zhongfu 貴中孚.

B111. *Beigu shanzhi* 北固山志
[Gazetteer of Beigu Mountain]
    12 *juan*, by monk Liaopu 了璞.
    1836. Harvard, UBC.
    The gazetteer of Ganlu Monastery 甘露寺.

B112. *Beigu shanzhi* 北固山志
[Gazetteer of Beigu Mountain]
    14 *juan*, by Zhou Boyi 周伯義 (cf. B124).
    1903. LC.
    1904 Jingkou edition; 1974 ZC reprint.

B113. *Helin sizhi* 鶴林寺志
[Gazetteer of Helin Monastery]
    1 *juan*, by monk Mingxian 明賢.
    1614. Columbia(m), Gest(m) Jimbun, LC(m), Naikaku, Taibei.
    1809 reprint. Harvard.
    1909 reprint. LC, Toyo.
    Early Republican-era reprint. Toyo.
    1980 ZF reprint.

B114. *Jiaoshan zhi* 焦山志
[Gazetteer of Jiao Shan Monastery]
    12 *juan*, by Lu Jianzeng 盧見曾 (1690-1768; cf. B121).
    1762. UBC.

B115. *Jiaoshan zhi* 焦山志
[Gazetteer of Jiao Shan Monastery]
    20 *juan*, by Wang Yu 王豫.
    1823. LC, Tobunken, Toyo.
    1839 reprint. BL.

B116. *Jiaoshan zhi* 焦山志
[Gazetteer of Jiao Shan Monastery]
    26 *juan*, by Wu Yun 吳雲 (1811-83).
    1874 (title page 1865). Cambridge, Columbia, Harvard,
    Jimbun, LC, Shifan, Tobunken, Toronto, Toyo, UBC.
    1904 Jingkou reprint; 1974 ZC reprint.

B117. *Jiaoshan xuzhi* 焦山續志
[Supplementary gazetteer of Jiao Shan Monastery]
    8 *juan*, by Chen Renchang 陳仁暘.
    1905 Jingkou edition; 1974 ZC reprint.

B118. *Jinshan ji* 金山集
[Anthology on Jin Shan Monastery]
    3 *juan*, by Registrar Jingtan Yuanji 圓濟.
    Jiajing era. Gest(m), LC(m), Taibei.
    1937 reprint. Jimbun.
    Only the first two *juan* survive. An early-sixteenth-century
    gazetteer of Jin Shan by Yang Xunji (1456-1544), with a
    preface by Li Dongyang (1447-1516), was destroyed in the
    Qianlong inquisition and is no longer extant. See L.
    Carrington Goodrich, *The Literary Inquisition of Ch'ien-Lung*
    (1935), p. 62, n. 1.

B119. *Jinshan zhilüe* 金山志略
[Abridged gazetteer of Jin Shan Monastery]
    4 *juan*, by monk Tiezhou Xinghai 鐵舟行海.
    1681. Beijing, Harvard, Shifan.
    1936 reprint with B120. LC, Shifan.
    1980 ZF reprint.

B120. *Jinshan zhi* 金山志
[Gazetteer of Jin Shan Monastery]
　　16 *juan*, by Liu Mingfang (cf. B22, B43).
　　1751.
　　1936 reprint with B119. LC.

B121. *Jinshan zhi* 金山志
[Gazetteer of Jin Shan Monastery]
　　10 *juan*, by Lu Jianzeng (cf. B114).
　　1762. Columbia, Harvard, LC, Shifan, Toyo, UBC.
　　1901 edition with B123. LC, Shifan, UBC.
　　1973 reprint with B123 under the title *Jinshan sizhi*
　　金山寺志 (Taibei: Xinwenfeng Chubanshe). Columbia, Gest.
　　1980 ZF reprint.

B122. *Xu Jinshan zhi* 續金山寺
[Supplementary gazetteer of Jin Shan Monastery]
　　20 *juan*, by Pan Ao 潘煥 .
　　1824. Columbia, Shifan.

B123. *Xu Jinshan zhi* 續金山志
[Supplementary gazetteer of Jin Shan Monastery]
　　2 *juan*, by monk Qiuya 秋崖 .
　　Daoguang era. Toyo.
　　1901 edition with B121. LC, Shifan, UBC.
　　1973 reprint with B121. Columbia, Gest.
　　1980 ZF reprint.

B124. *Jinshan zhi* 金山志
[Gazetteer of Jin Shan Monastery]
　　20 *juan*, by Zhou Boyi (cf. B112).
　　1904 Jingkou edition; 1974 ZC reprint.

B125. *Zhaoyin shanzhi* 招隱山志
[Gazetteer of Zhaoyin Mountain]

12 *juan*, by Miao Qian 繆潛 .
1925 (completed 1911). Harvard, Shifan, Toyo.
The gazetteer of Zhaoyin Monastery, also known as Luquan
Monastery 鹿泉寺.

Zhenjiang: Danyang

B126. *Lianhu zhi* 練湖志
[Gazetteer of Lian Lake]
　　10 *juan*, under the editorship of Li Shixu 黎世序
　　(1773-1824).
　　1810. Columbia, Harvard, LC, Naikaku.
　　1917 reprint, with addenda by Kong Zonglu and Sun Guojun
　　孫國鈞. LC, Tobunken.

C. South Zhili: Anhui

Luzhou: Hefei

C1. *Zifeng shanzhi* 紫蓬山志
[Gazetteer of Zifeng Mountain]
    1 *juan*, by Li Enshou 李恩綬, ed. Abbot Sanxing 三惺.
    1895.
    1931 reprint. Columbia, Shifan, Toyo.
    Gazetteer of Xilu Chan Monastery 西廬禪寺, southwest of
    the town of Hefei.

Luzhou: Lujiang

C2. *Yefu shanzhi* 冶父山志
[Gazetteer of Yefu Mountain]
    6 *juan*, by Chen Shi 陳詩.
    1936. Harvard.
    Previous gazetteer of 1704 by monk Yijian 一劍; a subse-
    quent 1829 edition was destroyed during the Taiping
    rebellion. The chief monastery on the mountain was Baoji Si
    寶際寺, colloquially known as Yefu Si.

Luzhou: Liuan zhou

C3. *Shaobei jishi* 勺陂紀事
[A record of events concerning Shao Dike]
    2 *juan*, by Xia Shangzhong 夏尚忠.
    1801.
    1877 reprint. Columbia.
    Shao Dike dates from the Spring and Autumn Period.

Anqing: Huaining

C4. *Daguan tingzhi* 大觀亭志
[Gazetteer of Daguan Pavilion]

2 *juan*, by Li Guomo 李國摸, ed. Li Bingrong 李丙榮.
1911. LC, Shifan.
1913 reprint. LC.
1916 reprint. Shifan, Toyo.
The gazetteer of a temple to Yu Que 余闕 (1302-57), a
Yuan official who died defending Anqing against the forces of
Zhu Yuanzhang; Zhu later canonized him as a paragon of
loyalty to his dynasty.

Anqing: Tongcheng

C5. *Fushan zhi* 浮山志
[Gazetteer of Fu Mountain]
    10 *juan*, by Abbot Shanzu Xingfu 山足興斧.
    1680; enlarged 1788.
    1873 reprint. Columbia, LC, Toyo.
    The main monastery on Fu Mountain was Huayan Si
    華嚴寺. Shanzu was dispatched to Huayan by native-son
    Fang Yizhi 方以智- (1611-71; cf. I39) to compile this
    gazetteer.

Anqing: Qianshan

C6. *Tianzhu shanzhi* 天柱山志
[Gazetteer of Tianzhu Mountain]
    11 *juan*, by Wu Yifeng 烏以風.
    1984 (Hefei: Anhui Jiaoyu Chubanshe). LC.
    Tianzhu Mountain, sacred to Daoist cosmology, was the origi-
    nal Southern Peak (Nanyue) prior to the imperial period and
    the expansion of the Chinese state into Hunan. Written in a
    modern classical style, this gazetteer was recompiled by the
    author after the original draft was destroyed in 1967.

Taiping: Wuhu

C7. *(Wuhu) Jiaoji shanzhi* 蕪湖蟆矶山志
[Gazetteer of Jiaoji Mountain in Wuhu county]
    4 *juan*, by Ke Yuan 柯愿.
    1689.
    1757 revised edition. Dili.

Chizhou: Guichi

C8. *Qishan zhi* 齊山志
[Gazetteer of Qi Mountain]
    7 *juan*, by Li Tao 李燾.
Qing. Keji.

C9. *Qishan yandong zhi* 齊山巖洞志
[Gazetteer of Qi Mountain Grotto]
    26 *juan*, by Chen Wei 陳蔚 (cf. C14).
1805. Harvard, Jimbun, LC, Seikado, Shifan, UBC, Zhejiang.
1901 Guichi edition.
Previous edition late Kangxi. Chen also has a one-*juan* essay by this same title collected in XF (4).

C10. *Xiushan zhi* 秀山志
[Gazetteer of Xiu Mountain]
    18 *juan*, by Chen Hong 陳竑, ed. Chang An 常安.
1772. Keji, LC.
Xuantong-era reprint. Dili.
1915 reprint. Toyo.
1917 Guichi reprint.
The mountain is noted for a shrine built in 1482 at the grave of a Liang-period prince.

Chizhou: Qingyang

C11. *Jiuhua shanzhi* 九華山志
[Gazetteer of Jiuhua Mountain]
    6 *juan*, by Wang Yihuai 王一槐.
1528. Columbia(m), Gest(m) LC(m), Taibei.
Jiuhua Mountain was the site of a major Buddhist monastic complex.

C12. *Jiuhua shanzhi* 九華山志
[Gazetteer of Jiuhua Mountain]
    8 *juan*, by Magistrate Cai Lishen 蔡立身.

1595. Columbia(m) LC(m), Taibei.
1629 reprint, edited by Gu Yuanjing 顧元鏡 . Toyo.
Bibliographic notice: Sun 8a.
Previous gazetteer in 6 *juan*, 1579, by Magistrate Su
Wanmin 蘇萬民 .

C13. *Jiuhua shanzhi* 九華山志
[Gazetteer of Jiuhua Mountain]
    12 *juan*, by Prefect Li Can 李燦 , ed. Prefect Yu Chenglong
    喩成龍 .
    1690. Columbia.
    1749 reprint. Naikaku, Seikado, Toyo, Zhejiang.

C14. *Jiuhua jisheng* 九華紀勝 .
[Record of the sights on Jiuhua Mountain]
    21 *juan*, by Chen Wei (cf. C9).
    1821. Harvard, LC, Toyo, UBC.

C15. *Jiuhua shanzhi* 九華山志
[Gazetteer of Jiuhua Mountain]
    10 *juan*, by Zhou Yun 周贇 (cf. C17) and Magistrate Xie
    Weijie 謝維喈 .
    1900. Harvard, LC, Shifan, Tobunken, Zhejiang.
    Based on C13.

C16. *Jiuhua shanzhi* 九華山志
[Gazetteer of Jiuhua Mountain]
    8 *juan*, by Abbot Desen 德森 .
    1938. Harvard, Toronto, Zhejiang.
    1978 Sida reprint.

C17. *Jiulian shanzhi* 九蓮山志
[Gazetteer of Jiulian Mountain]
    1 *ce*, by Zhou Yun (cf. C15).
    1904. Zhejiang.

Chizhou: Shidai

C18. *Shidai xian shanchuan zhi chugao* 石埭縣山川志初稿
[Draft gazetteer of the mountains and rivers of Shidai county]
    By Ni Wenshuo 倪文碩 and Chen Shuoliang 陳碩梁.
    1934. Anhui.

Huizhou: She

C19. *Huangshan zhi* 黃山志
[Gazetteer of Huang Mountain]
    10 *juan*, by monk Hongmei 弘眉.
    1667. Anhui, LC, Toyo.

C20. *Huangshan zhi dingben* 黃山志定本
[Standard gazetteer of Huang Mountain]
    7 *juan*, ed. Wang Muri 汪沐日 and Magistrate Min Linsi
閔麟嗣.
    1679. Anhui, Hangzhou, Harvard, Jimbun, LC, Shifan.
    1686 reprint. Gest, Zhejiang.
    1935 Anhui reprint of 1686 reprint.
    Based on C19. According to Anhui, p. 232, monk Hongji
弘濟 produced an edition of this work; a copy is in the
Huizhou Regional Museum.

C21. *Huangshan zhi* 黃山志
[Gazetteer of Huang Mountain]
    2 *juan*, by Xu Shankang 徐山康 and Zhang Peifang 張佩芳
(js. 1757).
    1770. Shifan, UBC, Zhejiang.

C22. *Huangshan lingyao lu* 黃山領要錄
[Record of important sights on Huang Mountain]
    2 *juan*, by Wang Hongdu 汪洪度.
    1774 Zhibuzu edition.
    1862 Japanese edition. Naikaku (2 copies).
    1936 Congshu edition; 1937 Huangshan edition.
    There are several other collectanea editions. The original

edition is lost.

C23. *Huangshan dao* 黃山導
[Guide to Huang Mountain]
    4 *juan*, by Shen Gaoshi 沈碻士, ed. Wang Ji 汪琪.
    1762. Harvard, Naikaku.
    Intended more as a portable guidebook than a gazetteer, this is a collection of renowned literary pieces on Huang Mountain.

C24. *Huangshan xiaozhi, xuzhi* 黃山小志, 續志
[Brief gazetteer of Huang Mountain, with supplement]
    2 *juan*, by Jiang Tan 蔣坦.
    1894. Zhejiang.

C25. *Huangshan xuji* 黃山續集
[Supplementary anthology on Huang Mountain]
    6 *juan*, by Wang Shihong 汪士鈜 .
    Late Qing. Naikaku, Toyo.
    1935 Anhui reprint.

C26. *Huangshan jisheng* 黃山紀勝
[Record of the sights on Huang Mountain]
    4 *juan*, by Xu Ao 徐璈 (1779-1841).
    Late Qing. Anhui, Toyo.
    1969 Biji reprint.
    1980 reprint (Shanghai: Shanghai Guji Chubanshe). LC.
    A travelogue that draws from earlier gazetteers.

Huizhou: Xiuning

C27. *Huangu shuyuan zhi* 還古書院志
[Gazetteer of Huangu Academy]
    18 *juan*, by Shi Huang 施璜.
    1741. Hefei, Jimbun, LC.
    1843 reprint. Anhui.
    Shi Huang also compiled an 18-*juan* gazetteer of an academy

in Hangzhou, entitled *Ziyang shuyuan zhi* 紫陽書院志 (HHC 185).

C28. *Qiyun shanzhi* 齊雲山志
[Gazetteer of Qiyun Mountain]
    5 *juan*, by Magistrate Lu Dian   魯點.
    1599. Harvard, Keji, LC(m), Taibei, Toyo.
    1666 reprint. Anhui, LC, Naikaku, Shifan.
    Bibliographic notice: Wang 207.
    Primarily a collection of literary works on this Daoist mountain.

C29. *Yangshan sheng* 仰山乘
[Gazetteer of Yang Mountain]
    5 *juan*, by Cheng Wenju   程文擧.
    1611. Gest(m) LC(m), Taibei.
    1980 ZF reprint.

C30. *Ziyun shuyuan zhi* 紫雲書院志
[Gazetteer of Ziyun Academy]
    5 fascicles, by Li Laizhang 李來章, ed. Wu Zhantai   吳瞻泰.
    Kangxi-era Lishan edition; Qianlong-era reprint.
    The academy was named for a peak in the Huang Mountains. Wu also wrote a postscript for a collection of woodblock prints of the Huang Mountains entitled *Huangshan tu* 黃山圖 and dated 1698 (UBC).

Huizhou: Wuyuan

C31. *Cheng Zhu queli zhi* 程朱闕里志
[Gazetteer of the natal homes of Cheng Yi, Cheng Hao, and Zhu Xi]
    6 *juan*, by Zhao Pang   趙滂, ed. Bao Ying'ao 鮑應鰲.
    1615. Naikaku (also has an Edo manuscript copy).
    Harvard has a manuscript copy of 1870 of the first volume (preface, table of contents, list of contributors, and illustrations).
    Wuyuan was the natal home of Zhu Xi 朱熹 (1130-1200), though he was actually born in Fujian. The family shrine in

the southern part of the county seat was converted to a temple in his honor by Lizong (r. 1225-64), who conferred on it the title *queli*, otherwise used only for the birthplace of Confucius. This gazetteer records other Huizhou sites associated with the Cheng brothers and Zhu, and includes historical material concerning their lives, disciples, and teachings. Cf. F5, N24, N25.

Huizhou: Qimen

C32. *Fenghuang shanzhi* 鳳凰山志
[Gazetteer of the Fenghuang Mountains]
     3 *juan*, by Hu Guangzhao 胡光釗.
     1939. Anhui.

Xuzhou

C33. *Lüliang hongzhi* 呂梁洪志
[Gazetteer of the Lüliang Rapids]
     1 *juan*, by Feng Shiyong 馮世雍.
     1561 Jinsheng edition; 1959 reprint.
     Bibliographic notice: Franke 8.2.2.

Chuzhou

C34. *Langya shanzhi* 瑯琊山志
[Gazetteer of Langya Mountain]
     8 *juan*, by Zhang Xinpei 章心培.
     1929. Anhui, Harvard, Jimbun, LC, Shifan, Toyo.

Hezhou

C35. *Xiangquan zhi* 香泉志, *Tangquan zhi* 湯泉志, *Bantang zhi* 半湯志
[Gazetteers of the Xiangquan, Tangquan, and Bantang springs]
     By Li Wei 李渭.
     1575, appended to the subprefectural gazetteer *Hezhou zhi* 和州志. Sonkeikaku.

Guangde zhou

C36. *Cishan zhi* 祠山志
[Gazetteer of Shrine Mountain]
   10 *juan*, by Zhang Guangcao 張光藻.
   1886. Jimbun, Keji, LC, Toyo, UBC.
   1895 reprint, ed. Zhou Bingxiu 周秉秀. Zhejiang.
   This mountain had a shrine to a soldier canonized as Zhang
   Zhenjun 張眞君.

D. Shandong

Jinan, Yuezhou, Dongchang

D1. *Shandong yunhe beilan* 山東運河備覽
[Complete conspectus of the Grand Canal in Shandong]
   12 *juan*, ed. Provincial Surveillance Commissioner Lu Yao
   陸耀 and Minister of War Yao Lide 姚立德.
   1776. Columbia.
   1971 Shuili reprint of 1871 edition with subsequent additions
   to 1901.
   The first *juan* is a series of rough maps of the Grand Canal,
   the second a complete chart of officials appointed to supervise
   the canal between 1279 and 1901 (in the later edition).

Jinan: Licheng

D2. *Baotu quanzhi* 趵突泉志
[Gazetteer of Baotu Spring]
   2 *juan*, by Ren Hongyuan 任弘遠.
   1742. Columbia.
   Includes illustrations dated 1650 and 1714.

Jinan: Zouping

D3. *Changbai shanlu* 長白山錄
[Record of Changbai Mountain]
   1 *juan*, by Wang Shizhen (cf. A18, K24).
   1697. LC, Seikado, Shifan, Toyo.
   Qianlong-era Yuyang edition.
   Changbai Mountain was sacred to Daoism. This gazetteer
   includes pre-Ming texts concerning its history.

Jinan: Changqing

D4. *Lingyan ji* 靈巖集
[Writings on Lingyan Mountain]
    6 *juan*, anonymous.
    Latest internal date 1440. Naikaku.
    Poems and stele texts.

D5. *Lingyan zhi* 靈巖志
[Gazetteer of Lingyan Mountain]
    6 *juan*, by Li Xingzu 李興祖.
    1696. Harvard, LC.
    Unlike D4, this is more a Buddhist monastic gazetteer.

Jinan: Qingcheng

D6. *Wufeng shanzhi* 五峰山志
[Gazetteer of Wufeng Mountain]
    2 *juan*, by Liu Tong 劉侗.
    1895 Anle edition.
    Gazetteer of the Daoist monastery Dongzhen Guan 洞眞觀,
    known as Longshou Gong 隆壽宮 in the Ming.

Jinan: Taian zhou

D7. *Taishan zhi* 泰山志
[Gazetteer of Tai Mountain]
    4 *juan*, by Wang Ziqing 汪子卿.
    1555. Beijing, Cambridge, Gest(m), LC, LC(m), Naikaku,
    Sonkeikaku, Taibei (2 copies).
    Bibliographic notice: Wang 206.
    Primarily literary pieces; the earliest Tai Mountain
    gazetteer.

D8. *Dai shi* 岱史
[History of Tai Mountain]
    18 *juan*, by Zha Zhilong 查志隆 (js. 1559).
    1587. Naikaku.

1654 reprint. Harvard, Shifan, Tobunken, Toyo.
1699 reprint. Hangzhou, LC, Tobunken.
Republican-era Daozang edition.
Bibliographic notice: Wang 206.

D9. *Taishan daoli ji* 泰山道里記
[An itinerary of Tai Mountain]
    1 *juan*, by Nie Wen 聶鈫.
    1775. SOAS (2 copies), Tobunken, UBC.
    1866 reprint. Columbia.
    1878 reprint. BL, Cambridge, Harvard, Shifan.
    1895 XF edition.
    1897 reprint. Tobunken.
    1922 reprint. Shifan.
    1935 reprint (Shanghai: Shangwu Yinshuguan). BL.
    ZC reprint, 1971 ZM reprint.

D10. *Taishan xiaoshi* 泰山小史
[Short history of Tai Mountain]
    1 *juan*, by Xiao Xiezhong 蕭協中 (d. 1644), edited by Song
    Siren 宋思仁.
    1789. Cambridge, SOAS, UBC.
    1932 reprint, with one *juan* of annotations by Zhao Xinru
    趙新儒. Gest, Harvard, Jimbun, LC, Shifan, Tobunken.
    1971 ZM reprint of 1932 edition.

D11. *Taishan shuji* 泰山述記
[Records of Tai Mountain]
    10 plus 2 *juan*, by Song Enren 宋恩仁.
    1790. Columbia, Toyo.
    The two extra *juan* at the end contain imperial poetry and
    edicts concerning Tai Mountain. Quotes extensively from D8.
    Published by the Taian magistrate.

D12. *Dai lan* 岱覽
[An overview of Tai Mountain]
    32 *juan*.
    1747. LC.

1793 edition, ed. Tang Zhongmian 唐仲冕 (cf. K18). Harvard.
1805 reprint. Toyo.
1807 reprint. Naikaku, Shifan, UBC.

D13. *Taishan zhi* 泰山志
[Gazetteer of Tai Mountain]
> 20 *juan*, by Jin Qi 金棨.
> 1801. Jimbun.
> 1810 reprint. Harvard, Shifan, SOAS, Tobunken, Toyo, UBC.
> 1898 reprint. Columbia, Gest, LC, Shifan, SOAS.
> Fanshu, p. 176, mentions a *Taishan tuzhi* in 8 *juan* by Zhu Xiaochun 朱孝純 (jr. 1762) dated 1774. Dwight Baker, *T'ai Shan: An Account of the Sacred Eastern Peak of China* (Shanghai: Commercial Press, 1925), xi, mentions a 12-*juan* edition.

Yuezhou: Qufu

D14. *Louxiang zhi* 陋巷志
[Gazetteer of a back alley]
> 8 *juan*, by Yang Guangxun 楊光訓, ed. Yan Yinxiang 顏胤祥.
> 1507. Beijing.
> 1601 revised edition, ed. Lü Zhaoxiang 呂兆祥 (cf. D20, D24). Gest(m), Jimbun, LC (2 copies), Naikaku, Shifan, Sonkeikaku, Taibei.
> 1632 revised edition, ed. Yan Guanglu 顏光魯, with material to 1666 (3.5b). Columbia, Harvard (2 copies), Naikaku, Toronto.
> Bibliographic notice: Wang 139.
> The figure on whom this gazetteer is based is Yan Hui, the disciple whom Confucius praised for living in obscurity in a "back alley" (*Analects* 6:9). It contains both information about his shrine outside the county seat and extensive genealogical matter.

D15. *Queli zhi* 闕里志
[Gazetteer of the burial place (of Confucius)]
      13 *juan*, by Assistant Surveillance Commissioner Chen Hao
      陳鎬 (js. 1487; cf. D14).
      1506. Beijing, LC (2 copies), Taibei.
      1552 edition. Beijing
      1609 edition in 12 *juan*, ed. Kong Zhencong 孔貞叢. LC (2
      copies), Naikaku, Shifan.
      Undated edition in 14 *juan*. Sonkeikaku.
      Bibliographic notice: Wang 138.
      Naikaku also has a Korean printing of this work.

D16. *Dacheng tongzhi* 大成通志
[Comprehensive gazetteer of the sage of great accomplishment]
      18 *juan*, by Yang Qing 楊慶.
      1669. Columbia, LC, Shifan, Sonkeikaku.

D17. *Queli guangzhi* 闕里廣志
[Encyclopedic gazetteer of the burial place (of Confucius)]
      20 *juan*, by Song Ji 宋際 and Song Qingchang 宋慶長
      1673. Beijing, LC, Naikaku.

D18. *Queli zhi* 闕里志
[Gazetteer of the burial place (of Confucius)]
      24 *juan*, ed. Kong Yinzhi 孔胤植 (cf. D20, D24).
      Compiled in Chongzhen era (?), includes material to 1669,
      with an appendix dated 1724. Beijing, Columbia, Gest, LC (2
      copies), Naikaku, Shifan, Tobunken (2 copies), Toronto.
      Bibliographic notice: Wang 139.
      An expanded edition of D15. The editor, a descendant of
      Confucius in the sixty-fifth generation, includes two
      documents that he has signed and dated 1631 (24.69a, 72a):
      this is clearly the work of several consecutive compilers.
      Further information on the shrine to Confucius may be found
      in Kong Jifen 孔繼汾, *Queli wenxian kao* 闕里文獻考 [Study
      of documents concerning the burial place (of Confucius)]
      (1762).

Yuezhou: Zou

D19. *Sanqian zhi* 三遷志
[Gazetteer of the thrice-moved home (of Mencius)]
    6 *juan*, by Assistant Surveillance Commissioner Shi E 史鶚
    1552. Beijing, Gest(m), Naikaku, Sonkeikaku.
Mencius' mother moved three times in order to find a place
suitable for raising her son, hence the title of this gazetteer of
his birthplace, temple, and tomb, and of his mother's shrine
as well. It also includes extensive biographical material,
imperial edicts conferring titles, and other documents. The
temple was founded in 1037, was moved to its present location in 1121, and had reached its full extent by 1623. An
official residence for his descendants was attached to the
west side of the temple.

D20. *Meng zhi* 孟志
[Gazetteer of Mencius]
    5 *juan*, by Pan Zhen, 潘榛, ed. Zhou Xikong 周希孔.
    1611. Gest(m), Sonkeikaku, Taibei.
    1628 edition under the title *Sanqian zhi*, ed. Lü Yuanshan
    呂元善 (1569-1619), Lü Zhaoxiang (cf. D14, D24) and Lü
    Fengshi 呂逢時 (cf. D24). Beijing, Harvard, LC.
    1654 reprint, with slight revision, ed. Gao Min 高旻. LC.
    1669 reprint. LC.
    Bibliographic notice: Wang 140.
Includes prefaces by Li Rihua 李日華 (1565-1635) and Kong
Yinzhi (cf. D18, D24), among others. Naikaku has an
Edo-period manuscript copy.

D21. *Sanqian zhi* 三遷志
[Gazetteer of the thrice-moved home (of Mencius)]
    8 *juan*, by Wang Texuan 王特選, ed. Kong Chuanshang
    孔傳商 and Zhong Yunjin 仲蘊錦.
    Ca. 1725. Beijing, Gest, Toronto.
There are no contemporary prefaces to this edition; the latest
internal date is 1725 (1.13a, 5.28d). An expanded version of
D20.

D22. *Sanqian zhi* 三遷志
[Gazetteer of the thrice-moved home (of Mencius)]
    10 *juan*, by Meng Guangjun, ed. Chen Jin 陳錦 and Sun
Baotian (1840-1911).
    1887 (Shandong Shuju). Beijing, Harvard, LC, Shifan,
Tobunken.
    Shifan also has a 6-*juan* abbreviation of this work by Sun
Baotian entitled *Meng shi bianlüe* [Notes on the *Gazetteer of
Mencius*] (1888).

Yuezhou: Jining zhou: Jiaxiang

D23. *Zeng zhi* 曾志
[Gazetteer of Zeng Zi]
    4 *juan*, by Li Tianzhi 李天植 (js. 1571).
    1595. Gest(m), LC, Taibei.
    Gazetteer of Zongsheng Temple, the shrine to Confucius'
disciple Zeng Zi, plus his genealogy and other historical
materials.

D24. *Zongsheng zhi* 宗聖志
[Gazetteer of Zongsheng Temple]
    12 *juan*, by Lü Zhaoxiang (cf. D14, D20), ed. Lü Weiqi
呂維祺 and Lü Fengshi (cf. D20).
    1629. Gest, Naikaku.
    Includes a preface by Kong Yinzhi (cf. D18, D20).

D25. *Zongsheng zhi* 宗聖志
[Gazetteer of Zongsheng Temple]
    20 *juan*, by Wang Dingan 王定安.
    1890. Columbia, Gest, Jimbun, LC.
    1968 reprint (Taibei: Shangwu). Gest.
    Published under the auspices of the statesman Zeng Guofan
曾國蕃 (1811-72), who claimed Zeng Zi as his ancestor. His
younger brother, Guoquan 國荃 (1824-90), is listed as an
honorary editor.

Yuezhou: Dongping zhou

D26. *Beihe ji* 北河紀
[Record of the northern part of the Grand Canal]
　　8 *juan* plus 4-*juan* supplement, by Xie Zhaozhe　謝肇淛
　　(1567-1624; cf. N1, N11, N33), ed. Prefect Wang Zhao
　　王沼, Shouzhang Magistrate Li Yang　李仰, and Yanggu
　　Magistrate Luo Can　羅璨.
　　1614. LC.
　　Bibliographic notice: Wang 210.

Dongchang: Puzhou

D27. *Yaoling kao* 堯陵考
[Study of the tomb of Emperor Yao]
　　2 *juan*, by Master Nanjian　南澗先生, ed. posthumously by
　　Duan Songling　段松苓.
　　1786 manuscript. Harvard.

Qingzhou: Zhucheng

D28. *Wulian shanzhi* 五蓮山志
[Gazetteer of Wulian Mountain]
　　5 *juan*, by monk Haiting　海霆.
　　1681. LC, Toyo.
　　1757 edition, with extensive additions. Harvard.

Laizhou: Jiaozhou: Jimo

D29. *Laoshan zhi* 勞山志
[Gazetteer of Lao Mountain]
　　8 *juan*, by Huang Zongchang　黃宗昌　(js. 1622, d. 1645), ed.
　　by his son Huang Tan　黃坦.
　　Ca. 1659.
　　1916 reprint. LC.
　　1971 ZM reprint of 1916 reprint.

Includes preface by Gu Yanwu (cf. A16), written during his sojourn in Shandong in 1657-59. *Jimo xianzhi* 即墨縣志 (1764), 10b.63b, notes a two-*juan* Ming edition of *Laoshan zhi* by Huang Zongchang.

Dengzhou: Huang

D30. *Shixiang shuyuan zhi* 士鄉書院志
[Gazetteer of Shixiang Academy]
    1 *juan*, by Yin Jimei 尹繼美.
    1872, appended to the county gazetteer *Huangxian zhi* 黃縣志. Tobunken.

Liaodong: Shenyang wei

D31. *Beiling zhilüe* 北陵志略
[Abridged gazetteer of the Northern Tomb]
    By Miao Wenhua 苗文華.
    1929. Columbia.
    The tomb of Abahai (1592-1643) is on the northern edge of the city of Shenyang. Zhang Xueliang 張學良 sponsored the publication of what is more a picture book than a proper gazetteer.

E. Shanxi

Taiyuan: Taiyuan

E1. *Qiyan shanzhi* 七岩山志
[Gazetteer of Qiyan Mountain]
    By monk Mingxuan 明玄 .
    1935. LC, Toyo.
    This is the gazetteer of a Buddhist monastery. It was
    preceded by a Daoguang-era edition, no longer extant.

Taiyuan: Daizhou: Wutai

E2. *Qingliang shanzhi* 清涼山志
[Gazetteer of Qingliang Mountain]
    10 *juan*, by monk Zhencheng 鎭澄 (1547-1617).
    1596.
    1661 reprint. Naikaku.
    1694 emended edition entitled *Qingliang shan xinzhi*, ed.
    lama Laozang Danba 老藏丹巴. Jimbun.
    1701 imperial reprint of 1694 edition, with emendations.
    Gest, LC, Palace (2 copies), SOAS, Toronto.
    1707 reprint of 1694 edition. Naikaku.
    1755 reprint of 1596 edition. BL, Cambridge, Columbia,
    Gest, Harvard, LC, Naikaku, Toyo.
    19th-century reprint. Author's collection.
    1887 reprint. Harvard, Jimbun, Shifan, SOAS, Tobunken,
    Toyo.
    1936 reprint (Shanghai: Shanghai Foxue Shuju). LC,
    Michigan.
    1971 ZM reprint.
    Gazetteer of the Lamaist monasteries on Wutai Mountain,
    and the most frequently reprinted monastic gazetteer in
    China. Based on a 20-*juan* draft gazetteer of the Zhengde era
    by Abbot Qiuya 秋厓 . While living on Wutai Shan,
    Zhencheng also authored a commentary on the writings of
    Chan Master Yongjia (*Chanzong Yongjia ji zhujie* 禪宗永嘉集

註解), published in 1595 (copy in Gest).

E3. *(Qinding) Qingliang shanzhi* 欽定清涼山志
[Imperially sponsored gazetteer of Qingliang Mountain]
  22 *juan.*
  1785 MS. Palace.
  1811. LC, Palace, Seikado, SOAS.
  An imperially sponsored expansion of E2, compiled in 1785
  but not printed until 1811.

E4. *Qingliang shanzhi* 清涼山志
[Gazetteer of Qingliang Mountain]
  8 *juan*, by monk Yinguang 印光 (1861-1940; cf. H20, L59).
  1933. Gest, Shifan, Tobunken, UBC.
  1971 ZM reprint; 1978 Sida reprint; 1980 ZF reprint.
  Adapted from E2.

E5. *Qingliang shanzhi jiyao* 清涼山志輯要
[Shortened gazetteer of Qingliang Mountain]
  2 *juan*, by Wang Benzhi 汪本直.
  Ca. 1780. Harvard, LC, Toyo.

Pingyang: Jiezhou

E6. *(Hanqian jiangjun) Guan gong cizhi* 漢前將軍關公祠志
[Gazetteer of the shrine to the Han general Guan Yu]
  9 *juan*, by Zhao Qintang 趙欽湯 (js. 1568).
  1603. Gest(m), LC, Sonkeikaku, Taibei; Naikaku has an
  Edo-period manuscript copy.
  Bibliographic notice: Wang 201.
  This gazetteer is of both the shrine in Jiezhou and another
  temple to Guan Yu in Dangyang county, Hubei (cf. J8).
  Further information on these and other shrines to Guan Yu
  may be found in *Guan di shengji tuzhi* 關帝聖蹟圖考 [Illus-
  trated gazetteer of the sacred vestiges of Emperor Guan]
  compiled by Lu Zhan 盧湛 in 1693 (expanded 1838, reprinted 1921).

Fenzhou: Fenyang

E7. *Longshan zhi* 龍山志
[Gazetteer of Long Mountain]
　　4 *juan*, by monk Xuean Derui 雪岸德睿.
　　1726. Columbia, Toyo.
　　The monastery on Long Mountain, also known as Longyin
　　龍隱山 Mountain, was called Huayan Si 華嚴寺.

Datong: Datong

E8. *Shanxi datong wuzhou shan shiku siji* 山西大同武州山石窟寺記
[Record of Shiku Monastery on Wuzhou Mountain in Datong,
Shanxi]
　　1 *juan*, by monk Lihong 力宏.
　　1922. Jimbun.

Datong: Hunyuan zhou

E9. *Beiyue bian* 北嶽編
[Anthology on the Northern Peak]
　　3 *juan*, by Quzhou Magistrate Huangfu Fang 皇甫汸
　　(1503-82).
　　1532, with fifteen pages subsequently added. LC.
　　Bibliographic notice: Wang 205.
　　Bei Yue is the sacrificial title of Heng Shan 恒山.

E10. *Beiyue miaoji* 北嶽廟集
[Anthology of the temple to the Northern Peak]
　　10 *juan*, by Wei Xueli 魏學禮.
　　1590, with additions to 1605. LC.
　　Bibliographic notice: Wang 205.
　　Based on E9.

E11. *Hengyue zhi* 恒嶽志
[Gazetteer of Heng Peak]
　　3 *juan*, by Wang Junchu 王濬初.
　　1612, with additional material to 1618. Sonkeikaku.

E12. *Hengshan zhi* 恒山志
[Gazetteer of Heng Mountain]
    6 *juan*, by Magistrate Gui Jingshun 桂敬順.
    1763. Columbia, Jimbun (2 copies), LC, Shifan (2 *juan*),
    SOAS.
    1819 reprint. UBC.
    1879 reprint with E13. Harvard, Toyo.

E13. *Hengshan xuzhi* 恒山續志
[Supplementary gazetteer of Heng Mountain]
    1 *juan*, by He Shuen 賀澍恩.
    1774.
    1879 reprint with E12. Harvard, Toyo.

Datong: Zezhou: Yangcheng

E14. *Wangwu shanzhi* 王屋山志
[Gazetteer of Wangwu Mountain]
    2 *juan*, anonymous.
    Ming.
    1927 Gaochang edition.

Datong

E15. *Qingzhong zhi* 青冢志
[Gazetteer of the Green Tumulus]
    12 *juan*, by Hu Fengdan (cf. B29, B40, G8, J1, J4, K11,
    M18).
    1877. Harvard.
    1914 Xiangyan edition.
    Gazetteer of the tomb of the Han imperial concubine, Ming
    Fei. The site was popular with poets, and the gazetteer is
    almost exclusively poetry.

F. Henan

Kaifeng, Henan

F1. *Yuhe zhi* 豫河志
[Gazetteer of the Yellow River in Henan]
28 *juan*, by Wu Yongxiang 吳詠湘.
1923. Columbia.
1969 Hehai reprint.
Published by the Henan River Affairs Bureau, this gazetteer
is principally about practical problems of river control.

F2. *Yuhe xuzhi* 豫河續志
[Supplementary gazetteer of the Yellow River in Henan]
20 *juan* plus one-volume appendix, ed. Wang Rongjin
王榮搢.
1926. Columbia, LC (2 copies), Toronto.

F3. *Yuhe sanzhi* 豫河三志
[Third gazetteer of the Yellow River in Henan]
12 *juan* plus one volume of maps and one of charts, ed. Dai
Meichuan 戴湄川.
1932. Columbia, LC.

Kaifeng

F4. *Huiji he jishuo* 惠濟河輯說
[Writings on the Huiji River]
4 *juan*, by Wang Ruxing 王儒行.
1870. Columbia.
A historical survey.

Kaifeng: Xiangfu

F5. *Mingdao shuyuan zhi*　明道書院志
[Gazetteer of Mingdao Academy]
　　10 *juan*, by Lü Yonghui　呂永輝.
　　1900. LC.
　　Mingdao is the studio name of Cheng Hao　程顥　(1032-85;
　　cf. C31), for whom sacrifices were carried out at this
　　academy, founded 1461.

Henan: Luoyang

F6. *Luoyang longmen zhi*　洛陽龍門志
[Gazetteer of the Longmen Grottoes at Luoyang]
　　By Lu Chaolin　路朝霖.
　　1898 reprint of 1887 edition. Toyo.

Henan: Dengfeng

F7. *Shaolin sizhi*　少林寺志
[Gazetteer of Shaolin Monastery]
　　8 *juan*, by Jiao Qinchong　焦欽寵, ed. Shi Yizan　施奕簪.
　　1748. Harvard, Toyo.

F8. *Songyue zhi*　嵩嶽志
[Gazetteer of Song Peak]
　　11 *juan*, by Lu Jian　陸柬.
　　1571, with additional material to 1589. Sonkeikaku.
　　Primarily a collection of pre-Ming literary writings.

F9. *Song shu*　嵩書
[The book on the Song Mountains]
　　22 *juan*, by Magistrate Fu Mei　傅梅　(d. 1645).
　　1612. Beida, Beijing, Gest(m), LC, Naikaku, Taibei, Toyo.
　　Bibliographic notice: Wang 208.

F10. *Songgao zhi* 嵩高志
[Gazetteer of the Song Mountains]
　　8 *juan*, ed. Qiu Yuan 丘園, revised by Jiao Biheng 焦賁亨.
　　1661. Sonkeikaku.
　　Adapted from F9. Compiled earlier in the Shunzhi era.

F11. *Songshan zhi* 嵩山志
[Gazetteer of the Song Mountains]
　　20 *juan*, by Magistrate Ye Feng 葉封 (js. 1659).
　　1661. LC.
　　1679 reprint. UBC.

F12. *Songyue miaozhi* 嵩嶽廟志
[Gazetteer of the Temple to the Song Mountains]
　　10 *juan*, by Jing Rizhen 景日昣 (js. 1691; cf. F13).
　　1696. Harvard, Jimbun, LC, Toyo.

F13. *Shuo song* 說嵩
[On the Song Mountains]
　　32 *juan*, by Jing Rizhen (cf. F12).
　　1721 (author's preface dated 1716). Gest, Harvard, Jimbun,
　　LC, Naikaku, Shifan (2 copies), Tobunken, Toronto, Toyo,
　　UBC.
　　1971 ZM reprint.
　　An entirely original work emphasizing scenic sights on the
　　mountain. *Juan* 14 includes a good collection of stele texts.

Runing: Xinyang zhou

F14. *Chuangjian yunan shuyuan cunlüe* 創建豫南書院存略
[Brief account of the founding of the Southern Henan Academy]
　　1 *juan*, by Zhu Shouyong 朱壽鏞.
　　1891. Shifan, Tobunken.

Nanyang: Nanyang

F15. *Wolong gangzhi* 卧龍崗志
[Gazetteer of the Wolong Range]
    2 *juan*, by Luo Jing 羅景.
    1712. Gest, Jimbun, LC (2 copies), Shifan, Toyo.
    The Wolong Ridge was the site of a shrine and academy
    dedicated to Zhuge Liang (181-234; cf. G16, H8).

Nanyang: Dengzhou: Xichuan

F16. *Xiangyan lüeji* 香巖略紀
[Abridged record of Xiangyan Monastery]
    2 *juan*, by monk Chaogu 超古.
    Ca. 1746. Harvard.
    The monastery's first gazetteer was compiled about 1675.

Weihui: Hui

F17. *Baiquan shuyuan zhi* 百泉書院志
[Gazetteer of Baiquan Academy]
    4 *juan*, by Ma Shulin 馬書林.
    1533. Columbia(m), Gest(m), LC(m), Taibei.

Zhangde: Linzhang

F18. *(Linzhang xian) Zhangshui tujing* 臨漳縣漳水圖經
[Illustrated record of the Zhang River in Linjiang county]
    1 *juan*, by Magistrate Yao Jianzhi 姚束之.
    1837. Columbia, UBC.
    Composed almost entirely of historical texts; numerous
    maps. The gazetteer was compiled to document the river's
    change of course, which occurred in 1823.

Zhangde: Tangyin

F19. *Tangyin jingzhong miaozhi* 湯陰精忠廟志
[Gazetteer of the Temple to Purity and Loyalty in Tangyin]

10 *juan*, by Zhang Yingdeng 張應登.
1587. Columbia(m), Gest(m), LC(m), Taibei.
1735 reprint, ed. Zhang Mengkui 張夢夔. Seikado (2 copies),
Shifan, Toyo.
Bibliographic notice: Wang 201.
The temple was dedicated to the Song military hero Yue Fei
(1103-1142). For other gazetteers of sites connected with
Yue Fei, see L53, L54.

G. Shaanxi

G1. *Guanzhong shengji tuzhi* 關中聖蹟圖志
[Illustrated gazetteer of the major sites in Shaanxi]
    30 *juan*, by Bi Yuan 畢沅 (1730-97).
    Completed 1776, undated. Harvard, Jimbun, Toyo.
    1934 reprint. Harvard, Seikado, Shifan.
    Comprehensive record of tombs, shrines, monasteries, and
    other important structures in the province.

Xi'an and Hanzhong

G2. *Shaanxi nanshan gukou kao* 陝西南山谷口考
[Study of the valleys in the mountains of southern Shaanxi]
    1 *juan*, by Mao Fengzhi 毛鳳枝.
    1868. LC.
    1908 Wenying edition; Republican-era Guanzhong edition.
    Mao wrote this study out of concern for regional security
    after Taiping forces had used these mountains as a base area
    in 1862.

Xi'an: Chang'an

G3. *Guanzhong shuyuan zhi* 關中書院志
[Gazetteer of Guanzhong Academy]
    9 *juan*, by He Zaitu 何載圖.
    1613. Columbia(m), Gest(m), LC(m), Taibei.
    The academy was founded in 1613. The documents
    concerning its founding are printed in the first *juan*, student
    regulations in the third, and the academy's land records in
    the seventh.

Xi'an: Xianyang

G4. *Zhouling zhi* 周陵志
[Gazetteer of the tomb (of King Wen) of the Zhou]

10 *juan*, by Wu Tingxi 吳廷錫.
1934. LC, Shifan, Tobunken, Toyo.
King Wen (d. 1132? BC) was the father of the founding ruler
of the Zhou dynasty.

Xi'an: Jingyang

G5. *Jingqu zhi* 涇渠志
[Gazetteer of the Jingyang Canal]
    2 *juan*, preface by Wang Taiyue 王太岳 (1722-85).
    Ca. 1767. Beijing, UBC.

G6. *Hou jingqu zhi* 後涇渠志
[Later gazetteer of the Jingyang Canal]
    3 *juan*, by Jiang Xiangnan 蔣湘南 (cf. G14).
    Qing.
    1925 Jingyang edition.
    Jiang also compiled a 5-*juan* monograph on the rivers of
    Jiangxi, entitled *Jiangxi shuidao kao* 江西水道考.

G7. *Shaan Gan weijing shuyuan zhi* 陝甘味經書院志
[Gazetteer of the Weijing Academy of Shaanxi and Gansu]
    8 *juan*, by Liu Guangfen 劉光蕡.
    1894. Jimbun, LC, Shifan, Tobunken.
    Republican-era Yanxia edition; Guanzhong edition.

Xi'an: Xingping

G8. *Mawei zhi* 馬嵬志
[Gazetteer of Mawei]
    16 *juan*, by Hu Fengdan (cf. B29, B40, E15, J1, J4, K11,
    M18).
    1877. Columbia, Harvard, Toyo.
    Gazetteer of the tomb of Tang imperial concubine Yang
    Guifei (d. 756).

Xi'an: Lantian

G9. *Wangchuan zhi* 輞川志
[Gazetteer of the Wanggu River]
    6 *juan*, by Hu Yuanying　胡元煐.
    1837. Tobunken, Toyo.

Xi'an: Sanyuan

G10. *Hongdao shuyuan zhi*　弘道書院志
[Gazetteer of Hongdao Academy]
    Incomplete Ming edition. Fu.

Xi'an: Huazhou: Huayin

G11. *Huayue quanji* 華嶽全集
[Complete anthology on Hua Peak]
    13 *juan*, by Magistrate Ma Mingqing　馬明卿.
    1596 (compiled 1562). LC.
    1597 reprint. LC.
    1602 reprint with additional material by Magistrate Feng
    Jiahui　馮嘉會. Naikaku, Tobunken, Toyo.
    Early Qing reprint. Gest, LC.
    1705 reprint with minor revisions by Tang Bin　湯斌.
    Naikaku.
    Bibliographic notice: Wang 205.
    Previous works on Hua Mountain: *Xiyue huashan zhi*, a
    single-*juan* work of the twelfth century by Wang Chuyi (a
    Ming-period reprint is in Taibei, microfilm in Gest); a 14-*juan*
    Yuan gazetteer by Wang Edong　王鶚洞; a 10-*juan* Ming
    edition (1562?) by Magistrate Li Shifang　李時芳　(js. 1574)
    (Huang 8.14b).

G12. *Taihua xiaozhi*　太華小志
[Short gazetteer of the great Hua Peak]
    6 *juan*, by Feng Minchang　馮敏昌　(1747-1806).
    1887. LC.

G13. *Huayue zhi* 華嶽志
[Gazetteer of Hua Peak]
    8 *juan*, by Li Rongyin 李榕蔭.
    1831. Harvard, LC (3 copies), Shifan, Toyo.
    1841 reprint. UBC.
    1883 reprint. Columbia, Gest, Jimbun, LC (2 copies),
    Michigan, Shifan, Tobunken, Toyo.
    1904 reprint. SOAS.
    1970 ZC reprint of 1883 edition.
    Printed at Yuquan Cloister, a shrine to the Northern Song
    Daoist scholar Chen Tuan (ca. 906-989). Previous
    Qianlong-era gazetteer in 12 *juan* by Yao Yuandao 姚遠翮 .

G14. *Huayue tujing* 華嶽圖經
[Illustrated gazetteer of Hua Peak]
    2 *juan*, by Jiang Xiangnan (cf. G6).
    1851. LC.
    The first *juan* is of drawings, the second of text.

G15. *Huashan youji* 華山遊記
[Traveler's record of Hua Mountain]
    1 *juan*, by Shi Linfeng 石林鳳.
    1881. UBC.

Hanzhong: Mian

G16. *Zhongwu cimu zhi* 忠武祠墓志
[Gazetteer of the shrine and tomb of "the loyal and martial"]
    8 *juan* plus an introductory *juan*, by Xubai Daoren 虛白道人.
    1823. Gest.
    1881 reprint. Columbia.
    "The loyal and martial" was the posthumous title given to
    Zhuge Liang (181-234; cf. F15, H8).

Yan'an: Fuzhou: Zhongbu

G17. *Huangling zhi* 黃陵志
[Gazetteer of the tomb of the Yellow Emperor]

By Li Jinxi 黎錦熙.
1944. Columbia, LC.

Pingliang: Pingliang

G18. *Kongtong zhi* 崆峒志
[Gazetteer of Kongtong Mountain]
　　1 *juan*, by Xu Deng 許登.
　　1621 manuscript. Gest(m), Taibei
　　Kongtong's first printed gazetteer was by Li Yingxiao
　　李應孝, published in 1589.

G19. *Kongtong shanzhi* 崆峒山志
[Gazetteer of Kongtong Mountain]
　　8 *juan*, by Zhang Bokui 張伯魁.
　　1819. LC, UBC.
　　1872 reprint. Jimbun, LC, Toyo (2 copies).
　　1970 ZC reprint.
　　Previous gazetteers 1671 and 1797.

H. Sichuan

H1. *Shuzhong mingsheng ji* 蜀中名勝記
[Record of the famous sights of Sichuan]
    30 *juan*, by Cao Xuequan 曹學佺 (js. 1595; cf. P1).
    1618.
    1875 Yueya edition.
    1910 reprint. Jimbun, Tobunken.
    1936 Tushu reprint.
    1937 reprint (Shanghai: Shangwu). Chicago, LC, Toronto.
    1984 reprint (Chongqing: Chongqing Chubanshe). LC.
    Cao also wrote a massive provincial survey entitled
    Shuzhong guangji 蜀中廣記 [Comprehensive notes on
    Sichuan] in 108 *juan*.

H2. *Shushui jing* 蜀水經
[Classic of the rivers of Sichuan]
    16 *juan*, by Li Yuan 李元.
    1800. UBC.
    This gazetteer of Sichuan's rivers is organized by county.

H3. *Shushui kao* 蜀水考
[Study of the rivers of Sichuan]
    4 *juan*, by Chen Denglong 陳登龍 and Zhu Xigu 朱錫穀.
    1825. Columbia, LC (2 copies).
    1890 reprint. LC.
    1896 reprint. UBC.
    1969 Yudi reprint.
    This gazetteer is organized according to the structure of the
    Min River system.

Chengdu: Chengdu

H4. *Wanhua caotang zhi* 浣花草堂志
[Gazetteer of the Thatched Hall beside Wanhua Stream]
    8 *juan*, by He Mingli 何明禮 (b. 1715, js. 1759).

1764.
1923 reprint. LC.
Cao Tang was a monastery, also the former residence of the poet Du Fu (712-70).

H5. *Zhaojue sizhi* 昭覺寺志
[Gazetteer of Zhaojue Monastery]
      8 *juan*, by Luo Yonglin 羅用霖, ed. Abbot Zhongxun 中恂.
1896. Toyo.
Previous gazetteer compiled in the 1680s.

Chengdu: Huayang

H6. *Jinjiang shuyuan jilüe* 錦江書院紀略
[Abridged record of Jinjiang Academy]
      3 *juan*, by Li Chengxi 李承熙 .
1858. Nanda.
1871, ed. Tan Tidai 譚體迫 . Jimbun, Nanda.

H7. *Wangjiang louzhi* 望江樓志
[Gazetteer of Wangjiang Pavilion]
      By Peng Yisun 彭藝蓀 (d. 1966), ed. posthumously by Wang
Wencai 王文才 (cf. H9).
1980 (Chengdu: Sichuan Renmin Chubanshe). Author's
collection.
The pavilion was built by a well dedicated to the memory of
the Tang poetess Xue Tao 薛濤 (d. ca. 834). This is a
modern gazetteer, but written in classical language.

H8. *Zhaolie zhongwu lingmiao zhi* 昭烈忠武陵廟志
[Gazetteer of the temple of the martyred "loyal and martial"]
      10 *juan*, by Pan Shitong 潘時彤 .
1829. LC.
More about Zhuge Liang (cf. F15, G16) than his tomb.

Chengdu: Guan

H9. *Qingcheng shanzhi* 青城山志
[Gazetteer of Qingcheng Mountain]
    2 *juan*, by Peng Xun 彭洵 (d. 1896).
    1895, entitled *Qingcheng shanji*, Toyo.
    1928 edition, ed. Luo Yuanfu 羅元黼.
    1976 Biwu reprint.
    1982 reprint (Chengdu: Sichuan Renmin Chubanshe) of 1928
    edition, ed. Wang Wencai (cf. H7). LC (2 copies), Toronto.
    Qingcheng was principally a Daoist mountain.

Baoning

H10. *Jialing jiangzhi* 嘉陵江志
[Gazetteer of Jialing River]
    By Ma Yiyu 馬以愚.
    1947 (Shanghai: Shangwu Yinshuguan). Columbia, LC,
    Toronto.
    The Jialing River is the major tributary flowing into the
    Yangzi at Chongqing.

Shunqing: Guang'an zhou: Yuechi

H11. *Huayin shanzhi* 華銀山志
[Gazetteer of Huayin Mountain]
    18 *juan*, by monk Changyan 昌言.
    1865. Shifan, Toyo (2 copies).
    The gazetteer of Guangming Monastery 光明寺.

Chongqing: Ba

H12. *Jinyun shanzhi* 縉雲山志
[Gazetteer of Jinyun Mountain]
    1 *juan*, ed. monk Chenkong 塵空.
    1942. EAHSL, Gest, Shifan.
    The gazetteer of Chongjiao Monastery 崇教寺.

Chongqing: Zhongzhou: Fengdu

H13. *Pingdu shanzhi* 平都山志
[Gazetteer of Pingdu Mountain]
    1 *juan*, by Ran Gao 冉皋, ed. Yang Shilong 楊時隆.
    1615. Columbia(m), Gest(m), LC(m), Taibei.

Longan: Jiangyou

H14. *Kuangshan tuzhi* 匡山圖志
[Illustrated gazetteer of the Kuang Mountains]
    4 *juan*, by Jiang Dejun 蔣德鈞.
    1890. LC, Toyo.
    Primarily a collection of poems about the Dakuang
Mountains in Jiangyou county and the Xiaokuang Mountains
in neighbouring Zhangming county, Chengdu.

Jiading zhou: Emei

H15. *Emei shanzhi* 峨眉山志
[Gazetteer of Emei Mountain]
    12 *juan*, by Jiang Chao 蔣超.
    1672. Beijing.
    1834 reprint. Shifan.
    1929 reprint of 1849 edition. Shifan.
    H16, H17, and H18 are adaptations of this edition; all three
should be considered monastic rather than just mountain
gazetteers.

H16. *Emei shanzhi* 峨眉山志
[Gazetteer of Emei Mountain]
    8 *juan*, edited by Cao Xiheng 曹熙衡.
    1689. Naikaku, Toyo.
    1929 reprint of 1834 edition.

H17. *Emei shanzhi* 峨眉山志
[Gazetteer of Emei Mountain]
    15 *juan*, by Zhang Yujia 張玉甲.
    1713.

1980 ZF partial reprint *(juan* 9, 10, 12-15).

H18. *Emei shanzhi* 峩眉山志
[Gazetteer of Emei Mountain]
    18 *juan*, by Li Yizhang 李肆樟.
    1688.
    1827 reprint. Seikado, UBC.

H19. *Eshan tuzhi* 峩山圖志
[Illustrated gazetteer of Emei Mountain]
    2 *juan*, by Huang Shoufu 黃綬芙 (d. 1886), illustrated by
    Tan Zhongyue 譚鐘嶽.
    1888. Columbia, Toyo.
    1891 reprint. Cambridge, Harvard, Jimbun, Shifan, Toyo,
    UBC.
    Undated reprint. Harvard.
    1971 ZM reprint; 1976 Biwu reprint.
    An English translation by Dryden Phelps was published by
    the Harvard-Yenching Institute in Peking in 1936, since
    reprinted in 1971 (Hong Kong: University of Hong Kong
    Press) and 1980 (ZF). Harvard, Shifan, Tobunken.

H20. *Emei shanzhi* 峩眉山志
[Gazetteer of Emei Mountain]
    8 *juan*, by monk Yinguang (1861-1940; cf. E4, L59).
    1934. Harvard, Toyo.
    1971 ZM reprint; 1978 Sida reprint; 1980 ZF reprint.
    A new edition based on H16.

H21. *Jiazhou ershan zhi* 嘉州二山志
[Gazetteer of the two mountains of Jiading subprefecture]
    6 *juan*, by Yuan Zirang 袁子讓.
    1605. Seikado.
    Primarily literary materials on Emei and Lingyun 凌雲
    mountains.

I. Jiangxi

Nanchang: Nanchang

I1. *Qingyun puzhi* 青雲譜志
[Gazetteer of Qingyun Monastery]
  2 *ce*, by Huang Hanrao 黃翰翹.
  1920. Shifan, Toyo.
  Previous edition of 1681 by Zhu Daolang 朱道朗. The use of
  the word *pu* to mean a Daoist monastery was coined by Zhu.

Nanchang: Xinjian

I2. *Huangtang longdao gongzhi* 黃堂隆道宮志
[Gazetteer of Huangtang Longdao Temple]
  14 *juan*, by Hu Zhifeng 胡執鳳.
  1840. Harvard.

I3. *Xiaoyao shan wanshou gongzhi* 逍遙山萬壽宮志
[Gazetteer of Wanshou Temple on Xiaoyao Mountain]
  20 *juan*, by Ding Bushang 丁步上.
  1740. Shifan.
  1846 reprint. Toyo.

I4. *Xiaoyao shan wanshou gongzhi* 逍遙山萬壽宮志
[Gazetteer of Wanshou Temple on Xiaoyao Mountain]
  22 *juan*, ed. Jin Guixin 金桂馨 and Qi Yuanbi 漆源弼.
  1878. Harvard (2 copies), LC, Shifan, Toyo.
  Slightly modified from I3.

I5. *Xishan zhilüe* 西山志略
[Abridged gazetteer of West Mountain]
  6 *juan*, by Wei Yuankuang 魏雲曠.
  1933 Weishi edition.
  West Mountain, also known as Nanchang Mountain, was a

Daoist holy place.

Jiujiang: Dehua

I6. *Lushan jishi*　廬山紀事
[Record of events pertaining to the Lu Mountains]
　　12 *juan*, by Sang Qiao　桑喬.
　　1561. Beijing, LC(m), Naikaku (2 copies), Taibei, Zhejiang.
　　1720 reprint. Columbia, UBC.
　　1916 Yuzhang reprint.
　　1920 reprint. LC.
This gazetteer is primarily a thorough collection of pre-Ming texts, with commentary by Sang; it served as the chief source for all later works on the Lu Mountains.

I7. *Lushan xiaozhi*　廬山小志
[Short gazetteer of the Lu Mountains]
　　24 *juan*, by Cai Ying　蔡瀛.
　　1572. Beijing.
　　1824 reprint. Harvard, LC, Seikado, Shifan, Toyo.

I8. *Lushan tongzhi*　廬山通志
[Comprehensive gazetteer of the Lu Mountains]
　　12 *juan*, by monk Dinghao Wenji　定昊聞極.
　　1661. LC.
　　Relies heavily on I6.

I9. *Lushan zhi*　廬山志
[Gazetteer of the Lu Mountains]
　　15 *juan*, by Xingzi Magistrate Mao Deqi　毛德琦 (cf. I20).
　　1719. Cambridge, LC, Tobunken, Toyo, UBC.
　　1794 reprint with emendations. Jimbun, Naikaku, Shifan, Tobunken.
　　1873 reprint. Shifan.
　　1910 reprint. LC, SOAS, Tobunken.
　　1915 reprint. Author's collection.
This became the most widely circulated of the Lu Shan

gazetteers, as the host of reprints suggests. A preface in the later editions suggests that the book was also reprinted in 1859. It is based in part on a 1668 *Lushan zhi* compiled by Wu Wei 吳煒, already rare in Mao's time and now apparently no longer extant.

I10. *Luxiu lu* 廬秀錄
[Record of the beauties of the Lu Mountains]
    4 *juan*, by Zhang Weiping 張維屏.
    1836. Columbia.
    A poetry anthology, arranged by site.

I11. *Lushan guji shixuan* 廬山古蹟詩選
[Selected poetry on ancient sites in the Lu Mountains]
    10 *juan*, ed. Xu Heling 徐鶴齡 and Wu Jingzhi 吳敬之.
    1870. Columbia.
    Written to supplement Mao Deqi's two gazetteers (I9, I20). The first *juan* is a survey of the main sites, the other nine are poetry.

I12. *Lushan zhi, fukan* 廬山志, 副刊
[Gazetteer of the Lu Mountains, with supplement]
    12 and 15 *juan*, by Wu Zongci 吳宗慈 (cf. I14).
    1933-34. Harvard, Gest, Jimbun, LC, Palace, Shifan, UBC.

I13. *Lushan xin daoyou* 廬山新導遊
[New travel guide to the Lu Mountains]
    By Jiang Zhicheng 蔣志澄.
    1935. UBC.
    Arranged according to routes through the mountains.

I14. *Lushan xuzhi gao* 廬山續志稿
[Draft supplementary gazetteer of the Lu Mountains]
    8 *juan*, by Wu Zongci (cf. I12).
    1947. Columbia, Gest.

Jiujiang: Hukou

I15. *Shizhong shanzhi* 石鐘山志
[Gazetteer of Shizhong Mountain]
16 *juan*, by Li Chengmou 李成謀.
1883. Columbia, Harvard, Jimbun, LC (3 copies), Shifan,
SOAS, Tobunken, Toyo, UBC.

Nankang: Xingzi

I16. *Bailu dong shuyuan xinzhi* 白鹿洞書院新志
[New gazetteer of White Deer Grotto Academy]
8 *juan*, by Li Mengyang 李夢陽 (1473-1529).
1513. Sonkeikaku.
1525 reprint, ed. Zhou Guang 周廣 . LC.
Bibliographic notice: Wang 202.
The academy in 1525 owned the blocks for both editions
(8.3b). The site was famous for its association with Zhu Xi
(1130-1200).

I17. *Bailu dong shuyuan zhi* 白鹿洞書院志
[Gazetteer of White Deer Grotto Academy]
12 *juan*, by Zhou Wei 周偉 and Dai Cexian 戴策獻.
1592. Beijing.

I18. *Bailu shuyuan zhi* 白鹿書院志
[Gazetteer of White Deer Grotto Academy]
17 *juan*, ed. Li Yingsheng.
1622. Columbia, Gest(m), Taibei.
Beijing has a partial copy (*juan* 12 to 15).

I19. *Bailu shuyuan zhi* 白鹿書院志
[Gazetteer of White Deer Grotto Academy]
16 *juan*, by Qian Zhengzhen 錢正振.
1673. LC, Shifan, Tobunken.

120. *Bailu shuyuan zhi* 白鹿書院志
[Gazetteer of the White Deer Grotto Academy]
    19 *juan*, by Magistrate Mao Deqi (cf. I9).
    1718. Jimbun, LC.
    1720 reprint. Hefei, Nanda.
    1795 reprint. LC.
    1871 reprint. Toronto.
    1883 reprint. Nanda, Shifan, Toyo.

Nankang: Jianchang

121. *Yunju shanzhi* 雲居山志
[Gazetteer of Yunju Mountain]
    20 *juan*, ed. Cen Xuelü 岑學呂 (cf. O23), ed. monk Xuyun
    虛雲 (1840-1959; cf. O23).
    1959 (Hong Kong). Columbia, Gest, Harvard.
    1980 ZF reprint.
    This gazetteer of Zhenru Chan Monastery 眞如禪寺 adapted
    from the 1673 edition by Abbot Yansou Yuanpeng 燕叟元鵬.

Raozhou: Fuliang

122. *Fuliang taozheng zhi* 浮梁陶政志
[Gazetteer of the porcelain industry in Fuliang county]
    1 *juan*, by Wu Yunjia 吳允嘉 (cf. L2).
    Kangxi era.
    1831 Xuehai edition; 1852 Xunmin edition; 1920 Xuehai
    reprint.
    Bibliographic notice: Franke 6.5.15.

Guangxin: Shangrao

123. *Lingshan yiai lu*　靈山遺愛錄
[Record of lingering beneficence at Ling Mountain]
　　　4 *juan*, by Xu Qian　徐謙.
　　　1793, with appended poem dated 1801. Toyo.
　　　This gazetteer to the shrine to Tang official Li Yuanming
　　　李元明　was first published in 1628.

124. *Xinjiang shuyuan zhi*　信江書院志
[Gazetteer of Xinjiang Academy]
　　　10 *juan*, by Zhong Shizhen　鐘世楨.
　　　1867. Shifan.

Guangxin: Yushan

125. *Huaiyu shanzhi*　懷玉山志
[Gazetteer of Huaiyun Mountain]
　　　8 *juan*, by Zhu Chengxu　朱承煦.
　　　1775. LC.
　　　Preceded by a lost Ming edition. Huaiyu Mountain was the
　　　site of Huaiyu Academy where Zhu Xi (1130-1200) and other
　　　Song Neo-Confucians lectured.

126. *Yushan yixiang*　玉山遺響
[Lingering echoes of Yu Mountain]
　　　6 *juan*, by Zhang Zhensheng　張貞生.
　　　Kangxi-era Kuishan edition.
　　　Yu Mountain was the colloquial name of Huaiyu Mountain.

Guangxin: Guixi

127. *Longhu shanzhi*　龍虎山志
[Gazetteer of Longhu Mountain]
　　　3 *juan*, by Yuan Mingshan　元明善, ed. Zhou Zhao　周召.
　　　Undated Ming expansion of Yuan edition. Gest(m), LC(m),
　　　Taibei.
　　　The latest internal date in the first two *juan* by Yuan is

1315. Longhu Mountain was the official residence of the Daoist patriarch of the Zhang family.

128. *Longhu shanzhi* 龍虎山志
[Gazetteer of Longhu Mountain]
    4 *juan*, by Lou Jinyuan 婁近垣.
    1740. Columbia, Jimbun, Shifan, Toronto, Toyo (2 copies), UBC.
    1770 reprint. Tobunken.
    1832 reprint. LC.

Guangxin: Qianshan

129. *Ehu shutian zhi* 鵝湖書田志
[Gazetteer of the academy at Ehu Mountain]
    4 *juan*, by Wu Songliang 吳嵩梁 (1766-1834).
    1843 Xiangsu edition.
    Ehu Mountain was the site of discussions among Zhu Xi 朱熹 (1130-1200), Lü Zuqian 呂祖謙 (1137-81), and Lu Jiuyuan 陸九源 (1139-93); the academy founded there later in the Song was called Wenzong 文宗 Academy. *Shutian*, "field of books," is simply a stylized term for a school.

Jianchang: Nancheng

130. *Magu ji* 麻姑集
[Anthology on Magu Mountain]
    4 *juan*, by Zheng Rong 鄭嶸.
    1543. Naikaku.
    Primarily a literary collection; previous edition 1478.

131. *Magu shan danxia dongtian zhi* 麻姑山丹霞洞天志
[Gazetteer of Danxia Sacred Place on Magu Mountain]
    17 *juan*, by Wu Minglei 烏鳴雷, ed. Zuo Zongying 左宗郢.
    1613. Naikaku.
    1718 reprint. LC, Shifan, Toyo.
    Bibliographic notice: Wang 209.

132. *Magu shanzhi*　麻姑山志
[Gazetteer of Magu Mountain]
    12 *juan*, ed. Huang Jiaju　黃家駒.
    1866. Jimbun, LC, Seikado, Shifan, Tobunken, Toyo.
    Based on an earlier work by Luo Sen　羅森.

133. *Wannian qiaozhi*　萬年橋志
[Gazetteer of Wannian Bridge]
    8 *juan*, by Xie Ganshang　謝甘賞.
    1896. LC.
    The bridge was built in 1893-95. The gazetteer records the engineering, costs, and process of construction.

Fuzhou: Linchuan

134. *Wenchang qiaozhi*　文昌橋志
[Gazetteer of Wenchang Bridge]
    8 *juan*, by Yimingga　伊明阿.
    1814.
    1882 reprint with 135. LC.

135. *(Xuxiu) Wenchang qiao zhilüe*　續修文昌橋志略
[Further abridged gazetteer of Wenchang Bridge]
    4 *juan*, by Wen Guang　文光.
    1844.
    1882 reprint with 134. LC.

Fuzhou: Chongren

136. *(Chongxiu jiangnan) Huagai shanzhi*　重修江南華蓋山志
[Revised gazetteer of Huagai Mountain south of the Yangzi]
    5 *juan*, by Xu Yunsheng　許雲昇.
    1555. LC.
    Bibliographic notice: Wang 206.
    Based on a Song Daoist work, edited in 1407 by Zhang Yuchu　張宇初.

Ji'an: Luling

137. *Bailu zhou shuyuan zhi*　白鷺洲書院志
[Gazetteer of Bailu Zhou Academy]
　　9 *juan*.
　　1871. Columbia, Nanda.

138. *Ji'an xian luoshan Song Wen chengxiang cizhi*　吉安縣螺山宋文丞
相祠志
[Gazetteer of the shrine to Minister Wen of the Song at Luo
Mountain in Ji'an county]
　　By Xiao Gengshao　肖賡韶.
　　1936. Shifan.

139. *Qingyuan zhilüe*　青原志略
[Abridged gazetteer of Qingyuan Mountain]
　　13 *juan*, by monk Xiaofeng Daran　笑峰大然　(d. 1659),
　　completed by Fang Yizhi方以智(1611-71; cf. C5), ed. Shi
　　Runzhang　施閏章　(js. 1649).
　　1669. Columbia, LC, Naikaku, Shifan, Toyo (2 copies).
　　Bibliographic notice: Ren, p. 257.
　　The monastery here, Jingju Si　淨居寺, was the
　　bodhimandala of the sixth and seventh patriarchs of Chan
　　Buddhism. The gazetteer was published as part of a
　　fund-raising effort.

140. *Qingyuan shanzhi*　青原山志
[Gazetteer of Qingyuan Mountain]
　　8 *juan*, by Peng Dashi　彭大融　and Luo Jingren　羅鏡仁.
　　1944. Shifan.

Ji'an: Taihe

141. *Taiyang zhou Xiao hou miaozhi*　太洋洲蕭侯廟志
[Gazetteer of the Temple to Duke Xiao on Taiyang Island]
　　7 *juan*, by Guo Zizhang　郭子章　(js. 1571; cf. M32).
　　1622. LC.
　　Bibliographic notice: Wang 201.

Xiao Tianren 蕭天任 was a local figure canonized in 1419 for spiritually aiding the maritime expedition of Zheng He 鄭和 (1371-1433). The gazetteer was published by Gan Yinqiu 甘胤虬 .

Linjiang: Qingjiang

142. *Huili sizhi* 慧力寺志
[Gazetteer of Huili Monastery]
    6 *juan*, by Zhao Runing 趙汝明 .
    1895. Columbia.
    Based on a 1681 gazetteer by Abbot Zizhi 自之 .

Ganzhou: Gan

143. *(Chongxiu) Lianxi shuyuan zhi* 重修濂溪書院志
[Revised gazetteer of Lianxi Academy]
    4 *juan*, by Yang Yujian 楊毓健 (cf. N25).
    1717. Shifan.

144. *Lianxi zhi* 濂溪志
[Gazetteer of Lianxi Academy]
    7 *juan* plus one *juan* of poetry, by Zhou Gao 周誥 (js. 1838).
    1839. LC, Shifan.

J. Huguang: Hubei

Wuchang: Jiangxia

J1. *Huanghu shanzhi* 黃鵠山志
[Gazetteer of Huanghu Mountain]
    12 *juan*, by Hu Fengdan (cf. B29, B40, E15, G8, J4, K11, M18).
    1874. Harvard (2 copies), Jimbun, LC, Shifan, Toyo, UBC.
    Primarily a collection of literary works about the mountain.

J2. *Shahu zhi* 沙湖志
[Gazetteer of Sand Lake]
    1 *juan*, by Ren Tong 任桐.
    1923. LC.

Wuchang: Chongyang

J3. *Jiugong shanzhi* 九宮山志
[Gazetteer of Jiugong Mountain]
    14 *juan*, by Fu Xieding 傅爕鼎.
    1883. Toyo.
    This is a Daoist monastic gazetteer; previous editions were published in 1568, 1656, and 1767.

Hanyang: Hanyang

J4. *Dabie shanzhi* 大別山志
[Gazetteer of Dabie Mountain]
    10 *juan*, by Hu Fengdan (cf. B29, B40, E15, G8, J1, K11, M18).
    1874. Columbia, Harvard, Jimbun, LC, Tobunken, Toyo.
    Primarily a compendium of short entries about the Buddhist institutions on this mountain, taken from other sources. The chief monastery here was Xingguo Si 興國寺.

J5. *Hankou Shan-Shaanxi huiguan zhi*　漢口山陝西會館志
[Gazetteer of the guildhall for Shanxi and Shaanxi merchants in Hankou]
2 *juan*, by Hou Peijun　侯倍峻　and Ji Linshu　冀麟書.
1896. Harvard(m), Jimbun, Toyo.

J6. *Hankou ziyang shuyuan zhilüe*　漢口紫陽書院志略
[Abridged gazetteer of Ziyang Academy at Hankou]
8 *juan*, by Dong Guifu　董桂敷　(js. 1805).
1806. Shifan.
Though nominally an academy gazetteer, this is a history of a merchant guild that incorporated an educational institution to serve as its more dignified public persona.

Huangzhou: Huangpi

J7. *Wenjin yuanzhi*　問津院志
[Gazetteer of Wenjin Academy]
6 *juan*, by Wang Huili　王會釐　(js. 1894).
1905. Columbia, Shifan.

Chengtian: Dangyang

J8. *Guan sheng lingmiao jilüe*　關聖陵廟紀略
[Abridged record concerning the mortuary temple of the sage, Guan Yu]
4 *juan*, by Wei Rang　魏勷.
1700, with addenda in the third *juan* to 1853. LC.
The gazetteer records the names of those officials who contributed to the temple's restoration in 1696 and at earlier times, inserted before the table of contents. Most of the gazetteer has to do with Guan Yu himself, though there is also information specific to this temple, such as its landholdings (2.42a-43a), and to other prominent Guan Yu temples. Cf. E6.

J9. *Yuquan shan sizhi*　玉泉山寺志
[Gazetteer of the monastery on Yuquan Mountain]

3 *juan*, by Piao Yinzhi 栗引之, ed. Magistrate Li Fang
李芳 (js. 1661).
1671. Shifan.
1694 reprint. LC, Toyo.
Preceded by a Wanli-era gazetteer.

J10. *Yuquan sizhi* 玉泉寺志
[Gazetteer of Yuquan Monastery]
6 *juan*, by Li Yuancai 李元才.
1885. Harvard, Shifan, Toyo.
An expanded version of J9.

Dean: Suizhou

J11. *Pinglin yixue zhi* 平林義學志
[Gazetteer of the charitable school of Pinglin]
By Zhou Shilian 周士連 (cf. L1).
1819. Tobunken.

Yuezhou

J12. *Dongting huzhi* 洞庭湖志
[Gazetteer of Dongting Lake]
14 *juan*, by Qi Shiji 綦世基, ed. Shen Juntang 沈筠堂 and
Wan Nianchun 萬年淳.
1828. Columbia, Harvard, Jimbun, LC (2 copies), Seikado,
Toyo.

Yuezhou: Linxiang

J13. *Linxiang shanzhi* 臨湘山志
[Gazetter of the mountains of Linxiang]
11 *juan*, by Xue Longqiu 薛隆裘.
1947. Shifan.

Yuezhou: Fengzhou

J14. *Wanshou gongzhi* 萬壽宮志
[Gazetteer of Wanshou Temple]
    12 *juan*, by Wu Menglan 伍夢蘭.
    1876. Toyo.

Jingzhou: Jiangling

J15. *(Jingzhou) Wancheng dizhi* 荊州萬城隄志
[Gazetteer of Wancheng Dike in Jingzhou]
    10 *juan*, by Ni Zhuocen 倪犳岑.
    1876. Columbia, Toyo.
    The dike extended for over 100 kilometers along the bank of
    the Yangzi River.

J16. *(Jingzhou) Wancheng di xuzhi* 荊州萬城隄續志
[Supplementary gazetteer of Wancheng Dike in Jingzhou]
    10 *juan*, by Shu Hui 舒惠.
    1894. Columbia, Toyo.

Jingzhou: Yiling zhou: Yidu

J17. *Xiajiang jiusheng chuanzhi* 峽江救生船志
[Gazetteer of the rescue boats on the upper Yangzi River]
    2 *juan*, by He Jinshen 賀縉紳.
    1877. Tobunken.
    1893 reprint. Tobunken.
    1969 Yudi reprint of 1906 edition (with 6.3.2 and 6.3.3).
    A motley collection of illustrations and texts concerning the
    river, the rescue service, and the temple at Yichang (Yidu in
    the Ming) to the spirit of the Yangzi River.

Xiangyang: Junzhou

J18. *Dayue taihe shanzhi* 大嶽太和山志
[Gazetteer of the Great Peak, Taihe Mountain]
    15 *juan*, by Ren Ziyuan 任自垣.

Ming. LC(m), Taibei.
The gazetteer of the Daoist mountain Wudang Shan 武當山.

J19. *Dayue zhilüe* 大嶽志略
[Abridged gazetteer of the Great Peak]
    5 *juan*, by Fang Sheng 方升.
    1536. LC(m), Taibei.

J20. *Dayue taihe shanzhi* 大嶽太和山志
[Gazetteer of the Great Peak, Taihe Mountain]
    8 *juan*, by Lu Chonghua 盧重華.
    1572. LC.
    1596 reprint, ed. Ling Yunyi 凌雲翼. Naikaku.
    Bibliographic notice: Wang 208.

J21. *Dayue taihe shan jilüe* 大嶽太和山紀略
[Abridged record of the Great Peak, Taihe Mountain]
    8 *juan*, edited by Wang Gai 王棨.
    1744. Harvard, Jimbun, LC (2 copies), Naikaku, Shifan,
    SOAS, Toyo, UBC.

J22. *(Xuxiu) Dayue taihe shanzhi* 續修大嶽太和山志
[Revised gazetteer of the Great Peak, Taihe Mountain]
    8 *juan*, by Zhao Kui 趙夔.
    1922. Jimbun, LC.

K. Huguang: Hunan

Changsha: Changsha

K1. *Changsha xian xuegong zhi* 長沙縣學宮志
[Gazetteer of the Changsha county school]
    8 *juan*, by Yu Zhenghuan 余正煥 , ed. Zhou Yuqi.
    1868. Harvard, LC (2 copies), Shifan.
    Previous gazetteers were published in 1514 and 1633. Yu's
original edition was compiled after the school's restoration in
1840; the 1868 edition includes minor addenda. Of particular
interest are the music texts in *juan* 5 and the contracts
regarding school property in *juan* 6.

K2. *Longtan shanzhi* 龍潭山志
[Gazetteer of Longtan Mountain]
    8 *juan*, by Kang Fu 康阜.
    1880. Harvard, Jimbun.
    1880, with material to 1883. Toyo.
    1880, with material to 1890. LC, Toyo.
    Longtan Mountain had a temple to Li Yuwan 李育萬
(1310-41).

K3. *Yuelu shuyuan tuzhi* 嶽麓書院圖志
[Illustrated gazetteer of Yuelu Academy]
    10 *juan*, by Prefect Wu Daoxing 吳道行 (js. 1577).
    1594. Gest(m), Taibei.
    Based on a 1514 gazetteer by Headmaster Chen Lun
陳論 , revised by Prefect Sun Cun 孫存 in 1528. Wu
became headmaster subsequent to publication. *Juan* 5
provides a detailed description of the academy's landholdings.
Wu's sons republished the gazetteer in 1633.

K4. *Yuelu zhi*　嶽麓志
[Gazetteer of Yuelu Academy]
　　　8 *juan*, by Zhao Ning　趙寧.
　　　1687. Naikaku.
　　　1867 reprint with K5 under the title *Yuelu shuyuan zhi*. LC.

K5. *Yuelu shuyuan zhi*　嶽麓書院志
[Gazetteer of Yuelu Academy]
　　　5 *juan*, by Headmaster Ding Shanqing　丁善慶　(1790-1869)
　　　and Liu Yue　劉岳.
　　　1867, with K4. LC, Toyo.

Changsha: Shanhua

K6. *Ding wang taizhi*　定王臺志
[Gazetteer of Prince Ding's Terrace]
　　　2 *juan*, by Xia Xianyun　夏獻雲　(cf. K8).
　　　1881. Columbia, Jimbun.
　　　The terrace commemorates a Han-dynasty prince.

Changsha: Ningxiang

K7. *Ningxiang yunshan shuyuan zhi*　寧鄉雲山書院志
[Gazetteer of Yunshan Academy of Ningxiang county]
　　　2 *juan*, by Zhou Ruisong　周瑞松.
　　　1874. LC.
　　　The second *juan* is devoted almost entirely to land records
　　　and contracts.

Changsha: Xiangxiang

K8. *(Changsha) Jia taifu cizhi*　長沙賈太傅祠志
[Gazetteer of the shrine in Changsha to Grand Councillor Jia]
　　　4 *juan*, by Xia Xianyun (cf. K6).
　　　1878. Shifan, Toyo.
　　　Grand Councillor Jia is Jia Yi　賈誼　(200-168 B.C.).

Changde: Taoyuan

K9. *Taoyuan dongzhi* 桃源洞志
[Gazetteer of the cave at Peach Blossom Spring]
    1 *juan*, edited by monk Lanyan Yixiu 蘭巖一休．
    1754. Harvard, LC.
    Peach Blossom Spring (Taohua Yuan or Taoyuan) is the supposed setting of the famous utopian tale by Tao Qian 陶潛 (376-427).

K10. *Taohua yuan zhilüe* 桃花源志略
[Abridged gazetteer of Peach Blossom Spring]
    13 *juan*, by Tang Kaishao 唐開韶．
    1844. Columbia, LC (2 copies), Shifan.
    1891 reprint. Harvard, Toyo.
    1976 reprint (Taibei: Guangwen Shuju). Gest.
    Previous gazetteer 1816.

K11. *Taohua yuanzhi* 桃源園志
[Gazetteer of Peach Blossom Spring]
    24 *juan*, by Hu Fengdan (cf. B29, B40, E15, G8, J1, J4, M18).
    1877. Harvard, LC, Shifan.

Hengzhou: Hengyang

K12. *Lianfeng zhi* 蓮峰志
[Gazetteer of Lianhua Mountain]
    5 *juan*, by Wang Fuzhi 王夫之 (1619-92).
    1842 (1865, 1933) Chuanshan edition.
    Compiled in 1646; previous gazetteer compiled in 1552. Wang wrote this gazetteer after taking refuge on the mountain in the winter of 1643-44 when Zhang Xianzhong's troops swept through Hunan.

K13. *Shigu shuyuan zhi* 石鼓書院志
[Gazetteer of Shigu Academy]
    2 *juan*, by Prefect Li Anren 李安仁 (js. 1571), ed. Wang

Dashao 王大韶.
1579. Beida.
Bibliographic notice: Wang 202.
Previous gazetteer published in the Jiajing era by Zhou Zhao 周詔 and Wang Wanceng 汪玩曾 on the basis of an older gazetteer.

Hengzhou: Hengshan

K14. *Hengyue zhi* 衡嶽志
[Gazetteer of Heng Peak]
    13 *juan*, by Yao Hongmo 姚弘謨, ed. Mao Bin 毛彬.
    1571. Sonkeikaku.
    Previous gazetteer 1528 by Magistrate Peng Zan 彭簪 (cf. K21) (Huang 8.15a).

K15. *Hengyue zhi* 衡嶽志
[Gazetteer of Heng Peak]
    8 *juan*, by Zeng Fengyi 曾鳳儀 (js. 1583), ed. Assistant Surveillance Commissioner Deng Yunxiao 鄧雲霄 (js. 1598).
    1612. Toyo.

K16. *Hengyue zhi* 衡嶽志
[Gazetteer of Heng Peak]
    8 *juan*, by Yuan Huan 袁奐.
    1664. Columbia, LC.
    1710 reprint. Naikaku (2 copies).
    Later Qing reprint. Tobunken.
    Based on K15.

K17. *Nanyue zhi* 南嶽志
[Gazetteer of the Southern Peak]
    8 *juan*, by Gao Ziwei 高自位.
    1754. Harvard, Jimbun, LC (3 copies), Naikaku, Seikado, Shifan, SOAS (2 copies), Toyo (2 copies).
    The Southern Peak (Nanyue) was the formal title of Heng Mountain.

K18. *Nanyue zongsheng ji* 南嶽總勝集
[Comprehensive record of the sites of the Southern Peak]
    3 *juan*, by Tang Zhongmian (cf. D12).
    1802. Columbia.

K19. *(Chongxiu) Nanyue zhi* 重修南嶽志
[Revised gazetteer of the Southern Peak]
    26 *juan*, by Li Yuandu 李元度 (1821-87).
    1883. BL, Columbia, Gest, Harvard, LC (2 copies), SOAS, Toyo, UBC.
    1924 reprint. Jimbun, LC, Toyo.

K20. *(Xuzeng) Nanyue zhi* 續增南嶽志
[Further addenda to the gazetteer of the Southern Peak]
    2 *juan*, by Wang Xiangyu 王香余.
    1924 (appended to 1924 reprint of K19). Jimbun, Toyo.

K21. *Jinggu zhi* 靜谷志
[Gazetteer of Jing Valley]
    1 *juan*, by Magistrate Peng Zan (cf. K14).
    1533. Gest(m), Taibei.

Hengzhou: Ling

K22. *Yanling zhi* 炎陵志
[Gazetteer of Emperor Yan's tomb]
    8 *juan*, by Peng Zhitan 彭之曇, ed. Wang Kaizhuo 王開琸.
    1828. LC.
    The tomb was dedicated to the mythical emperor Shennong. Peng's original edition was published in 1721.

K23. *Yanling zhi* 炎陵志
[Gazetteer of Emperor Yan's tomb]
    10 *juan*, expanded from K22 by an anonymous author.
    1858. LC.

Yongzhou: Qiyang

K24. *Wuxi kao*   浯溪考
[Study of the Wuxi River]
　　2 *juan*, by Wang Shizhen (cf. A18, D3).
　　Kangxi era.
　　Qianlong-era Yuyang edition; Guangxu-era Xike edition.

K25. *Wuxi xinzhi*   浯溪新志
[New gazetteer of the Wuxi River]
　　14 *juan*, by Song Rong   宋溶.
　　1770. Jimbun, Naikaku.
　　1773 reprint. Toyo.

Yongzhou: Daozhou: Ningyuan

K26. *Jiuyi shanzhi*   九疑山志
[Gazetteer of Jiuyi Mountain]
　　9 *juan*, by Jiang Huang   蔣鐄.
　　1633. Harvard.
　　The gazetteer of the shrine to the legendary Emperor Shun.

K27. *Jiuyi shanzhi*   九疑山志
[Gazetteer of Jiuyi Mountain]
　　4 *juan*, by Xu Xudan   徐旭旦.
　　1709. LC.

K28. *Jiuyi shanzhi*   九疑山志
[Gazetteer of Jiuyi Mountain]
　　4 *juan*, by Magistrate Fan Zaiting   樊在廷.
　　1796. Columbia, Harvard, LC (3 copies), UBC.
　　1864. Shifan, Tobunken.
　　1883 reprint by Magistrate Zhang Ming   張銘. Jimbun,
　　Toyo.
　　Based on K27.

Chenzhou: Xupu

K29. *Qinglong shanzhi* 靑龍山志
[Gazetteer of Qinglong Mountain]
    1 *juan*, by Chen Baoshou 陳寶壽.
    1900. Shifan.

Chenzhou: Yizhang

K30. *Shihu shan wuling houzhi* 石虎山武陵侯志
[Gazetteer of Duke Wuling's tomb at Shihu Mountain]
    18 *juan*, by Huang Mingyan 黃名彥.
    1875. Harvard.
    First published 1841. The shrine honored a Tang aristocrat
named Huang Shihao 黃師浩 (b. 822). Though officially a
state shrine, this was very much a Huang kinship enterprise.

L. Zhejiang: Hangzhou Prefecture

Hangzhou and Jiaxing

L1. *Hang Jia yixue hezhi* 杭嘉義學合志
[Joint gazetteer of charitable schools in Hangzhou and Jiaxing]
By Zhou Shilian (cf. J11).
1819. Nanjing.
Bibliographic notice: ZFK 17.133.

Hangzhou

L2. *Wulin fanzhi* 武林梵志
[Gazetteer of Buddhist monasteries in Hangzhou]
12 *juan*, by Wu Zhijing 吳之鯨.
Ca. 1615. Beijing.
1780 Siku edition; 1934 Zhenben edition (1973 reprint).
Bibliographic notice: Hong 384, HHC 186, ZFK 17.18, Wu 26b.
Brief historical notices of 426 monasteries in urban and suburban Hangzhou. There was also a *Wulin gongguan zhi* 武林宮觀志 by Wu Yunjia (cf. I22) (Wu 27a).

Hangzhou: Qiantang

L3. *Cang sheng miaozhi* 倉聖廟志
[Gazetteer of the Shrine to the Sage Cang Jie]
1 *juan*, by Ding Bing 丁丙 (1832-99; cf. L7, L50) and Zhuo Bingsen 卓炳森 (cf. L56).
1881. Tobunken.
Cang Jie 倉頡 was the mythical subordinate of the Yellow Emperor credited with the invention of the Chinese script. The gazetteer was compiled to commemorate the refounding of the shrine by the authors in a converted stately residence. The Tobunken copy includes two handwritten postfaces by a descendant in the next generation of the family that sold its residence for this purpose.

L4. *Cui fujun cilu* 崔府君祠錄
[Gazetteer of the Shrine to Master Cui]
    1 *juan*, by Zheng Lang 鄭烺.
    1832. Nanjing.
    1881 WZ edition; Guangxu-era Huaiyou edition.
    Bibliographic notice: Hong 411, HHC 195, Wu 27b, ZFK
    17.102.
    The gazetteer of a shrine in honor of the Han official, Cui
    Yuan 崔瑗.

L5. *Da zhaoqing lüsi zhi* 大昭慶律寺志
[Gazetteer of Great Zhaoqing Vinaya Monastery]
    10 *juan*, by monk Zhuanyu 篆玉 (cf. L75).
    1764 (first published 1742). Nanjing, Shifan, SOAS.
    1882 WZ edition.
    Bibliographic notice: Hong 386, HHC 187, ZFK 17.29.

L6. *(Xihu) Guan di miao guangji* 西湖關帝廟廣記
[Encyclopedic record of the Temple to Emperor Guan Yu in West
Lake]
    8 *juan*, by Jin Jiahui 金嘉會.
    1624. Naikaku.

L7. *Guangshou huiyun sizhi* 廣壽惠雲寺志
[Gazetteer of Guangshou Huiyun Monastery]
    7 *juan*, by Ding Bing (cf. L3, L50), ed. monk Zujin 祖勤.
    1868. Zhejiang.
    1928 reprint. Shifan.
    Bibliographic notice: Hong 389, HHC 189, ZFK 17.43.
    Previous edition 1649 by monk Xingsheng 行盛.

L8. *Gushan zhi* 孤山志
[Gazetteer of Gu Mountain]
    1 *juan*, by Wang Fuli 王復禮 (cf. M14, N22).
    1719.
    1881 WZ edition.
    Republican-era reprint. Toyo.
    Bibliographic notice: Hong 305, HHC 179, ZFK 14.9.

This "mountain" is actually an island in West Lake, the site of a small Buddhist temple. There was also a 5-*juan* gazetteer by Wang Zengxiang 王曾祥.

L9. *Hangzhou san shuyuan jilüe* 杭州三書院紀略
[Abridged record of three academies in Hangzhou]
5 *juan*, by Wang Tong 王同.
Unpublished manuscript. Zhejiang.
Bibliographic notice: Hong 418, HHC 185, ZFK 17.121.
Gazetteer of Fuwen 敷文, Chongwen 崇文, and Ziyang 紫陽 academies (cf. L70).

L10. *Huiyin sizhi* 慧因寺志
[Gazetteer of Huiyin Monastery]
12 *juan*, by Li Zhu 李翥.
1627. UBC (probably a later reprint).
Chongzhen-era edition. Nanjing.
1881 WZ edition; 1980 ZF reprint.
Bibliographic notice: Hong 387, HHC 188, ZFK 17.35.

L11. *Hupao dinghui sizhi gao* 虎跑定慧寺志稿
[Draft gazetteer of Dinghui Monastery on Hupao Mountain]
1900 manuscript by abbot Shengguang 聖光.
1980 ZF reprint.
The previous gazetteer of 1704 was destroyed when the monastery was burned down during the Taiping rebellion.

L12. *Hupao fozu cangdian zhi* 虎跑佛祖藏殿志
[Gazetteer of the Buddhist Patriarch Hall on Hupao Mountain]
10 *juan*, by the staff of Hupao Monastery.
1921. Fudan.
Bibliographic notice: Hong 391, HHC 190, ZFK 17.52.

L13. *Hushan bianlan* 湖山便覽
[Overview of West Lake and the surrounding mountains]
12 *juan*, by Zhai Hao 翟灝 (js. 1754; cf. L65, L71).
1765. LC, Shifan.

1875 reprint. Harvard, Jimbun, LC (3 copies), Naikaku, Toyo.
1891 XF (4) edition.
1895 reprint. Columbia.
1969 Yudi reprint.
Bibliographic notice: ZFK 14.218.

L14. *Jinlong si dawang cimu lu* 金龍四大王祠墓錄
[Record of the shrine and tomb of the fourth prince of Jinlong Mountain]
     5 *juan*, by Zhong Xuelu 仲學輅.
1896 WZ edition.
Bibliographic notice: Hong 416, HHC 196, ZFK 17.109.
The tomb of Xie Xu 謝緒 of the late Song.

L15. *Li'an sizhi* 理安寺志
[Gazetteer of Li'an Monastery]
     8 *juan*, by monk Binyue Zhilang 賓月智朗.
1762, with material to 1789.
1878 WZ edition.
Bibliographic notice: Hong 391, HHC 190, Wu 28a, ZFK 17.54.
Previous gazetteer (*Li'an siji*) by monk Rusong Zhongguang 如嵩仲光 published in the Wanli era.

L16. *Lianju anzhi* 蓮居庵志
[Gazetteer of Lianju Chapel]
     10 *juan*, by Sun Jun 孫峻 (cf. L22, L27, L29) and monk Zhanming.
1930. LC, Zhejiang.
Bibliographic notice: Hong 395, HHC 192, ZFK 17.67.
Sun Jun also compiled an eight-*juan* gazetteer of Hupao Monastery, which was never published (HHC 190).

L17. *Lingfeng zhi* 靈峰志
[Gazetteer of Lingfeng Monastery]
     5 *juan*, by Zhou Qingyun 周慶雲 (cf. L48, M12).
1912. Columbia, Gest, Harvard, Jimbun, LC, Shifan,

Tobunken, Toyo.
Bibliographic notice: Hong 305, HHC 165, 178, ZFK 14.7.
No previous gazetteer.

L18. *Lingfeng sizhi* 靈峰寺志
[Gazetteer of Lingfeng Monastery]
      9 *juan*, by Wang Hua 王華.
      1935. Jimbun, Shifan.

L19. *Lingyin sizhi* 靈隱寺志
[Gazetteer of Lingyin Monastery]
      8 *juan*, by Sun Zhi 孫治.
      1663. LC.
      1672 reprint. Harvard.
      1888 WZ edition.
      Bibliographic notice: Hong 385, HHC 187, Wu 27a, ZFK
      17.25.
      Previous edition 1592.

L20. *Yunlin sizhi* 雲林寺志
[Gazetteer of Yunlin Monastery]
      8 *juan*, edited by Zhang Zeng 張熷.
      1829 reprint of 1744 edition.
      1888 WZ edition; 1980 ZF reprint.
      Bibliographic notice: Hong 386, HHC 187, Wu 27a, ZFK
      17.26.
      Yunlin Monastery was the official name given to Lingyin
      Monastery in the Kangxi era.

L21. *Yunlin si xuzhi* 雲林寺續志
[Supplementary gazetteer of Yunlin Monastery]
      8 *juan*, by Shen Huangbiao 沈鎤彪.
      1829.
      1888 WZ edition; 1980 ZF reprint.
      Bibliographic notice: Hong 386, HHC 187, ZFK 17.27.

L22. *Liuhe tazhi gao* 六和塔志稿
[Draft gazetteer of Liuhe Pagoda]
    By Sun Jun (cf. L16, L27, L29).
    Unpublished manuscript. Zhejiang.
    Bibliographic notice: Hong 379, HHC 379, ZFK 17.16.

L23. *Liuxiang yilan* 流香一覽
[A survey of monasteries along the Liuxiang River]
    1 *juan*, by monk Mingkai Juyi 明開具宜, ed. Zhu Zongwen
    朱宗文.
    1679 (first compiled ca. 1651).
    Ca. 1879 WZ edition.
    Bibliographic notice: Wu 25b.
    A collection of brief notices concerning small monasteries on
    Fahua Mountain, bordered on its eastern edge by the
    Liuxiang River.

L24. *Shengguo sizhi* 聖果寺志
[Gazetteer of Shengguo Monastery]
    1 *juan*, by monk Chaoqian Shitang 超乾石堂.
    1662.
    1722 edition. Nanjing.
    1881 WZ edition.
    Bibliographic notice: Hong 390, HHC 189, Wu 27b, ZFK
    17.46.

L25. *Shengyin jiedai sizhi* 聖因接待寺志
[Gazetteer of Shengyin Jiedai Monastery]
    4 *juan*, by Qiu Jun 邱峻.
    Qing. Nanjing has a two-*juan* manuscript.
    Bibliographic notice: Hong 389, HHC 189, ZFK 17.40.

L26. *Tianzhu shanzhi* 天竺山志
[Gazetteer of Tianzhu Mountain]
    12 *juan*, by Guan Tingfen 管庭芬 (1797-1880).
    1875 (compiled in the Daoguang era). Harvard, LC,
    Tobunken.
    Bibliographic notice: Hong 304, HHC 178, Wu 25b, ZFK

14.4.

A joint gazetteer of the three Tianzhu monasteries. Guan also wrote a record of a journey in 1839 to eastern Zhejiang entitled *Yueyou xiaolu* 越遊小錄 (Chen 114).

L27. *Tianzhu xuzhi beigao* 天竺續志備稿
[Complete draft of a supplementary gazetteer of the Tianzhu monasteries]
　　By Sun Jun (cf. L16, L22, L29).
　　Qing manuscript. Zhejiang.
　　Bibliographic notice: Hong 304, HHC 165, 178, 186, ZFK 14.5.

L28. *Shang tianzhu jiangsi zhi* 上天竺講寺志
[Gazetteer of Upper Tianzhu Doctrine Monastery]
　　15 *juan*, by monk Bichu Guangbin 苾芻廣賓 (cf. L99).
　　1646 (compiled Chongzhen era). LC, Nanjing.
　　1897 WZ edition; 1983 ZC reprint.
　　Bibliographic notice: Hong 303, 384, HHC 178, 186, Wu 25b, ZFK 17.21, 17.31.
　　According to L26 (12.25b), Guangbin also authored a monastic gazetteer entitled *Lingshan sizhi* 靈山寺志, no longer extant. Hong (391, 399) credits him with *Tianlong sizhi* 天龍寺志 and *Jingshan zhi* 徑山志.

L29. *Zhong tianzhu fajing sizhi beigao* 中天竺法淨寺志備稿
[Draft gazetteer of Middle Tianzhu Fajing Monastery]
　　By Sun Jun (cf. L16, L22, L27).
　　Qing manuscript. Zhejiang.
　　Bibliographic notice: Hong 385, HHC 186, ZFK 17.22.

L30. *(Wushan) Wang wang miao zhilüe* 吳山汪王廟志略
[Abridged gazetteer of the Temple to Prince Wang]
　　1 *juan*, by Wang Wenbing 汪文炳.
　　1905. Harvard, LC.
　　1936 reprint. Harvard.
　　Bibliographic notice: HHC 194, ZFK 17.94.
　　This temple was dedicated to Wang Hua of the Tang.

L31. *Wenlan gezhi* 文蘭閣志
[Gazetteer of Wenlan Pavilion]
  3 *juan*, by Sun Shuli 孫樹禮 (cf. L79).
  1883 WZ edition.
  1898 reprint. Toyo (2 copies).
  Bibliographic notice: Hong 380, HHC 185, ZFK 17.17.
  The pavilion was built to house one of the copies of the *Siku quanshu* library.

L32. *Wushan chenghuang miaozhi* 吳山城隍廟志
[Gazetteer of the City God Temple on Wu Mountain]
  8 *juan*, by Lu Song 廬崧 and Zhu Wencao 朱文藻 (cf. L62, L67, L73, L76, L91, M19).
  1789. Nanjing.
  1878 reprint. LC, Tobunken, Toyo, Zhejiang.
  Bibliographic notice: Hong 408, HHC 193, ZFK 17.92.
  Previous gazetteers were published in the mid-Ming, 1638, and 1704.

L33. *Wushan Wu gong miaozhi* 吳山伍公廟志
[Gazetteer of the Temple to Duke Wu on Wu Mountain]
  6 *juan*, by Jin Zhizhang 金志章, ed. Hang Shijun 杭世駿 (1696-1776; cf. L85).
  1754. Toyo.
  1876. Gest, LC, Shifan, Tobunken.
  Bibliographic notice: Hong 409, HHC 193, ZFK 17.94.
  Wu Zixu 伍子胥 took refuge here during the Spring and Autumn Period. Jin's original edition was published in the Qianlong era. Jin also authored a 20-*juan Wushan zhi*.

L34. *Xiaoci anji* 孝慈庵集
[Anthology from Xiaoci Chapel]
  1 *juan*, by Zhou Zhiyun 周芷筠.
  Kangxi era. Nanjing.
  1881 WZ edition.
  Bibliographic notice: Hong 395, HHC 192, ZFK 17.68.
  A collection of literary writings.

L35. *Xihu youlan zhi*　西湖遊覽志
[Tourist gazetteer of West Lake]
　　24 *juan*, by Tian Rucheng　田汝成　(js. 1526; cf. L36).
　　1547. Naikaku, Shifan.
　　1584 reprint. Beijing, Columbia, Gest, LC.
　　1619 reprint, edited by Shang Jun (cf. 5.1.1, L36). Beijing,
　　LC(m), Naikaku, Seikado, Sonkeikaku, Taibei, Zhejiang.
　　1896 WZ edition.
　　Recent reprints: 1958 (Beijing, Shanghai), 1960 (Taibei),
　　1963 (Taibei), 1974 (Taibei), 1980 (Hangzhou, Shanghai).
　　Columbia, Gest (3 copies), Harvard, Jimbun, LC (4 copies),
　　SOAS.
　　Bibliographic notice: HHC 180, Wang 211, ZFK 18.12.

L36. *Xihu youlan zhiyu*　西湖遊覽志餘
[Addenda to the tourist gazetteer of West Lake]
　　26 *juan*, by Tian Rucheng (js. 1526; cf. L35).
　　1547. Hangzhou, Naikaku, Taibei.
　　1584 reprint. Columbia, Gest, LC.
　　1619 reprint, edited by Shang Jun (cf. 5.1.1, L35). Beijing,
　　LC(m), Naikaku, Seikado, Sonkeikaku, Taibei, Zhejiang.
　　1896 WZ edition.
　　1958 reprint (Beijing: Zhonghua Shuju), 1980 reprint
　　(Shanghai: Guji Chubanshe). Columbia, Harvard, Jimbun,
　　LC, SOAS.
　　Bibliographic notice: HHC 180, Wang 211, ZFK 18.12.

L37. *Xihu zhi leichao*　西湖志類鈔
[Draft gazetteer of West Lake]
　　3 *juan*, by Yu Sichong　余思沖.
　　1579. Gest(m), Taibei.
　　1615 reprint. LC, Zhejiang.
　　1660 reprint. Naikaku.
　　Bibliographic notice: Hong 345, HHC 180, Wang 211, ZFK
　　14.203.
　　Excerpts from L35 and L36.

L38. *Xihu zhi zhaicui buyi xinang bianlan*　西湖志摘粹補遺奚囊便覽
[Complete overview of West Lake based on gleanings from its

gazetteer]
>   12 *juan*, by Gao Yingke   高應科.
>   1601. Gest, Harvard, LC, Suzhou.
>   Bibliographic notice: Hong 345, HHC 183, Wang 211, ZFK
>   14.206.

L39. *Xihu mengxun*   西湖夢尋
[Searching in dreams for West Lake]
>   5 *juan*, by Zhang Dai   張岱 (1597-1684).
>   1671.
>   1717 edition. Beijing.
>   1881 *Xihu jilan* (L46) edition; 1883 WZ edition.
>   1957 edition (Shanghai: Gudian Wenxue Chubanshe).
>   Beijing, Shanghai, Shifan.
>   1984 edition (Hangzhou: Zhejiang Wenyi Chubanshe), ed.
>   Sun Jiasui   孫家遂. LC.
>   Primarily a literary collection of writings, both early and con-
>   temporary, arranged according to seventy-two sites in the
>   West Lake area, for each of which Zhang has written a brief
>   historical essay. According to the preface by Wang Yuqian
>   王雨謙,   this work was intended to make up for lacunae in
>   L35.

L40. *Xihu zhi*   西湖志
[Gazetteer of West Lake]
>   26 *juan*, ed. Yao Jing   姚靖.
>   1689. Beijing, Naikaku, Zhejiang.
>   Bibliographic notice: Hong 346.
>   Based on L35 and L36.

L41. *Xihu zhi*   西湖志
[Gazetteer of West Lake]
>   48 *juan*, by Fu Wanglu   傅王露.
>   1731. Fudan, Sonkeikaku, Toronto.
>   1735 reprint. Gest (2 copies), Harvard, LC, Naikaku (2
>   copies), Shifan, Toronto (2 copies).
>   1878 reprint. Columbia, Harvard, Jimbun, LC (5 copies),
>   Seikado (2 copies), Shifan, Toronto.
>   1983 ZC reprint.

Bibliographic notice: Hong 346, HHC 181, ZFK 14.207.
Toyo has several of these editions. The two Gest copies were printed from the same blocks but on different sized paper; the phrase "blocks deposited in the storehouse of the Office of Salt Administration for Eastern China" has been removed from the title page of the later printing.

L42. *Xihu zhizuan* 西湖志纂
[Edited gazetteer of West Lake]
> 12 *juan*, by Liang Shizheng 梁詩正 (1697-1763) and Shen Deqian 沈德潛 (1673-1769).
> 1755. Fudan, Gest, Harvard, LC, Shifan, UBC.
> 1758 reprint. Hangzhou, Naikaku.
> 1762 enlarged edition (15 *juan*). Columbia, Jimbun, LC (2 copies), Nanjing, Seikado (2 copies), Shifan, Toyo, Zhejiang.
> Recent reprints: 1971 (Taibei), 1978 (Taibei). Harvard, LC, Toronto.
> Bibliographic notice: Hong 346, HHC 181, ZFK 14.208, 14.209, Wu 24b.

L43. *Xihu lansheng zhi* 西湖攬勝志
[Tourist gazetteer of West Lake]
> 14 *juan*, by Xia Ji 夏基.
> 1772. Zhejiang.
> Bibliographic notice: HHC 198, ZFK 18.19.

L44. *Xihu shiyi* 西湖拾遺
[Miscellany concerning West Lake]
> 48 *juan*, by Chen Shuji 陳樹基.
> 1791 preface.
> 1811 reprint. Columbia, Harvard.
> 1824 reprint under the title *Xihu zhi*, ed. Li Wei 李衛.
> 1847 reprint. Harvard.
> 1969 Biji reprint of 1824 edition.
> Bibliographic notice: HHC 206, ZFK 18.35.

L45. *Xihu quanan* 西湖全案
[Complete documents on West Lake]

2 *juan*, by Huang Bei 黃陂 and Liu Binshi 劉彬士.
1830. LC, Nanjing.
Bibliographic notice: Hong 348, HHC 182, ZFK 14.217.

L46. *Xihu jilan* 西湖集覽
[Anthology on the sights of West Lake]
    32 fascicles, ed. Xu Zeng 許增.
    1881. Columbia, LC.
    A collection of writings on West Lake, Song to Qing.

L47. *Xihu xinzhi* 西湖新志
[New gazetteer of West Lake]
    14 *juan*, by Hu Xianghan 胡祥翰.
    1921. Columbia, Gest, Jimbun, LC, Shifan.
    1971 reprint (Taibei: Wenhai Chubanshe). Harvard.
    Bibliographic notice: Hong 347, ZFK 14.213.

L48. *Xixi qiuxue anzhi* 西溪秋雪庵志
[Gazetteer of Qiuxue Chapel in West Valley]
    4 *juan*, by Zhou Qingyun (cf. L17, M12).
    1918 Chenfeng edition.
    Bibliographic notice: ZFK 17.69.

L49. *Xixi fanyin zhi* 西紹梵隱志
[Gazetteer of monastic retreats in West Valley]
    4 *juan*, by Wu Bentai 吳本泰.
    1651. LC, Nanjing.
    1881 WZ edition.
    Bibliographic notice: Hong 385, HHC 186, Wu 26b, ZFK 17.23.

L50. *Yu zhongsu gong cimu lu* 于忠肅公祠墓錄
[Record of the shrine and tomb of Yu Qian, the loyal and stern]
    12 *juan*, by Ding Bing (cf. L3, L7).
    1900 WZ edition.
    Bibliographic notice: Hong 415, ZFK 17.107.
    Shrine to Yu Qian 于謙 (1398-1457), founded by petition of

his eldest son in 1489. The posthumous title Zhongsu ("loyal and stern") was not conferred until 1590.

L51. *Yuanmiao guanzhi* 元妙觀志
[Gazetteer of Yuanmiao Monastery]
    4 *juan*, by Daoist Yangheng Qingyu 仰蘅青嶼.
    1824 (first published 1818).
    1881 WZ edition.
    Bibliographic notice: Hong 394, HHC 191, ZFK 17.61.

L52. *Yuanmiao guanzhi* 元妙觀志
[Gazetteer of Yuanmiao Daoist Monastery]
    12 *juan*, by Gu Yuan 顧沅 (cf. B61).
    1927. Jimbun, Shifan, Toyo.

L53. *Yue miao zhilüe* 岳廟志略
[Abridged gazetteer of the Temple to Yue Fei]
    10 *juan*, by Feng Pei 馮培.
    1803. Jiaxing.
    1879 edition. Harvard (2 copies), Jimbun, LC, Shifan, Tobunken.
    Bibliographic notice: Hong 410, ZFK 17.99.
    Concerning Yue Fei (1103-42), see also F19. Tang Xianzu 湯顯祖 (1550-1616) wrote a preface to an apparently lost Ming edition in 6 volumes entitled *Yue wang cizhi* 岳王祠志 (*Tang Xianzu ji* [Shanghai: Shanghai Renmin Chubanshe, 1973], pp. 1057-58).

L54. *Yue zhongwu wang chuyi zhi* 岳忠武王初瘞志
[Gazetteer of the first burial place of Prince Yue Fei, the loyal and martial]
    1 *juan*, by Wu Tingkang 吳廷康.
    Tongzhi-era reprint, together with *Yue miao gongyan* 岳廟公言, also by Wu Tingkang. Nanjing.
    Bibliographic notice: Hong 410, ZFK 17.100.

L55. *Yueyuan zhi* 約園志
[Gazetteer of Yue Garden]
    1 *juan*, by Xu Shuming 徐樹銘.
    1897. Shifan, Tobunken, Toronto, Toyo.
    Poems about famous pavilions around West Lake.

L56. *Yuhuang shan miaozhi* 玉皇山廟志
[Gazetteer of the temple on Yuhuang Mountain]
    1 *juan*, by Zhuo Bingsen (cf. L3).
    1881. Jimbun.
    This is the gazetteer of a Daoist temple.

L57. *Yunju shengshui sizhi* 雲居聖水寺志
[Gazetteer of Yunju-Shengshui Monastery]
    6 *juan*, by monk Minglun 明倫.
    1773. Nanjing.
    1892 WZ edition.
    Bibliographic notice: Hong 392, HHC 191, ZFK 17.56.
    Previous gazetteers 1649, 1729.

L58. *Yunqi jishi* 雲棲紀事
[Record of the affairs of Yunqi Monastery]
    8 *juan*, by Abbot Lianchi Zhuhong 蓮池袾宏 (1535-1615; cf.
    L81).
    Compiled ca. 1609, first published in 1624.
    1879 WZ edition based on 1735 edition.
    1899 edition in his collected works, *Yunqi fahui* 雲棲法彙.
    Bibliographic notice: Hong 388, HHC 188, ZFK 17.36.

L59. *Yunqi zhi* 雲棲志
[Gazetteer of Yunqi Monastery]
    10 *juan*, by Xiang Shiyuan 項士元, ed. monk Yinguang (cf.
    E4, H20).
    1934. Harvard, Jimbun, LC, Shifan.
    Bibliographic notice: Hong 388, HHC 188, ZFK 17.37.

L60. *Zhaodan tai zhilüe*　照膽臺志略
[Abridged gazetteer of Zhaodan Terrace]
　　1 *juan*, by Zou Zaiyin　鄒在寅.
　　1896 WZ edition.
　　Bibliographic notice: Hong 416, HHC 185, ZFK 17.110.
　　Gazetteer of a temple to Guan Yu on West Lake's Gushan
　　Island.

L61. *Zhaoxian si lüeji*　招賢寺略記
[Abridged record of Zhaoxian Monastery]
　　By monk Ruhuan　如幻.
　　1920. LC, Zhejiang.
　　Bibliographic notice: HHC 191, ZFK 17.58.

L62. *Zhige Zhu gong cimu lu*　直閣朱公祠墓錄
[Record of the shrine and tomb of Master Zhu Zhige]
　　2 *juan*, by Zhu Wencao　朱文藻　(cf. L32, L67, L73, L76,
　　L91, M19).
　　1895 WZ edition.
　　Bibliographic notice: Hong 417, HHC 198, ZFK 17.115.
　　Gazetteer of a shrine to Zhu Bian　朱弁　of the Song.

L63. *(Xihu) Zhou yuangong cizhi*　西湖周元公祠志
[Gazetteer of the shrine to Zhou Dunyi on West Lake]
　　4 *juan*, by Zhou Xunmao　周勳懋.
　　1822 manuscript. Taibei.
　　1983 ZC reprint.
　　This shrine to the Song philosopher Zhou Dunyi (1017-73)
　　was rebuilt in 1821 after a fifteen-year fund-raising. The
　　gazetteer includes a detailed list of donors (4.65a-82a) and
　　contains additionally both genealogical material and informa-
　　tion on other shrines to Zhou in northern Zhejiang.

L64. *Ziyang anji*　紫陽庵集
[Anthology from Ziyang Chapel]
　　1 *juan*, by Ding Wu　丁午　(1852-80; cf. L66, L82).
　　1882 WZ edition.
　　Bibliographic notice: Hong 395, HHC 192, ZFK 17.60.
　　The gazetteer of a Daoist temple.

Hangzhou: Renhe

L65. *Bianli yuanzhi*　犇利院志
[Gazetteer of Bianli Cloister]
    3 *juan*, by Zhai Hao (cf. L13, L71).
    1765. Zhejiang.
    1830 reprint. Harvard, LC, Shifan, Toyo.
    Bibliographic notice: Hong 394, HHC 192, Wu 27b, ZFK
    17.64.
    Preceded by a one-*juan* gazetteer by a resident monk in the
    early Qing, which the abbot in 1750 gave to Zhai Hao to
    expand into this edition.

L66. *Chengbei tianhou gongzhi*　城北天后宮志
[Gazetteer of the Temple to the Empress of Heaven in the north part
of the city]
    1 *juan*, by Ding Wu (cf. L64, L82).
    1881 WZ edition; Guangxu-era Tianyuan edition.
    Bibliographic notice: Hong 408, HHC 193, Wu 27b, ZFK
    17.93.

L67. *Chongfu sizhi*　崇福寺志
[Gazetteer of Chongfu Monastery]
    4 *juan*, by Zhu Wencao (cf. L32, L62, L73, L76, L91, M19).
    1842 (compiled 1801). Nanjing.
    1881 WZ edition, with addenda to 1885.
    Bibliographic notice: Hong 392, HHC 191, Wu 27b, ZFK
    17.57.

L68. *Xu chongfu sizhi*　續崇福寺志
[Supplementary gazetteer of Chongfu Monastery]
    1 *juan*, by Zhang Tingyu　章庭棫 .
    1842. Nanjing.
    1882 WZ edition.
    Bibliographic notice: Hong 392, HHC 191, ZFK 17.57.

L69. *Chongyang anji* 重陽庵集
[Anthology from Chongyang Chapel]
　　1 *juan*, by Mei Zhixian 梅志暹, ed. Yu Dazhang 俞大彰.
　　1534 adaptation of 1475 edition. Nanjing.
　　1877 WZ edition.
　　Bibliographic notice: Hong 394, HHC 192 ZFK 17.65.
　　Chongyang was a Daoist chapel.

L70. *Fuwen shuyuan zhilüe* 敷文書院志略
[Abridged gazetteer of Fuwen Academy]
　　4 *juan*, by Wei Songtang 魏頌唐.
　　1935. Jimbun, LC.
　　Bibliographic notice: Hong 418, ZFK 17.122.
　　The academy was founded in 1498 under the name Wansong
　　萬松　Shuyuan; the name was changed in 1716. An account
　　of the academy is included in L9.

L71. *Genshan zazhi* 艮山雜志
[Gazetteer of miscellany on Gen Mountain]
　　2 *juan*, by Zhai Hao (cf. L13, L65).
　　1896 WZ edition.
　　Bibliographic notice: Hong 306, HHC 179, Wu 25a, ZFK
　　14.15.
　　This gazetteer was compiled about 1750 but never previously
　　published. Wu (25a) lists it as the work of Huang Zhu　黃柱.

L72. *Guangfu miaozhi* 廣福廟志
[Gazetteer of Guangfu Temple]
　　1 *juan*, edited by Tang Hengjiu 唐恒九.
　　1846 (first published 1741).
　　1877 WZ edition.
　　Bibliographic notice: Hong 410, HHC 194 ZFK 17.98.
　　Guangfu Miao was a temple to Jiang Chongren of the twelfth
　　century who once provided relief grain in a time of famine.

L73. *Hanhai tangzhi* 捍海塘志
[Gazetteer of the Hanhai Sea Wall]
　　1 *juan*, by Qian Wenhan 錢文瀚, preface by Zhu Wencao (cf.

L32, L62, L67, L76, L91, M19).
1797. Nanjing (manuscript copy).
Guangxu-era WZ edition.
Bibliographic notice: Wu 25a, ZFK 14.183.

L74. *(Nanping) Jingci sizhi* 南屏淨慈寺志
[Gazetteer of Jingci Monastery at Nanping Mountain]
　　10 *juan*, by Abbot Dahe Xunshu 大壑薰沐.
　　1615, with material to 1665 in the fourth *juan*. LC.
　　Bibliographic notice: Wu 26b, ZFK 17.32.

L75. *Jingci sizhi* 淨慈寺志
[Gazetteer of Jingci Monastery]
　　28 *juan*, by monk Jixiang 際祥.
　　1805.
　　1888 WZ edition; 1980 ZF reprint.
　　Bibliographic notice: Hong 387, HHC 188, ZFK 17.33.
　　Previous gazetteer compiled in the Qianlong era by monk
　　Zhuanyu (cf. L5).

L76. *Jingu dongzhi* 金鼓洞志
[Gazetteer of Jingu Grotto]
　　8 *juan*, by Zhu Wencao (cf. L32, L62, L67, L73, L91, M19).
　　1807. Fudan.
　　1877 WZ edition.
　　1879 edition. LC, Shifan.
　　Bibliographic notice: Hong 397, Wu 25a, ZFK 17.79.
　　This is a Daoist monastic gazetteer.

L77. *Linping anyin sizhi* 臨平安隱寺志
[Gazetteer of Linping Anyin Monastery]
　　4 *juan*, by Shen Qian 沈謙 .
　　Qing. Nanjing.
　　Bibliographic notice: Hong 393, HHC 191, Wu 27a, ZFK
　　17.59.

L78. *Longxing xiangfu jietan sizhi* 龍興祥福戒壇寺志
[Gazetteer of Longxing, Xiangfu, and Jietan monasteries]
    12 *juan*, by Zhang Dachang 張大昌.
    Qing manuscript edition. Nanjing.
    1894 WZ edition. Jimbun, Toyo.
    Bibliographic notice: Hong 392, HHC 190, ZFK 17.55.

L79. *Fan gong cilu* 樊公祠錄
[Record of the Shrine to Master Fan]
    2 *juan*, by Sun Shuli (cf. L31).
    1899 WZ edition.
    Bibliographic notice: Hong 411, HHC 195, ZFK 17.104.
    This shrine was to Yuan official Fan Zhijing 樊執敬.

L80. *Tongren cilu* 同仁祠錄
[Record of Tongren Shrine]
    2 *juan*, by Sun Bingkui 孫炳奎.
    1897 WZ edition.
    Bibliographic notice: Hong 411, HHC 195, ZFK 17.103.
    This shrine was dedicated to Hu Shining 胡世寧, Sun Sui
    孫燧, and Wang Shouren 王守仁 (1472-1529).

L81. *Xiaoyi wuai anlu* 孝義無碍庵錄
[Gazetteer of Xiaoyi Wuai Chapel]
    6 *juan*, by monk Lianchi Zhuhong (cf. L58).
    Compiled ca. 1611, first published 1624.
    Guangxu-era WZ edition based on 1735 edition.
    1899 edition in his collected works *Yunqi fahui.*
    Bibliographic notice: Hong 388.

L82. *Yangqing cizhi* 楊清祠志
[Gazetteer of Yangqing Shrine]
    1 *juan*, edited by Ding Wu (cf. L64, L66).
    1881. Nanjing.
    Guangxu-era Tianyuan edition; 1904 WZ edition.
    Bibliographic notice: Hong 409, HHC 194, ZFK 17.97.
    This shrine commemorated two Ming officials, Wang Qi and
    Xiang Qi.

Hangzhou: Haining

L83. *Baima miaozhi* 白馬廟志
[Gazetteer of Baima Temple]
  1 *juan*, by monk Dashou 達受.
  Qing manuscript. Zhejiang.
  Bibliographic notice: Hong 410, ZFK 17.117.

L84. *Haitang lu* 海塘錄
[A record of the sea wall]
  26 *juan*, by Zhai Junlian 翟均廉 (jr. 1765).
  1765 Siku edition; Zhenben reprint.
  Bibliographic notice: ZFK 14.178.

L85. *Liangzhe haitang tongzhi* 兩浙海塘通志
[Comprehensive gazetteer of the Zhejiang sea wall]
  20 *juan*, by Fang Guancheng 方觀承 (1698-1768), Zha
  Xiang 查祥 (js. 1718), and Hang Shijun (cf. L33).
  1751. Columbia, LC, Nanjing, Zhejiang (MS).
  Bibliographic notice: ZFK 14.174; see also ECCP 276.
  Hang also authored *Zhejiang shanchuan guji ji* 浙江山川古
  蹟記 [Record of the mountains, rivers, and ancient sites of
  Zhejiang] in 6 *juan*, of which Beijing holds a manuscript copy.

L86. *Haitang xinzhi* 海塘新志
[New gazetteer of the sea wall]
  6 *juan*, by Changbai Langgan 長白琅玕.
  Ca. 1791. LC, Nanjing.
  Jiaqing-era reprint. LC, Nanjing.
  1970 ZC reprint with L88.
  Bibliographic notice: ZFK 14.175.

L87. *Haitang lanyao* 海塘攣要
[A general survey of the sea wall]
  12 *juan*, by Ruan Yuan (cf. B32, B105, M1, M67).
  1810 (compiled 1808). Columbia, Gest.
  The first *juan* includes extensive maps and illustrations of
  the sea wall.

L88. *Xu haitang xinzhi* 續海塘新志
[Supplement to the new gazetteer of the sea wall]
    4 *juan*, by Funiyangga 富呢楊阿.
    1839. Fudan.
    1970 ZC reprint with L86.
    Bibliographic notice: ZFK 14.176.

L89. *Jiawu haitang tuji* 甲午海塘圖記
[Illustrated record of the sea wall as of 1834]
    By Yan Lang 嚴烺.
    1844. Nanjing.
    Bibliographic notice: ZFK 14.182.

L90. *Xiashi shanshui zhi* 峽石山水志
[Topographical gazetteer of Xiashi]
    1 *juan*, by Jiang Hongren 蔣宏任.
    1728.
    1923 Biexia reprint; 1936 Congshu reprint.
    Bibliographic notice: Wu 24a, ZFK 14.19.
    A gazetteer of the northeast corner of Haining county.

Hangzhou: Yuhang

L91. *Dongxiao gongzhi* 洞霄宮志
[Gazetteer of Dongxiao Daoist Monastery]
    5 *juan*, by Wen Renru 聞人儒.
    1753. Zhejiang.
    Bibliographic notice: Hong 397, ZFK 17.77.
    The first edition of this gazetteer, compiled in 1305 by Deng
Mu 鄧牧 , is reprinted in Zhibuzu and Congshu. Wu (27b)
says Zhu Wencao (cf. L32, L62, L67, L73, L76, M19)
compiled a supplement in 6 *juan*.

L92. *Jingshan zhi* 徑山志
[Gazetteer of Jing Mountain]
    2 *juan*, by Magistrate Gao Zexun 高則巽.
    1585. Sonkeikaku.

L93. *Jingshan ji* 徑山集
[Anthology on Jing Mountain]
    3 *juan*, by monk Zongjing   宗淨.
    1570s. Nanjing.
    Bibliographic notice: Hong 398, ZFK 17.81.

L94. *Jingshan zhi*   徑山志
[Gazetteer of Jing Mountain]
    14 *juan*, by Song Kuiguang   宋奎光 (jr. 1612).
    1624. Beijing, Gest(m), Taibei.
    Bibliographic notice: Huang 8.22a, ZFK 17.83.
    Principally a monastic gazetteer of Xingsheng Wanshou
    Chan Monastery 興聖萬壽禪寺, with considerable informa-
    tion on eminent monks associated with the monastery.
    Landholdings are given in *juan* 14.

L95. *Jingshan zhi*   徑山志
[Gazetteer of Jing Mountain]
    5 *juan*, attributed to Zhang Zhicai 章之采 (cf. L96).
    1636. Naikaku.
    This gazetteer was printed together with L96 and L98 under
    the inappropriate title *Xihu hezhi* 西湖合志 [Joint gazetteer
    of West Lake].

Hangzhou: Lin'an

L96. *Dong tianmu shanzhi*   東天目山志
[Gazetteer of East Tianmu Mountain]
    4 *juan*, by Zhang Zhicai (cf. L95).
    1624. Gest(m), Naikaku, Taibei.
    1636 reprint in *Xihu hezhi* (Hong 307; cf. L95, L98).
    Naikaku.
    Bibliographic notice: Hong 308, ZFK 14.22.
    Zhang's surname is replaced by a homophone (張), sug-
    gesting that the 1636 reprint was a pirate edition.

L97. *Dong tianmu shan zhaoming chansi zhi*   東天目山昭明禪寺志
[Gazetteer of Zhaoming Chan Monastery on East Tianmu Mountain]

2 *juan*, by Song Hua   松華, ed. Chen Chaoyuan   陳兆元.
1914. Harvard, Jimbun, Toyo.
Bibliographic notice: Hong 399, ZFK 17.84.

L98. *Xi tianmu shanzhi*   西天目山志
[Gazetteer of West Tianmu Mountain]
    4 *juan*, by Sun Changyi   孫昌裔.
1621. Gest(m), LC(m), Naikaku, Taibei.
1636 reprint in *Xihu hezhi* (Hong 307; cf. L95, L96).
Naikaku.
Bibliographic notice: Hong 308, ZFK 14.22.
The first gazetteer of this mountain was compiled in 1581 by
Chen Zihou   陳子厚   and Tan Tingfu   譚廷輔, the second in
1614 by Xu Jiatai   徐嘉泰.

L99. *Xi tianmu zushan zhi*   西天目祖山志
[Gazetteer of West Tianmu Mountain]
    8 *juan*, by monk Bichu Guangbin (cf. L28), ed. Abbot Jijie
際界.
Compiled 1638.
1806. SOAS.
1876 reprint. Cambridge, Columbia, Harvard, LC, Seikado,
Shifan, Tobunken, Toyo.
1926 reprint. Jimbun.
Bibliographic notice: Hong 309, ZFK 14.26.

L100. *Tianmu shan mingsheng zhi*   天目山名勝志
[Gazetteer of the famous sights of Tianmu Mountain]
    By Qian Wenxuan   錢文選.
1936 (Zhengkai Shuju). LC.
Bibliographic notice: HHC 166, ZFK 14.27.
Based on L95 and L97.

L101. *Linglong zhi*   玲瓏志
[Gazetteer of Linglong Mountain]
    3 *juan*, by Tong Yideng   童以登, ed. Tong Cuixian   童萃先.
Kangxi era. Nanjing.
Bibliographic notice: Hong 306, ZFK 14.17.

The first two *juan* were written by Yideng in the Ming, the third added by Cuixian in the early Qing.

M. Zhejiang: Other Prefectures

M1. *Liangzhe fanghu lingqin cimu lu*　兩浙防護陵寢祠墓錄
[Record of the tombs and shrines of military heroes in Zhejiang]
　　　8 *ce*, by Ruan Yuan (cf. B32, B105, L87, M67).
　　　1802. LC.
　　　1889 reprint. Jimbun, Shifan, Tobunken.
　　　Bibliographic notice: Hong 415, ZFK 17.88.

Jiaxing: Jiaxing

M2. *Nanhu yanyu louzhi gao*　南湖煙雨樓志稿
[Draft gazetteer of Yanyu Pavilion by South Lake]
　　　2 *juan*, by Dong Xunguan　董巽觀.
　　　Qing manuscript. Jiaxing.
　　　Bibliographic notice: Hong 381, ZFK 17.128.

Jiaxing: Pinghu

M3. *Jingxian cizhi*　景賢祠志
[Gazetteer of Jingxian Shrine]
　　　4 *juan*, by Lu Jizhong　陸基忠.
　　　1605. Nanjing.
　　　Bibliographic notice: Hong 412, ZFK 17.131.
　　　A lineage shrine consecrated to Lu Zhi　陸贄　of the Tang.

M4. *(Pinghu Lu shi) Jingxian cizhi*　平湖陸氏景賢祠志
[Gazetteer of Jingxian Shrine to Master Lu of Pinghu]
　　　No *juan* divisions, no editor indicated.
　　　1880. Columbia, Jiaxing, Toyo.
　　　Bibliographic notice: Hong 399, ZFK 17.130 (in which the
　　　title is mistranscribed as *Jingxian sizhi*).
　　　Combines the text of M3 with a longer series of appendices.

M5. *Nongzhu louzhi* 弄珠樓志
[Gazetteer of Nongzhu Pavilion]
> 6 *juan*, by Zhang Jinyun 張錦雲.
> 1742. Shanghai.
> Bibliographic notice: ZFK 17.125.

M6. *Zhapu jiushan buzhi* 乍浦九山補志
[Emended gazetteer of the nine mountains at Zhapu]
> 12 *juan*, by Li Que 李確 (d. 1672), ed. Wei Bingshu 魏冰叔.
> 1757 (compiled 1665).
> 1831 reprint. Zhejiang.
> 1916 reprint. Jimbun, Shifan, Toyo.
> 1918 reprint. LC.
> 1926 reprint. Harvard.
> Bibliographic notice: Hong 310, ZFK 14.30.
> Beijing has a manuscript copy.

M7. *Shizhu ji jianshi* 石柱記箋釋
[Explications of the *Stone Pillar Record*]
> 5 *juan*, edited by Zheng Yuanqing 鄭元慶.
> 1702. Beijing, LC, Seikado, Shifan.
> Bibliographic notice: ZFK 17.135.
> A record of the mountains, shrines, and tombs of Huzhou prefecture, loosely based on a Tang work by Yan Zhenqing 顏眞卿.

M8. *Bao Qian liangxi zhilüe* 寶前兩溪志略
[Abridged gazetteer of the Bao and Qian rivers]
> 12 *juan*, by Wu Yushu 吳玉樹 (cf. M11).
> 1807. Nanda.
> 1922 Wuxing edition.
> Bibliographic notice: ZFK 14.240.

Huzhou: Wucheng

M9. *Jin'gai shanzhi* 金蓋山志
[Gazetteer of Jingai Mountain]

4 *juan*, by Li Zonglian 李宗蓮 (js. 1874), plus supplementary *juan* by Wen Tiaofu 文苕敷.
1883. Shifan.
1896 reprint. Columbia, Harvard, Toyo.
Bibliographic notice: ZFK 14.42.
The first gazetteer of this mountain was compiled in 1809 when the Daoist Chunyang Gong 純陽宮 was founded.

M10. *Jinjing zhi* 金井志
[Gazetteer of Jinjing Cave]
    4 *juan*, by Jiang Qiulü 姜虬綠.
    1750.
    1823 edition, entitled *Jinjing dongzhi* 洞志. Harvard, LC, Toyo.
    Bibliographic notice: Hong 312, ZFK 14.41.
    By 1823 the cave was known as Huanglong 黃龍 Cave.

Huzhou: Guian

M11. *Donglin shanzhi* 東林山志
[Gazetteer of Donglin Mountain]
    24 *juan*, by Wu Yushu (cf. M8).
    1818. Nanjing.
    1923 reprint. Harvard, Jimbun, LC, Shifan, Toyo.
    Bibliographic notice: Hong 312, ZFK 14.40.
    Previous gazetteers published in 1465, 1611, and the Kangxi era. This is the gazetteer of a Daoist monastery consecrated to Patriarch Lü 呂祖.

Huzhou: Wukang

M12. *Mogan shanzhi* 莫干山志
[Gazetteer of Mogan Mountain]
    13 *juan*, by Zhou Qingyun (cf. L17, L48).
    1927. Cambridge, Columbia, Jimbun, LC, Shifan, Toronto, Toyo.
    1936 Chenfeng reprint.
    Bibliographic notice: Hong 313, HHC 166, ZFK 14.45.
    Mogan Shan was a resort mountain for the wealthy of

Shanghai.

Shaoxing: Shanyin

M13. *Keshan xiaozhi* 柯山小志
[Short gazetteer of Ke Mountain]
    2 *juan*, by Zhou Mingding 周銘鼎.
    1855.
    1911 Yuezhong edition; 1936 Shaoxing edition.
    Bibliographic notice: Chen 95, Hong 321, ZFK 14.79.

M14. *Lanting zhi* 蘭亭志
[Gazetteer of Orchid Pavilion]
    11 *juan*, by Wu Gaozeng 吳高增.
    1752. LC, UBC.
    Bibliographic notice: Chen 78.
    Orchid Pavilion was made famous by the calligrapher Wang
    Xizhi 王羲之 (ca. 307-365). A one-*juan* gazetteer by Wang
    Fuli (cf. L8, N22) was published in 1695.

M15. *Lanting zhi* 蘭亭志
[Gazetteer of Orchid Pavilion]
    4 *juan* plus appendix, by Zhang Ruoxia 張若霞.
    1936. Gest.

M16. *Meng an youshang xiaozhi* 夢庵遊賞小志
[Short touring gazetteer of Meng Chapel]
    1 juan, by Li Ciming 李慈銘 (1830-94).
    Guangxu-era manuscript. Shanghai.
    Bibliographic notice: Chen 97.
    A collection of touring records to several places including the
    Buddhist chapel Meng An. Li also authored an 1885
    catalogue of shrines in Shaoxing entitled *Yuezhong xianxian*
    cimu 越中先賢祠目 (Tobunken).

M17. *Yushan zhi* 寓山志
[Gazetteer of Yu Mountain]

3 *juan*, by Qi Biaojia 祁彪佳 (1602-1645).
1638. Beijing, Zhejiang (manuscript copy).
Bibliographic notice: Chen 102.
Yu Mountain was Qi's private garden 14 km. southeast of the city. Shanghai also has his *Yushan shiliu jing* 寓山十六景 [The sixteen prospects of Yu Mountain] in manuscript.

Shaoxing: Guiji

M18. *Cao E jiangzhi* 曹娥江志
[Gazetteer of the Cao E River]
8 *juan*, by Hu Fengdan (1823-90; cf. B29, B40, E15, G8, J1, J4, K11).
1877. Toyo.
Bibliographic notice: Chen 162, Hong 351, ZFK 14.268.
The river is named after Cao E (131-44), who drowned herself there after her father had drowned accidentally.

M19. *Caojiang xiaonü miaozhi* 曹江孝女廟志
[Gazetteer of the temple at Cao E River to the filial daughter]
8 *juan*, by Jin Tingdong 金廷棟.
1808.
1882 reprint. Jimbun, LC (2 copies), Shifan, Tobunken, Toyo, Zhejiang (MS).
Bibliographic notice: Chen 320, Hong 414, ZFK 17.173.
Shen Zhili 沈志禮 produced an earlier gazetteer in 1687. Chen, p. 320, also mentions a Jiaqing-era edition by Zhu Wencao (cf. L32, L62, L66, L72, L75, L90).

M20. *Chenshan chenxin sizhi* 傴山傴心寺志
[Gazetteer of Chenxin Monastery on Chen Mountain]
5 *juan*, by Zhao Xun 趙旬 and Zhang Shifa 章士法.
Jiaqing era. Nanjing.
Bibliographic notice: Hong 415, ZFK 17.176.

M21. *(Guiji) Chenshan zhi* 會稽傴山志
[Gazetteer of Chen Mountain in Guiji]

2 *juan*, edited by Zhang Yue 章鑰 .
1758 manuscript. Hangzhou.
Bibliographic notice: Chen 101, ZFK 14.69.
Based on M20.

M22. *Yunmen xiansheng sizhi* 雲門顯聖寺志
[Gazetteer of Xiansheng Monastery on Yunmen Mountain]
    16 *juan*, by Zhao Dian 趙甸 .
    1659. Beijing.

M23. *Yunmen zhiliie* 雲門志略
[Abridged gazetteer of Yunmen Mountain]
    5 *juan*, by Zhang Yuanbian 張元忭 (1538-88).
    Wanli era (composed ca. 1576). Gest(m), Nanjing, Shanghai,
    Taibei.
    Bibliographic notice: Chen 89, Hong 319, ZFK 14.67.

Shaoxing: Xiaoshan

M24. *Xianghu shuili zhi* 湘湖水利志
[Gazetteer of the water resources of Xiang Lake]
    3 *juan*, by Mao Qiling 毛奇齡 (1623-1716).
    1720 Xihe edition; 1770 Xihe reprint; Xiaoshan edition.
    Bibliographic notice: ZFK 14.264.

M25. *Xianghu kaoliie* 湘湖考略
[Brief investigation of Xiang Lake]
    1 *juan*, by Yu Shida 於士達 and Wang Xu 王煦 .
    1798. Zhejiang.
    Bibliographic notice: Hong 352, ZFK 14.266.

M26. *Xiaoshan xianghu zhi* 蕭山湘湖志
[Gazetteer of Xiang Lake in Xiaoshan county]
    10 *juan*, by Zhou Yicao 周易藻 .
    1927. Columbia, Fudan, Harvard, LC, Shifan, Tobunken,
    Toyo.
    Bibliographic notice: Hong 352, ZFK 14.267.

Shaoxing: Zhuji

M27. *Zhuluo zhi* 苧蘿志
[Gazetteer of Zhuluo Mountain]
    8 *juan*, by Zhang Tian 張天 and Lu Mai 路邁.
    Chongzhen era. Naikaku.
    Bibliographic notice: Hong 320, ZFK 14.74.

Shaoxing: Yuyao

M28. *Dongshan zhi* 東山志
[Gazetteer of Dong Mountain]
    19 *juan*, by Xie Minxing 謝敏行, edited by his grandson Xie
    Zhonghe 謝鐘和.
    1576. Toyo. Suzhou Municipal Library has *juan* 12-19.
    1666 reprint. Beijing.
    1826. LC, Nanjing (16 *juan*).
    Bibliographic notice: Hong 320, ZFK 14.76.
    This is a gazetteer of Xie lineage properties in the vicinity of
    Dong Mountain, where the chief ancestor was buried. Xie
    Minxing also compiled a separate lineage genealogy the same
    year.

M29. *Dongshan zhi* 東山志
[Gazetteer of Dong Mountain]
    10 *juan*, by Xie Qilong 謝起龍.
    1910. Jiaxing.
    Bibliographic notice: Hong 320, ZFK 14.77.
    First published in the Qianlong era.

M30. *Siming shanzhi* 四明山志
[Gazetteer of the Siming Mountains]
    9 *juan*, by Huang Zongxi 黃宗羲 (1610-95).
    1675 (first compiled 1642).
    1703 edition. LC.
    1936 Siming edition.
    1956 reprint (Taibei: Jicheng Tushu Gongsi). Gest, Jimbun,
    LC (2 copies), SOAS, UBC (2 copies).
    Bibliographic notice: Hong 314, ZFK 14.49.

The 1703 edition may be the earliest published edition. Huang's family home was by the north spur of the Siming Mountains.

M31. *Yangming xiansheng cizhi* 陽明先生祠志
[Gazetteer of the shrine to Master Yangming]
    3 *juan*, by Zhou Rudeng 周汝登 (1547-1629).
    Wanli era. Beijing.
    Wang Shouren 王守仁 (1472-1529), better known as Yangming, was a native of Yuyao county.

Ningbo: Yin

M32. *Ayu wang shanzhi* 阿育王山志
[Gazetteer of King Aśoka Mountain]
    10 *juan*, by Guo Zizhang (cf. I41).
    1619. Harvard, LC, Naikaku, Nanjing, Toyo, Zhejiang.
    Ca. 1758 reprint with M34. Gest(m), Harvard, LC, Naikaku, Shifan, Taibei, UBC, Zhejiang.
    1977 reprint (Taibei: Xinwenfeng); 1980 ZF reprint.
    Bibliographic notice: Hong 318, Wang 208, ZFK 14.62.

M33. *Ayu wang shan zhilüe* 阿育王山志略
[Abridged gazetteer of King Aśoka Mountain]
    2 *juan*, ed. monk Daoqian 道謙.
    1624. Gest(m), Taibei, Toyo.
    1983 ZC reprint.
    An edited-down version of M32.

M34. *Ayu wang shan xuzhi* 阿育王山續志
[Supplementary gazetteer of King Aśoka Mountain]
    6 *juan*, by Abbot Wanquan Songlai 畹荃嵩來.
    Ca. 1758 (printed together with M32). Gest(m), Harvard, LC, Naikaku, Shifan, Taibei, UBC, Zhejiang.
    1977 reprint (Taibei: Xinwenfeng); 1980 ZF reprint.
    Bibliographic notice: Hong 318, ZFK 14.63.
    This work has been dated by the last entry in the penultimate *juan*; there is no preface or postface by the

abbot. Other dates are given in other bibliographies, usually 1747 or 1755.

M35. *Dongqian huzhi* 東錢湖志
[Gazetteer of Dongqian Lake]
    4 *juan*, by Wang Rongshang 王榮商.
    1916. Jiaxing.
    Bibliographic notice: Hong 351, ZFK 14.254.

M36. *Qita sizhi* 七塔寺志
[Gazetteer of Qita Monastery]
    8 *juan*, by Chen Liaoshi 陳廖士.
    1937. Jimbun, LC, Shifan.
    1980 ZF reprint.

M37. *Sanmao puan sizhi* 三茅普安寺志
[Gazetteer of Puan Monastery on Sanmao Mountain]
    2 *juan*, by monk Wuzhu 無住.
    1935. Toyo.
    Bibliographic notice: Hong 403, ZFK 17.156.
    Previous gazetteers under the title *Maoshan zhi* published in 1350, 1654, and 1726.

M38. *Tiantong sizhi* 天童寺志
[Gazetteer of Tiantong Monastery]
    6 *juan*, by monk Tongbu 通布, ed. Zhang Tingbin 張廷賓.
    1633. Sonkeikaku.
    Bibliographic notice: Hong 401, ZFK 17.147.
    The publication format is identical to that of N9. Previous gazetteer compiled 1559.

M39. *Tiantong sizhi* 天童寺志
[Gazetteer of Tiantong Monastery]
    10 *juan*, by monk Dejie 德介 and Wen Xingdao 聞性道.
    1712. Zhejiang.
    Yongzheng-era reprint. Nanjing.
    1811 reprint with minor revisions. Cambridge, Harvard,

Tobunken, Toyo.
1851 reprint. Jimbun, LC (2 copies).
1969 Japanese reprint. Jimbun.
1976 Biwu reprint; 1980 ZF reprint.
Bibliographic notice: Hong 401, ZFK 17.149.
Naikaku and Shifan have Qing editions I have not dated.
Previous gazetteer 1641 by Huang Yuqi 黃毓奇. Wen also
authored a two-*juan* mountain gazetteer entitled *Dongyang
zhilüe* 東陽志略, cited in *Yinxian zhi* 鄞縣志 (1788), 21.41b,
but no longer extant.

M40. *Tiantong si xuzhi* 天童寺續志
[Supplementary gazetteer of Tiantong Monastery]
2 *juan*, by monk Lianping 蓮萍.
1920. Fudan, Jimbun, LC, Toyo.
Bibliographic notice: Hong 401, ZFK 17.150.

M41. *Yongshang shuili zhi* 甬上水利志
[Gazetteer of the water resources of the Yong River system]
6 *juan*, by Zhou Daozun 周道遵 (cf. M56).
1848. Fudan.
1936 Siming edition.
1970 ZC reprint of 1848 edition.
Bibliographic notice: ZFK 14.250.

Ningbo: Ciqi

M42. *Baoguo sizhi* 保國寺志
[Gazetteer of Baoguo Monastery]
2 *juan*, by Yu Zhaohao 余兆灝, ed. Abbot Min'an Juexing
敏庵覺性.
1805, with additional material to 1813. LC.
Bibliographic notice: ZFK 17.163.

M43. *Du Bai erhu quanshu* 杜白二湖全書
[Complete book of Du and Baiyang lakes]
6 fascicles, by Wang Xiangneng 王相能.
1805. LC.

Bibliographic notice: ZFK 14.255.
An earlier edition of 1590 was entitled *Minghe Du Bai er guanhu jishi* [Record of matters pertaining to the two state-owned lakes Du and Baiyang of Minghe].

M44. *Xianjue si zhilüe* 先覺寺志略
[Abridged gazetteer of Xianjue Monastery]
    1 *juan*, by Abbot Xinming 心明.
    1705 (first published 1694). Naikaku.

Ningbo: Fenghua

M45. *Xuedou si zhilüe* 雪竇寺志略
[Abridged gazetteer of Xuedou Monastery]
    1 *juan*, by monk Lüping 履平.
    1645. Nanjing.
    1948 Xuansan edition.
    Bibliographic notice: Hong 402, ZFK 17.151.

M46. *Xuedou sizhi* 雪竇寺志
[Gazetteer of Xuedou Monastery]
    10 *juan*, by monk Daoyan 道嚴 .
    Qing (colophon dated *bingshen* 丙申). Nanjing, Toyo.
    Bibliographic notice: Hong 402, ZFK 17.152.

M47. *Yuelin sizhi* 岳林寺志
[Gazetteer of Yuelin Monastery]
    6 *juan*, by Dai Mingzong 戴明宗.
    1687. Beijing.
    1857 reprint. Jimbun.
    1980 ZF reprint; 1983 ZC reprint.
    Bibliographic notice: Hong 404, ZFK 17.167.

Ningbo: Dinghai

M48. *Putuoluojia shanzhi* 補陀洛伽山志
[Gazetteer of Potaraka Mountain]

6 *juan*, by Regional Commander Hou Jigao 侯繼高.
1598 (first published 1589). Naikaku.
Bibliographic notice: Hong 316, ZFK 14.53.
This is the earliest full gazetteer of the famous Buddhist
island off the coast of Ningbo. A one-*juan* account of Putuo
(*Putuoluojia shanzhuan* 山傳) was written by Sheng Ximing
盛熙明 in 1305 (SOAS and the Bibliothèque Nationale in
Paris have copies, and it is included in the Taishō Tripitaka).

M49. *Putuo shanzhi* 普陀山志
[Gazetteer of Potaraka Mountain]
    6 *juan*, by Zhou Yingbin 周應賓 (js. 1583).
    1607, with additions to 1611. Beida, LC, Naikaku,
    Sonkeikaku, Taibei.
    1980 ZF reprint.
    Bibliographic notice: Hong 316, Wang 207, ZFK 14.54.
    Zhou Yongbin also authored a monograph on the Hanlin
    Academy in Nanjing, entitled *Jiujing cilin zhi* 舊京詞林志,
    published in 1597 (Franke 6.2.9).

M50. *Putuo shanzhi* 普陀山志
[Gazetteer of Potaraka Mountain]
    15 *juan*, by Qiu Lian 裘璉 (js. 1715).
    1704 (completed 1698). Harvard, Naikaku, Nanjing,
    Sonkeikaku.
    1735 reprint (*Nanhai* 南海 *putuo shanzhi*). Jimbun, LC.
    Bibliographic notice: Hong 316, ZFK 14.55, 14.56.

M51. *Nanhai putuo shanzhi* 南海普陀山志
[Gazetteer of Potaraka Mountain in the southern ocean]
    20 *juan*, by Xu Yan 許琰.
    1740. LC, Naikaku, Tobunken, Toyo, UBC.
    Bibliographic notice: Hong 317, ZFK 14.57.
    Slightly expanded version of M50.

M52. *Nanhai putuo shanzhi* 南海普陀山志
[Gazetteer of Potaraka Mountain in the southern ocean]
    20 *juan*, by Qin Yaozeng 秦耀曾.

1832, with additions to 1843. Harvard (3 copies), Jiaxing,
Seikado, SOAS, Toyo (2 copies).
1915 reprint. Shifan.
1917 reprint. LC.
Bibliographic notice: Hong 317, ZFK 14.58.
Adapted from M49.

M53. *Putuo quansheng* 普陀全勝
[The sights of Potaraka Mountain]
    1 *juan*, by Zhu Defeng 祝德風.
Daoguang era. Nanjing.
Bibliographic notice: Hong 317, ZFK 14.59.

M54. *Nanhai shengjing putuoluojia shanzhi* 南海勝境普陀洛伽山志
[Gazetteer of the marvelous region of Potaraka Mountain in the
southern ocean]
    1 *juan*, anonymous.
Qing. BL.
More a tourist guide than a gazetteer, this crudely printed
short work provides information on routes and tides, a list of
the main sights and buildings, and a 5-page panoramic
drawing of the island.

M55. *Putuoluojia xinzhi* 普陀洛伽新志
[New gazetteer of Potaraka Mountain]
    12 *juan*, by Wang Hengyan 王亨彥.
1924. LC.
1928. Toyo.
1931. Harvard, Jimbun, Shifan, Toyo (2 copies).
1971 ZM reprint; 1978 Sida reprint: 1980 ZF reprint.
Bibliographic notice: Hong 317, HHC 166, ZFK 14.60.

M56. *Zhaobao shanzhi* 招寶山志
[Gazetteer of Zhaobao Mountain]
    2 *juan*, by Chen Jingpei 陳景霈, ed. Zhou Daozun (cf. M41).
1847. LC, Zhejiang.
Bibliographic notice: Hong 318, ZFK 14.64.
Zhaobao Mountain was located outside the northeast corner

of the city wall and afforded a breathtaking view of the ocean. Travelers to Putuo Island invariably visited Zhaobao before boarding the ferry. This part of Dinghai county was under the jurisdiction of Zhenhai county in the Qing.

M57. *Zhoushan zhi* 舟山志
[Gazetteer of the Zhoushan Archipelago]
    4 *juan*, by Asst. Regional Commander He Rubin 何汝賓 , ed.
Regional Commander Shao Fuzhong 邵輔忠 (js. 1595).
Early Qing manuscript. Gest(m), Taibei.
Bibliographic notice: ZFK 5.90.
He Rubin was posted as a military commander to Zhoushan in 1622.

Ningbo: Xiangshan

M58. *Xiangyi xiawang miaozhi* 象邑夏王廟志
[Gazetteer of the Temple to the King of the Xia in Xiangshan county]
    4 *juan*, by Ni Maibai 倪勱拜.
1829. Harvard.
Printed together with *Xicheng zalu* 西城雜錄 (2 *juan*), a record of other temples near the county seat.

Taizhou: Linhai

M59. *Donghu zhi* 東湖志
[Gazetteer of East Lake]
    2 *juan*, by Hong Zhenxuan 洪震煊 (1770-1815), Shen Hedou 沈河斗, and Guo Xieyin 郭協寅.
1808. UBC.
Bibliographic notice: Xiang 20b.
A literary collection on sites around the lake. Guo Xieyin also authored a 1-*juan* *Jinzi shanzhi* 巾子山志.

M60. *Tainan donglin zhi* 台南洞林志
[Gazetteer of the "Forest of Caves" in southern Taizhou]
    2 *juan*, by Feng Gengxue 馮賡雪.
1772.

1899 reprint with supplement by Ye Shu 葉書. LC.
Bibliographic notice: Hong 383, ZFK 17.188, Xiang 29b.
Feng also authored *Xianyan dazhong cilu* 僊巖大忠祠錄 in 6
juan, with preface by Qi Zhaonan 齊召南 (cf. M61, M66).

Taizhou: Huangyan

M61. *Huangyan hezha zhi* 黃巖河閘志
[Gazetteer of the riverine locks of Huangyan]
    9 *juan*, by Magistrate Liu Shining 劉世寧 (js. 1745).
    Ca. 1756. Nanjing.
    Bibliographic notice: Xiang 1a, ZFK 14.273.
    Preface by Qi Zhaonan (cf. M60, M66).

M62. *Weiyu shanzhi* 委羽山志
[Gazetteer of Weiyu Mountain]
    6 *juan*, by Hu Changxian 胡昌賢.
    1602.
    1870 reprint with M63. Harvard, Jimbun, LC, Shifan,
    Tobunken, Toyo, Zhejiang.
    Bibliographic notice: Hong 325, Xiang 16b, ZFK 14.91.

M63. *Weiyu shan xuzhi* 委羽山續志
[Supplementary gazetteer of Weiyu Mountain]
    6 *juan*, by Wang Weihan 王維翰.
    Compiled 1864.
    1870, printed with M62. Columbia, Harvard, Jimbun, LC,
    Shifan, Tobunken, Toyo, Zhejiang.
    Bibliographic notice: Hong 325, Xiang 23a, ZFK 14.92.
    Based on an unpublished gazetteer by Lu Tinggan 盧廷幹.
    Wang also authored *Santai shengji lu* (4 *juan*).

Taizhou: Tiantai

M64. *Tiantai shengji* 天台勝記
[Record of the sights of the Tiantai Mountains]
    6 *juan*, by Chen Xie 陳偕, ed. Magistrate Li Su 李素 .
    1591. Beijing.

Bibliographic notice: ZFK 18.64.
The first record of Tiantai dates from the Yuan and is included in Daozang. There was an earlier Ming gazetteer by Xu Biaoran (cf. N18); a collection of poems on the sights of Tiantai, *Tiantai shengji lu* 天台聖蹟錄 (4 *juan*), was published by Pan Zhen 潘榛 in 1546 (copy in Taibei, microfilm in Gest).

M65. *Tiantai shan fangwai zhi* 天台山方外志
[Gazetteer of the spiritual world of Tiantai Mountain]
    30 *juan*, by monk Chuandeng Wujin 傳燈無盡.
    1601. Naikaku, Nanjing.
    1612 reprint, with preface by Gu Qiyuan 顧起元. LC, Toyo.
    Chongzhen-era reprint. Naikaku.
    1894 reprint. Cambridge, Harvard, LC, Shifan, Tobunken.
    1922 reprint. Jimbun, Toyo, UBC.
    Bibliographic notice: Hong 323, Xiang 10a, Wang 207, ZFK 17.190.
    Chuandeng Wujin also compiled a 16-*juan* literary gazetteer of Tiantai's Gaoming Monastery 高明寺 and the You River on which it was located (*Youxi biezhi* 幽溪別志) in 1624 (not published until 1644); he compiled an eight-*juan* gazetteer of Yanqing Monastery (*Yanqing sizhi*) in Linhai county; and he is listed as editor of the eighth *juan* of *Ayu wang shanzhi* (M32).

M66. *Tiantai shan fangwai zhiyao* 天台山方外志要
[Abridged gazetteer of the spiritual world of Tiantai Mountain]
    10 *juan*, by Qi Zhaonan (cf. M60, M61).
    1767. Harvard, LC.
    Bibliographic notice: Hong 323, Xiang 19b, ZFK 17.191.
    A condensed version of M65.
    Qi is best known for his geography of China's rivers, *Shuidao tigang* 水道提綱 [Outline of water courses], published in 1761.

M67. *(Chongding) Tiantai shan fangwai zhiyao* 重訂天台山方外志要
[Re-edited abridged gazetteer of the spiritual world of Tiantai Mountain]

13 *juan*, ed. Ruan Yuan (cf. B32, B105, L87, M1).
1802. Shifan.
Bibliographic notice: Xiang 20a.
Expanded from M66.

M68. *Tiantai shan quanzhi* 天台山全志
[Complete gazetteer of Tiantai Mountain]
    18 *juan*, by Prefect Zhang Lianyuan 張聯元 (js. 1691).
    1711. Seikado, Toyo.
    1717 reprint. Columbia, Gest, Hangzhou, Harvard, Jimbun,
LC, UBC, Zhejiang.
    Bibliographic notice: Hong 324, ZFK 14.87.
    Zhang also authored *Qingsheng cizhi* 清聖祠志 (1723), a
6-*juan* gazetteer of a shrine to the ancients Bo Yi and Shu Qi.

M69. *Tiantai shanji jisheng* 天台山跡記勝
[Record of remarkable sites on Tiantai Mountain]
    By Yao Tinghe 姚廷和.
    Qing manuscript. Nanjing.
    Bibliographic notice: Hong 325, 383, Xiang 20b, ZFK
17.186.

M70. *Tiantai shan youlan zhi* 天台山遊覽志
[Touring gazetteer of Tiantai Mountain]
    6 chapters, by Chen Jialin 陳甲林.
    1937 (Shanghai: Zhonghua Shuju). UBC.
    Bibliographic notice: HHC 168, ZFK 18.77

Jinhua: Yongkang

M71. *Wufeng shuyuan zhi* 五峰書院志
[Gazetteer of Wufeng Academy]
    8 *juan*, by Cheng Shangpei 程尚斐.
    1781. Zhejiang.
    Bibliographic notice: Hong 420, ZFK 17.203.
    The academy dates from the Jiajing era.

Quzhou: Xi'an

M72. *Lanke shanzhi* 爛柯山志
[Gazetteer of Lanke Mountain]
    13 *juan*, by Zheng Yongxi 鄭永禧.
    1907. Columbia, Harvard, Shifan, Tobunken, Zhejiang.
    Bibliographic notice: Hong 330, ZFK 14.110.
    The gazetteer had three previous seventeenth-century
    editions.

Quzhou: Changshan

M73. *Sanqu Kong shi jiamiao zhi* 三衢孔氏家廟志
[Gazetteer of the Kong family temple at Sanqu Mountain]
    3 *juan*, by Shen Jie 沈杰.
    Jiajing era. Beijing.

Quzhou: Jiangshan

M74. *Xianxia zhilüe* 仙霞志略
[Abridged gazetteer of Xianxia Ridge]
    1 *juan*, by monk Zhenglong 正龍.
    1692, with material to 1695 (48b). LC.
    Gazetteer of a temple to Guan Yu.

M75. *Xianxia ling tianyu anzhi* 仙霞嶺天雨庵志
[Gazetteer of Tianyu Chapel on Xianxia Ridge]
    Kangxi era. Zhejiang.
    Bibliographic notice: Hong 405, ZFK 17.204.

Chuzhou: Lishui

M76. *Tongji yanzhi* 通濟堰志
[Gazetteer of Tongji Embankment]
    1 *juan*, by Wang Tingzhi 王庭芝.
    1870. LC.

Chuzhou: Qingtian

M77. *Nantian shanzhi* 南田山志
[Gazetteer of Nantian Mountain]
  14 *juan*, by Liu Yaodong 劉燿東.
  1935. LC, Shifan, Toyo.
  Bibliographic notice: Hong 342, HHC 167, ZFK 14.159.
  Essentially a local gazetteer for the mountainous
  southwestern part of Qingtian county, in which Nantian
  Shan is the principal peak.

Chuzhou: Jinyun

M78. *Xiandu zhi* 僊都志
[Gazetteer of Xiandu Mountain]
  5 *juan*, by Li Shifu 李時孚.
  1571. Naikaku.
  Bibliographic notice: ZFK 14.157.
  Manuscript copies of a two-*juan* Yuan gazetteer of this
  mountain by Chen Xingding 陳性定, ed. Wu Mingyi 吳明義,
  are held at Beijing, Kexue, and Seikado.

Chuzhou: Suichang

M79. *Nanming shan zhilüe* 南明山志略
[Abridged gazetteer of Nanming Mountain]
  4 *juan*, by Zheng Liaokang 鄭廖康, ed. Prefect Zheng
  Kuiguang 鄭奎光.
  1639. Naikaku.
  Bibliographic notice: Hong 320, ZFK 14.72.

Chuzhou: Yunhe

M80. *Daqing sizhi* 大慶寺志
[Gazetteer of Daqing Monastery]
  1 *juan*, by Mei Rong 梅榕.
  1852. Nanjing.
  Bibliographic notice: Hong 407, ZFK 17.219.

Wenzhou: Yongjia

M81. *Jiangxin zhi* 江心志
[Gazetteer of Jiangxin Monastery]
6 *juan*, by Wang Guangyun 王光蘊.
1590 manuscript. Kexue (Dili Yanjiusuo).
Bibliographic notice: Hong 406, Sun 24b, ZFK 17.211.
Previous gazetteer compiled early in the Chenghua era by
monk Hongbin 宏斌. The monastery was called Jiangxin
["Heart of the River"] because it was located on an island
called Guyu 孤嶼 in the Ou River in the middle of the
prefectural capital.

M82. *Jiangxin zhi* 江心志
[Gazetteer of Jiangxin Monastery]
6 *juan*, by Chen Jie 陳階.
1626. Naikaku.
Bibliographic notice: Hong 406, Sun 26b, ZFK 17.211.

M83. *Jiangxin zhi* 江心志
[Gazetteer of Jiangxin Monastery]
10 *juan*, by Lin Danwu 林丹五 and Huang Xinhou 黃信侯,
ed. monk Yuechuan Yuanqi 月川元奇.
1707. Hangzhou, Toyo, Zhejiang.
Bibliographic notice: Hong 406, Sun 28a, ZFK 17.213.

M84. *Guyu zhi* 孤嶼志
[Gazetteer of Guyu Island]
9 *juan*, by Chen Shunzi 陳舜咨.
1809. Columbia, Harvard, LC, Shifan, Tobunken, Toyo.
1934 reprint.
Bibliographic notice: Hong 406, Sun 29b, ZFK 17.214.
This also is a gazetteer of Jiangxin Monastery.

Wenzhou: Ruian

M85. *Xianyan zhi* 僊巖志
[Gazetteer of Xianyan Mountain]

10 juan, by Li Canqi 李燦箕.
1634. Naikaku.
1685 revised edition, ed. monks Foyan 佛彥 and Fogao 佛皋.
Bibliographic notice: Hong 340, 407, ZFK 14.148, 17.215.

M86. *Xianyan shanzhi* 儇巖山志
[Gazetteer of Xianyan Mountain]
    8 *juan*, by Zhang Yang 張揚.
    1933. Jimbun, LC, Shifan, Toyo.
    Bibliographic notice: Hong 340, HHC 167, ZFK 14.149.
    Based on a Song edition. A Qianlong-era gazetteer was compiled by Qi Zhouhua 齊周華 (1698-1768), according to his *Mingshan cang fuben* 名山藏副本 (1761), 2.7a.

Wenzhou: Leqing

M87. *Yanshan zhi* 雁山志
[Gazetteer of the Yandang Mountains]
    4 *juan*, by Zhu Lian 朱諫 (js. 1496).
    1526. LC(m), Taibei.
    1539 edition, ed. Pan Huang. Beijing.
    1601 reprint. LC(m), Taibei.
    Bibliographic notice: Hong 331, Sun 3a, ZFK 14.114.
    Based on a one-*juan* gazetteer by Ming monk Yongsheng 永昇.

M88. *Yanshan zhi* 雁山志
[Gazetteer of the Yandang Mountains]
    4 *juan*, ed. Hu Runing 胡汝寧.
    1581. Naikaku, Zhejiang.
    1601. Sonkeikaku.
    1976 reprint of Qing manuscript copy (Taibei: Zhulin Chubanshe). Gest, LC, Michigan.
    1980 ZF reprint.
    Bibliographic notice: Hong 332, ZFK 14.116.
    Based on the 1539 edition of M87. As of 1581 the mountain had eighteen Buddhist monasteries.

M89. *Yanshan zhisheng* 雁山志勝
[Gazetteer of the sights of the Yandang Mountains]
    2 *juan*, by Xu Daipin 徐待聘, ed. Yao Zongyi 姚宗儀.
    1606. Gest(m), Taibei.
The first *juan* describes the sights of the mountain, the second its thirteen Buddhist monasteries.

M90. *Yanshan zaji* 雁山雜志
[Notes on the Yandang Mountains]
    1 *juan*, by Han Zeyu 韓則愈.
    1695 Tanji edition; 1895 XF edition.
    Bibliographic notice: Hong 334, ZFK 14.121.

M91. *Yanshan zhigao* 雁山志稿
[Draft gazetteer of the Yandang Mountains]
    25 *juan*, by Li Xiangkun 李象坤.
    1708 manuscript (only 11 *juan* survive). Hangzhou.
    Bibliographic notice: Sun 12a, ZFK 14.120.

M92. *Yandang shanzhi* 雁蕩山志
[Gazetteer of the Yandang Mountains]
    2 *ce*, preface by Ni Hongfan 倪鴻範.
    1745. Toyo.

M93. *Yanshan zhi* 雁山志
[Gazetteer of the Yandang Mountains]
    4 *ce*, by Song Ao 宋鰲.
    1755. Harvard.
    An editorially confused expansion of M92.

M94. *Yanshan tuzhi* 雁山圖志
[Illustrated gazetteer of the Yandang Mountains]
    By monk Shixing 實行.
    Qianlong-era reprint. Nanjing.
    Bibliographic notice: Hong 335, ZFK 14.124.

M95. *Guang yandang shanzhi*　廣雁蕩山志
[Gazetteer of the greater Yandang Mountains]
　　28 *juan*, by Zeng Wei　曾唯.
　　1790. Cambridge, Columbia, Harvard, Jiaxing, SOAS,
　　Tobunken, Toyo (2 copies).
　　1808 reprint. LC.
　　1869 reprint with supplement. Jimbun, Shifan.
　　Bibliographic notice: Hong 335, Sun 18b, ZFK 14.127.

M96. *Yuzeng fengzhi*　玉甑峰志
[Gazetteer of Yuzeng Peak-Monastery]
　　10 *juan*, by Chen Chongya　陳崇雅.
　　1637 (preface dated 1629). Naikaku.
　　Bibliographic notice: Hong 339, ZFK 14.144.

Wenzhou: Pingyang

M97. *Nan yandang shanzhi*　南雁蕩山志
[Gazetteer of the South Yandang Mountains]
　　13 *juan*, by Zhou Wei　周喟.
　　1918. Columbia, Harvard, Jimbun, LC, Shifan, Toyo.
　　Bibliographic notice: Hong 338, HHC 167, ZFK 14.141.
　　Preceded by eight gazetteers from Song to Qing, none extant.

N. Fujian

Fuzhou: Min

N1. *Gushan zhi* 鼓山志
[Gazetteer of Drum Mountain]
12 *juan*, by Xie Zhaozhe (cf. D26, N11, N33).
1608. Beijing, Naikaku.
Early Qing reprint, ed. monk Yuanxian (cf. N30). Beijing.
1694 Japanese reprint. Naikaku.
Xie compiled this Buddhist monastic gazetteer from an
unpublished draft by Huang Yongzhong   黃用中, given to
him by Huang's nephew. Xie completed the work before
returning to Peking later that year.

N2. *Gushan zhi* 鼓山志
[Gazetteer of Drum Mountain]
14 *juan*, by Huang Ren   黃任.
1761. Gest, Jimbun, LC.
1774 reprint. SOAS, Toyo.
1876 reprint, ed. monk Qiiiang   奇量. Harvard, Shifan,
Tobunken.
1980 ZF reprint.

N3. *Xihu zhi* 西湖志
[Gazetteer of West Lake]
24 *juan*, by He Zhendai   何振岱.
1916. Columbia, Harvard, LC, Shifan.

Fuzhou: Houguan

N4. *Changqing sizhi* 長慶寺志
[Gazetteer of Changqing Monastery]
6 *juan*, by Provincial Commissioner of Education Shen Han
沈涵   (js. 1676).
1709.

1800 reprint, with additional material to 1807. Toyo.

N5. *Daoshan jilüe* 道山紀略
[Abridged record of Dao Mountain]
　　By Xiao Zhen 蕭震.
　　1672. Harvard, Naikaku, Toyo.
　　Dao Mountain was also known as Min Mountain 閩山 or
　　Wushi Mountain 烏石山.

N6. *Wushi shanzhi* 烏石山志
[Gazetteer of Wushi Mountain]
　　9 *juan*, by Guo Baicang 郭柏蒼 and Liu Yongsong 劉永松.
　　1842. Columbia, Jimbun, LC, Shifan, Tobunken.
　　1873 reprint. Toyo.
　　1881 reprint. Toyo.
　　1883 reprint. LC.
　　1886 reprint. Shifan.
　　1975 ZC reprint.

N7. *Jiufeng zhi* 九峰志
[Gazetteer of Jiufeng Mountain]
　　4 *juan*, by Chen Zuokang 陳祚康.
　　1867. Harvard, Jimbun, LC, Toyo.
　　The gazetteer of Zhenguo Chansi 鎮國禪寺.

N8. *Xuefeng zhi* 雪峰志
[Gazetteer of Xue Peak]
　　10 *juan*, by Xu Bo 徐煿 (1570-1642; cf. N11), ed. Lin
　　Hongyan 林弘衍.
　　1632. Sonkeikaku.
　　1754 reprint. Harvard, LC.
　　The gazetteer of Chongsheng Chan Monastery 崇聖禪寺.

Fuzhou: Fuqing

N9. *Huangbo sizhi* 黃檗寺志
[Gazetteer of the monastery on Huangbo Mountain]

3 *juan*, by monks Xingji 行璣 and Xingyuan 行元.
1637. Naikaku, Sonkeikaku.
The gazetteer of Wanfu Chan Monastery 萬福禪寺. This
gazetteer's layout is identical to that of M38.

N10. *Huangbo shan sizhi* 黃檗山寺志
[Gazetteer of the monastery on Huangbo Mountain]
8 *juan*, by monk Daoxian 道暹.
1922. Toyo.

Fuzhou: Yongfu

N11. *Fangguang yanzhi* 方廣巖志
[Gazetteer of Fangguang Cave-Monastery]
3 *juan*, by Xie Zhaozhe (cf. D26, N1, N33), ed. Xu Bo (cf.
N8).
1612. Naikaku.

N12. *Fangguang yanzhi* 方廣巖志
[Gazetteer of Fangguang Cave-Monastery]
4 *juan*, ed. Chen Zhengli 陳正立.
1735.
1885 reprint, ed. magistrate Lin Ying 林瀛. BL.
The first three *juan* are a reprint of N11.

Xinghua: Putian

N13. *(Chifeng) Tianhou zhi* 勅封天后志
[Gazetteer (of the temple) of the imperially enfeoffed empress of
heaven]
2 *juan*, by Lin Qingbiao 林清標.
1778. Columbia, Harvard, LC (2 copies).
1843 reprint, with additional material to 1810. Shifan, Toyo.
Further information on the Tianhou cult may be found in
Tianhou shengmu shengji tuzhi [Illustrated gazetteer of the
holy relics of the holy mother Tianhou] (1832), of which LC
has a copy. See also L65.

Xinghua: Xianyou

N14. *Jiuli huzhi* 九鯉湖志
[Gazetteer of Jiuli Lake]
    6 *juan*, by Huang Tianquan 黃天全.
    1586. Beijing, Columbia(m), Gest(m), LC(m), Taibei (2 copies).
    Bibliographical notice: Wang 211.

N15. *Jiuli huzhi* 九鯉湖志
[Gazetteer of Jiuli Lake]
    18 *juan*, by Kang Dangshi 康當世.
    Wanli era. Sonkeikaku.

N16. *Jiuli huzhi* 九鯉湖志
[Gazetteer of Jiuli Lake]
    By Xu Lijiu 徐鯉九.
    1942. Gest.

Jianning: Chongan

N17. *Wuyi jiuqu xiaozhi* 武夷九曲小志
[Short gazetteer of the nine sections of the Wuyi Mountains]
    1 *juan*, by Liu Er 劉而 (?).
    1558. Seikado.
    The Wuyi Mountains were sacred to Daoists. Their sights were traditionally divided into nine sections according to the nine arms of the ravine running through the mountains.

N18. *Wuyi zhilüe* 武夷志略
[Abridged gazetteer of the Wuyi Mountains]
    4 *juan*, by Xu Biaoran 徐表然 (cf. M64).
    1576. Toyo.
    1589 reprint. BL.
    1619 reprint. Columbia, Gest, Harvard, Naikaku, Shifan.
    Ca. 1627 reprint. LC.
    Bibliographic notice: Wang 208.
    The LC copy has been edited such that the dates of the

prefaces have been removed and the original four *juan* redivided into twelve, with a text by Ge Yinliang (cf. B1) dated 1627 appended at the end. Zhejiang has a Ming edition.

N19. *Wuyi shanzhi* 武夷山志
[Gazetteer of the Wuyi Mountains]
    4 *juan*, by Lao Kan 勞堪.
    1582, with additions to 1584. Naikaku, Sonkeikaku, UBC (reprint?).
    Said to be based on an older gazetteer.

N20. *Wuyi shanzhi* 武夷山志
[Gazetteer of the Wuyi Mountains]
    19 *juan*, by Zhong Zhongru 衷仲孺.
    1643. Gest(m), Harvard, Michigan, Naikaku, Taibei.
    Edo edition. Naikaku.

N21. *Wuyi shanzhi* 武夷山志
[Gazetteer of the Wuyi Mountains]
    28 *juan*, by Wang Zi 王梓.
    1710. LC.
    In addition to the three foregoing editions, Wang also cites a Zhengde-era edition by Yang Gen 楊亘.

N22. *Wuyi jiuqu zhi* 武夷九曲志
[Gazetteer of the nine sections of the Wuyi Mountains]
    16 *juan*, by Wang Fuli (cf. L8, M14).
    1718. LC, Michigan, Shifan.
    1876 reprint. Toyo.

N23. *Wuyi shanzhi* 武夷山志
[Gazetteer of the Wuyi Mountains]
    24 *juan*, by Dong Tiangong 董天工.
    1753. LC, SOAS, UBC.
    1760. Harvard, SOAS.
    1847 reprint. Cambridge, Columbia, Harvard, Jimbun, LC

(2 copies), Michigan, Seikado, Shifan, SOAS, Tobunken, Toronto, Toyo.
1971 ZM reprint.

Yanping: Youxi

N24. *Nanxi shuyuan zhi*   南溪書院志
[Gazetteer of Nanxi Academy]
    4 *juan*, by Ye Tingxiang.
    1594. Zhejiang.
    Tianqi-era reprint. Beijing.
    Nanxi Academy was at the site of the tomb and shrine to Zhu
    Xi (1130-1200). Cf. C31.

N25. *Nanxi shuyuan zhi*   南溪書院志
[Gazetteer of Nanxi Academy]
    4 *juan*, by Yang Yujian (cf. I43).
    1717. LC (2 copies), Nanda, Toyo.
    1870 reprint. Jimbun, Nanda, Toyo.

N26. *Lixi zhengshun miaozhi*   歷西正順廟志
[Gazetteer of Zhengshun Temple in west Meili]
    After 1728.
    Nongcun, pp. 47-50, 160-67, quotes extensively from the
    third *juan* of this gazetteer. The 1873 prefectural gazetteer,
    Yanping fuzhi   延平府志, 12.30b, refers to the temple as
    Zhengshun Wang   王 Miao.

Dingzhou: Qingliu

N27. *Yuhua dongzhi*   玉華洞志
[Gazetteer of Yuhua Cave]
    10 *juan*, by Lin Xichun   林熙春, ed. Wang Zhizhu   王之柱.
    1598. Naikaku (*juan* 7-10 missing).
    1623 reprint. Naikaku.

N28. *Yuhua dongzhi* 玉華洞志
[Gazetteer of Yuhua Cave]
    6 *juan*, by Liao Heling 廖鶴齡.
    1724. LC.
    The main text was compiled in 1711; a supplementary *juan*
    has been appended. Two earlier editions are mentioned.

Quanzhou: Jinjiang

N29. *Jiuri shanzhi* 九日山志
[Gazetteer of Jiuri Mountain]
    By Huang Bailing 黃柏齡.
    1983 (Quanzhou: Jinjiang Diqu Wenhuaju). LC.
    A modern work, but composed in keeping with traditional
    principles of mountain-gazetteer compilation. Published as
    the inaugural volume of a series entitled *Quanzhou wenwu
    zhi* 泉州文物志. The mountain is located 7 km. northwest of
    the city of Quanzhou. A 1620s gazetteer by Huang Wenzhao
    黃文炤 was reprinted in the Qing but seems to be no longer
    extant.

N30. *Kaiyuan sizhi* 開元寺志
[Gazetteer of Kaiyuan Monastery]
    2 *juan*, by monk Yuanxian 元賢 (cf. N1).
    1643.
    1927 edition. Toyo.
    1980 ZF reprint.

Quanzhou: Nan'an

N31. *Guoshan miaozhi* 郭山廟志
[Gazetteer of the temple on Guo's Mountain]
    8 *juan*, by Dai Fengyi 戴鳳儀, ed. Dai Shaoqi 戴紹箕.
    1897. Harvard, LC, Shifan.
    This gazetteer is of Weizhen Temple 威鎮廟 in Nan'an
    county, as well as of Longshan Temple 龍山宮 and Weizhen
    Temple in Qingxi county.

Zhangzhou: Haicheng

N32. *Xiamen nan putuo sizhi*　夏門南普陀寺志
[Gazetteer of the southern Potaraka Monastery in Xiamen]
    By monk Jichen　寄塵.
    1933.
    1980 ZF reprint.
    No previous gazetteers.

Funing zhou: Fuan

N33. *Tailao shanzhi*　太姥山志
[Gazetteer of Tailao Mountain]
    2 *juan*, by Xie Zhaozhe (cf. D26, N1, N11).
    1609.
    1889 reprint. LC.

O. Guangdong

Guangzhou: Nanhai

O1. *Xiqiao shanzhi* 西樵山志
[Gazetteer of Xiqiao Mountain]
      6 *juan*, by Ma Fulu 馬符錄, ed. Luo Guoqi 羅國器 and Chen
Zhangyi 陳張翼.
1814. UBC.
Ma's original edition was published in 1595.

O2. (*Xiqiao*) *Baiyun dongzhi* 西樵白雲洞志
[Gazetteer of Baiyun Cave on Xiqiao Mountain]
      5 *juan*, by Huang Heng 黄亨.
1839. Harvard, Toyo, UBC.
1887 reprint. LC.
1931 typeset edition. Gest, Shifan.
1932, 1933 reprints. UBC.

O3. *Xiqiao youlan ji* 西樵遊覽記
[Touring record of Xiqiao Mountain]
      14 *juan*, by Liu Nanyu 劉南畬.
1790 (compiled 1781-82).
1833 reprint. LC, UBC.

O4. *Guangxiao sizhi* 光孝寺志
[Gazetteer of Guangxiao Monastery]
      12 *juan*, by Gu Guang 顧光.
1769.
1935 edition. Harvard, Jimbun, LC, Toronto, Toyo, UBC (2
copies).
Previous gazetteer of 1640 by Zhang Zong 張悰.

O5. *Leizu zhi*　雷祖志
[Gazetteer of (the temple to) Patriarch Lei]
    2 *juan*, by Zhuang Yuanzhen　莊元貞, ed. Liu Shixing
劉世馨.
    1802. Jimbun, LC.
    Zhuang's original edition was 1637; subsequent edition
published in 1727.

O6. *Sangyuan weizhi*　桑園圍志
[Gazetteer of Sangyuan Embankment]
    14 *juan*, ed. Ming Zhigang　明之綱 (js. 1852).
    1870. Harvard, LC.
    1889 edition in 17 *juan*, ed. He Ruquan　何如銓. Columbia,
Tobunken, UBC.
    A compilation of several earlier editions, of which the earliest
is 1794.

O7. *Xu sangyuan weizhi*　續桑園圍志
[Supplement to the gazetteer of Sangyuan Embankment]
    16 *juan*, ed. He Bingkun　何炳堃.
    1932. Columbia.
    The first *juan* is a set of detailed maps. Much of the material
concerns conservancy work done after the great flood of
1914.

O8. *Yingyuan shuyuan zhilüe*　應元書院志略
[Abridged gazetteer of Yingyuan Academy]
    1 *juan*, by Wang Kaitai　王凱泰 (1823-75).
    1870. LC.

Guangzhou: Panyu

O9. *Boluo waiji*　波羅外紀
[Unofficial record of the Boluo River]
    8 *juan*, by Cui Bi　崔弼.
    1805 (preface dated 1800). Toyo.
    The gazetteer of Nanhai Temple　南海廟, where sacrifices
were made to the spirit of the Southern Ocean.

O10. *Luofeng jilüe* 蘿峰紀要
[Brief record of Luofeng Monastery]
    1 *juan*, by Zhong Feng　鐘鳳.
    Ca. 1888. Toyo, UBC.
    A collection of literary writings on Luofeng Monastery.

O11. *Xuehai tangzhi*　學海堂志
[Gazetteer of Xuehai Hall]
    1 *juan*, by Lin Botong　林伯桐.
    1838. Shifan, UBC.
    1844 Xiuben edition.
    1964 reprint (Hong Kong: Yadong Shushe). Jimbun.

Guangzhou: Xin'an

O12. *Dayu shanzhi*　大嶼山志
[Gazetteer of Dayu Mountain]
    7 chapters, by monk Minghui　明慧, ed. Abbot Fuke　符可.
    1958. Gest, UBC.
    Gazetteer of Baolian Chan Monastery　寶蓮禪寺 on Lantau
    Island, Hong Kong.

Guangzhou: Zengcheng

O13. *Huafeng shanzhi*　華峰山志
[Gazetteer of Huafeng Mountain]
    5 *juan*, by monk Jianchuan　鑑傳.
    1900. UBC.
    1980 ZF reprint.
    The gazetteer of Haimen Chan Cloister　海門禪院.

Guangzhou: Xinhui

O14. *Yashan zhi*　厓山志
[Gazetteer of Ya Mountain]
    5 *juan*, by Huang Chun　黃淳.
    1503.
    Manuscript copy. UBC.

1912 reprint, with annotations. LC.
Gazetteer of Quanjie Temple 全節廟 built at the end of the
Yuan to an empress and ministers of the Song.

Guangzhou: Qingyuan

O15. *Cangxia ji* 藏霞集
[Anthology on Cangxia Cave]
    3 *juan*, by Zhu Ruzhen 朱汝珍 (js. 1904).
    1915. Harvard.
    The cave, once visited by Bodhidharma, was located above
Feilai Monastery on Yuxia Mountain.

O16. *Yuxia shulüe* 禺峽疏略
[A short collection of texts on Yuxia Mountain]
    4 *juan*, by Zhu Xuexi 朱學熙, ed. Lu Xihou 魯晳後.
    1636, with material to 1643. Gest(m), Taibei.
    Yuxia's first gazetteer was published 1588. Zhu Xuexi was
involved in the construction of several buildings on the
mountain through the Wanli era.

O17. *Yuxia shanzhi* 禺峽山志
[Gazetteer of Yuxia Mountain]
    4 *juan*, by Sun Shengzu 孫繩祖.
    1721. Beijing, LC.
    1862 reprint. Naikaku, Toyo (their paginations differ
slightly).
    1884 reprint. LC, Shifan, Toronto, UBC (2 copies).

Zhaoqing: Gaoyao

O18. *Dinghu waiji* 鼎湖外紀
[Informal record of Dinghu Mountain]
    5 *juan*, by monk Kaiwei 開溈.
    Ca. 1690. UBC (2 copies).

O19. *Dinghu shanzhi*　鼎湖山志
[Gazetteer of Dinghu Mountain]
　　　8 *juan*, by Abbot Dongqiao Chengjiu　東樵成鷲.
　　　1711. Harvard.
　　　1717 reprint. Harvard, Jimbun, LC (4 copies), Shifan,
　　　SOAS, Toyo, UBC (2 copies).
　　　1980 ZF reprint.
　　　The gazetteer of Qingyun Monastery　慶雲寺. Originally the
　　　work included a supplementary *juan* on intramonastic
　　　disputes, which was removed in the Qianlong era (*Gaoyao
　　　xianzhi* (1826), 21.40b). No extant copy I have seen includes
　　　this supplement.

O20. *Duanxi shuyuan zhi*　端溪書院志
[Gazetteer of Duanxi Academy]
　　　1 *juan*, by Zhao Jingxiang　趙敬襄 (js. 1799).
　　　Ca. 1817 Zhugang edition.

Zhaoqing: Deqing zhou

O21. *Xiaotong zumiao zhi*　孝通祖廟志
[Gazetteer of Xiaotong Patriarch Temple]
　　　2 *juan*, by Wang Shihan　王士瀚.
　　　1760. LC.
　　　1887 reprint under the title *Yuecheng longmu miaozhi*
　　　悅城龍母廟志 [Gazetteer of the temple to the Dragon Mother
　　　in Yuecheng] under the editorship of Huang Peifang　黃培芳
　　　(cf. O33). LC, Toyo.
　　　1930s reprint under original title (Xinchang: Nanyue
　　　Yinshuguan). LC.
　　　Previous editions published in 1672 and 1740.

Shaozhou: Qujiang

O22. *Caoxi tongzhi*　曹谿通志
[Comprehensive gazetteer of Cao's Stream]

8 *juan*, ed. Prefect Ma Yuan 馬元 and Abbot Zhenpu 眞樸.
1672, including material to 1680. Naikaku, Toyo (their
paginations differ slightly).
1836 reprint. LC, Shifan, Toyo.
1932 reprint. Harvard, UBC.
The gazetteer of the prestigious Nanhua Monastery 南華寺.
There were four Ming editions by Huang Cheng 黃城, monk
Hanshan Deqing 憨山德淸 (1546-1623), Fu Xi 符錫, and
Gong Bangzhu 龔邦柱.
The stream on which Nanhua Monastery was located was
named after Cao Shuliang, who donated his residence to
found the monastery.

Shaozhou: Ruyuan

O23. *Yunmen shanzhi* 雲門山志
[Gazetteer of Yunmen Mountain]
9 chapters, ed. Cen Xuelü (cf. I21).
1951. Gest, Harvard.
1980 ZF reprint.
The material for this gazetteer was compiled by monks
Weixin 惟心 and Chengyuan 澄圓 under the direction of
Abbot Xuyun (cf. I21).

Huizhou: Guishan

O24. *Huiyang shanshui jisheng* 惠陽山水紀勝
[Topographical record of Huiyang]
4 *juan*, by Wu Qian 吳騫 (1733-1813).
1721. Columbia, Toyo.

O25. *Huizhou xihu zhi* 惠州西湖志
[Gazetteer of Huizhou's West Lake]
9 *juan*, by Zhang Youren 張友仁, ed. Liu Wanzhang
劉萬章.
1937. UBC.

UBC has the editor's personal copy. The first 8 *juan* are typeset, the handwritten ninth xylographed; 4 further *juan* were planned but never published.

Huizhou: Boluo

O26. *Luofu zhi*　羅浮志
[Gazetteer of the Luofu Mountains]
      12 *juan*, by Chen Lian　陳槤.
      Ca. 1412. Seikado.
      1848 Lingyan edition based on 1469 reprint; 1850 Yueya edition.
      1920 reprint, ed. Chen Botao　陳伯陶　(b. 1855, js. 1892; cf. O36, O37). LC.
      1936 Congshu edition.
      Previous gazetteer compiled in 1227.

O27. *Luofu shanzhi*　羅浮山志
[Gazetteer of the Luofu Mountains]
      12 *juan*, by Huang Zuo (1490-1566; cf. B8).
      1557. Gest(m), Taibei.

O28. *Luofu zhilüe*　羅浮志略
[Abridged gazetteer of the Luofu Mountains]
      2 *juan*, by Han Mingluan　韓鳴鸞.
      1611 (preface dated 1607). Naikaku.

O29. *Luofu yesheng*　羅浮野乘
[Unofficial gazetteer of the Luofu Mountains]
      6 *juan*, by Han Huangbin　韓晃賓.
      1639 preface, with additions past 1644. Tobunken.

O30. *Luofu shanzhi*　羅浮山志
[Gazetteer of the Luofu Mountains]
      12 *juan*, by Li Wanhou　李礪侯.
      1705 (preface dated 1699). Naikaku.

O31. *Luofu shanzhi huibian*　羅浮山志會編
[Combined gazetteer of the Luofu Mountains]
　　　22 *juan*, by Song Guangye　宋廣業.
　　　1717.　Cambridge, Columbia, EAHSL, Gest, Harvard,
　　　Jimbun, LC, Naikaku, Shifan, SOAS, Toyo.
　　　Republican-era reprint. Toyo.

O32. *Luofu waishi*　羅浮外史
[Unofficial history of the Luofu Mountains]
　　　1 *juan*, by Qian Yiqi　錢以塏.
　　　1786. Toyo, UBC.

O33. *Fushan xiaozhi*　浮山小志
[Short gazetteer of the Luofu Mountains]
　　　3 *juan*, by Huang Peifang (cf. O20).
　　　1809.
　　　1870s? reprint, ed. Jiang Benyuan　蔣本源. UBC.
　　　Beijing has a Qing MS copy.

O34. *Fushan xinzhi*　浮山新志
[New gazetteer of the Luofu Mountains]
　　　3 *juan*, by Lai Hongxi　賴洪禧 (b. 1772).
　　　1845.
　　　1860 edition. UBC.

O35. *Fushan zhi*　浮山志
[Gazetteer of the Luofu Mountains]
　　　5 *juan*, by Sulao Dongzhu　酥醪洞主 (Chen Minggui　陳銘珪).
　　　1881. Shifan, UBC (2 copies).
　　　Ca. 1930 Jude edition.
　　　Incorporates both O33 and O34. Chen Minggui is the
　　　identity of Sulao Dongzhu given in *Dongguan xianzhi*
　　　東莞縣志 (1911), 85.16a; Sulao Jushi is, however, the
　　　epithet of Jiang Benyuan (O33), so the author's identity here
　　　is open to question.

O36. *Luofu zhi* 羅浮志
[Gazetteer of the Luofu Mountains]
    16 *juan*, by Chen Botao (cf. O26, O37).
    1920. Jimbun, Shifan.
    Undated edition entitled *Luofu zhibu*, with O37, credited to
    Jiulong Zhenqi 九龍眞起. UBC.
    An expanded version of O26.

O37. *Luofu buzhi* 羅浮補志
[Emendations to the gazetteer of the Luofu Mountains]
    1 *juan*, by Chen Botao (cf. O26, O36).
    1930s, edited by his son Chen Liangshi 陳艮士. Harvard.
    Undated edition entitled *Luofu zhinan*, with O36. UBC.

Huizhou: Longchuan

O38. *Huoshan zhi* 霍山志
[Gazetteer of Huo Mountain]
    4 *juan*, by Wu Sanzhu 巫三祝.
    1644.
    1824 reprint, ed. Miao Gen 繆艮. Toyo.
    There was a 1765 edition, edited by Wu Rong 巫榮.

O39. *Huoshan zhi* 霍山志
[Gazetteer of Huo Mountain]
    6 *juan*, by monk Likong 力空.
    1933. Shifan, Toyo.

Chaozhou: Haiyang

O40. *Xihu shanzhi* 西湖山志
[Gazetteer of Xihu Mountain]
    10 *juan*, by Rao E 饒鍔.
    1924. UBC.
    1971 ZM reprint.
    Although published in the Republican period, this gazetteer
    was composed in imitation of *Huqiu shanzhi* (B77).

Chaozhou: Chengxiang

O41. *Yinna shanzhi* 陰那山志
[Gazetteer of Yinna Mountain]
      6 *juan*, by Li Langzhong 李閬中.
      1880 (first published 1862). LC, Shifan, Toyo.
      The gazetteer of Lingguang Monastery 靈光寺.
      Previous edition published in 1623 by Li Shichun 李士淳.

P. Guangxi

P1. *Guangxi mingsheng zhi* 廣西名勝志
[Gazetteer of the famous sights of Guangxi]
    10 *juan*, by Cao Xuequan (cf. H1).
    1622.
    1979 reprint (Shanghai: Guji Chubanshe). Columbia, Gest, LC.

Guilin

P2. *Guilin shanshui zhi* 桂林山水志
[Gazetteer of the Guilin landscape]
    2 *juan*, by Luo Chen 羅辰.
    1831. LC.
    Primarily illustrations, with accompanying texts.

P3. *Gui sheng*; *Gui gu* 桂勝, 桂故
[The sights of Guilin; the history of Guilin]
    16 + 8 *juan*, by Zhang Mingfeng 張鳴鳳.
    Undated manuscript. Seikado, Toyo.
    1765 Siku edition.
    Guxue (1912) has a four-*juan* version.
    This is a Ming work.

Guilin: Lingui

P4. *Qixia sizhi* 棲霞寺志
[Gazetteer of Qixia Monastery]
    2 *juan*, by Zhao Jiong 趙炯.
    1704. Jimbun.
    1881 reprint. Toyo.

Guilin: Quanzhou: Qingxiang

P5. *Xiangshan zhi* 湘山志
[Gazetteer of Xiang Mountain]
    4 *juan*, by Xie Jiufu 謝久復.
    1682. LC, Shifan, Toyo.
    The gazetteer of Shoufu Monastery 壽福寺, known as
    Guangxiao Monastery 光孝寺 in the Ming.

P6. *Xiangshan zhi* 湘山志
[Gazetteer of Xiang Mountain]
    2 *juan*, by Zhang Danyan 張澹煙.
    1708.
    1853 reprint. Toyo.
    Based on P5.

Q. Yunnan

Q1. *Yunnan shanchuan zhi* 雲南山川志
[Gazetteer of the mountains and rivers of Yunnan]
    1 *juan*, by Yang Shen 楊慎 (1488-1559).
    1646 Shuofu edition; Qianlong-era Qijin edition (1912
    reprint); Qianlong-era Hanhai edition (1809, 1825, and 1881
    reprints).

Q2. *Yun Mian shanchuan zhi* 雲緬山川志
[Gazetteer of the mountains and rivers of Yunnan and Burma]
    1 *juan*, by Li Rongjie 李榮陛 (cf. Q4).
    1908 Wenying edition.

Q3. *Yunnan shuidao kao* 雲南水道考
[Study of the water courses of Yunnan]
    5 *juan*, by Li Cheng 李誠 (gs. 1813).
    Republican-era Jiaye edition.
    Bibliographic notice: Xiang 7a.
    Li is the author of several works on China's geography.

Q4. *Heishui kaozheng* 黑水考證
[Notes on the Hei River]
    4 *juan*, by Li Rongjie (cf. Q2).
    Ca. 1918 Yuzhang edition.
    Originally published in the Qing.

Q5. *Yunnan wenquan zhibu* 雲南温泉志補
[Supplemented gazetteer of the hot springs of Yunnan]
    3 *juan*, by Tong Zhencao 童振藻.
    1919. LC (2 copies).

Yunnan: Kunming

Q6. *Yunnan shengcheng liuhe tushuo* 雲南省城六河圖說
[Illustrated study of the six rivers flowing through the provincial capital of Yunnan]
    1 *juan*, by Huang Shijie 黃士傑.
    1880.
    1974 ZC reprint.
    A series of maps and explanatory texts.

Q7. *Gaoyao zhi* 高嶢志
[Gazetteer of Gaoyao Mountain]
    2 *juan*, by You Yunlong 由雲龍 (b. 1887).
    1939. Fu.

Q8. *Panlong shan jiyao* 盤龍山紀要
[Abridged record of Panlong Mountain]
    4 *juan*, by Fang Bingxiao 方秉孝 (1835-94).
    1893.
    1918 Yunnan reprint.

Chuxiong: Dingyuan

Q9. *Heiyan jingzhi* 黑鹽井志
[Gazetteer of Black Salt Well]
    8 *juan* by Yang Xuan 楊璿, ed. Shen Maojie 沈懋价.
    1710. Palace.

Q10. *Langyan jingzhi* 琅鹽井志
[Gazetteer of Lang Salt Well]
    4 *juan*, compiled by Zhao Chun 趙淳 (cf. Q12), ed. Sun Yuanxiang 孫元相.
    1756 manuscript. Palace.

Yaoan: Dayao

Q11. *Baiyan jingzhi* 白鹽井志
[Gazetteer of White Salt Well]
    8 *juan*, by Liu Bangrui 劉邦瑞.
    1730 manuscript. Palace.
    1967 ZC reprint.
    The White Salt Well was not a single location but comprised nine separate wells.

Q12. *Baiyan jingzhi* 白鹽井志
[Gazetteer of White Salt Well]
    4 *juan*, compiled by Zhao Chun (cf. Q10), ed. Guo Cunzhuang 郭存莊.
    1758 manuscript. Palace.

Q13. *(Xuxiu) Baiyan jingzhi* 續修白鹽井志
[Later gazetteer of White Salt Well]
    11 *juan*, compiled by Wu Shizhao 吳式釗, ed. Li Xunhong 李訓鋐.
    1901. Fu.

Dali: Binchuan zhou

Q14. *Jizu zhi* 雞足志
[Gazetteer of Jizu Mountain]
    8 *juan*, by Xu Hongzu 徐弘祖 (1585-1640).
    Compiled 1640. Not extant, probably never published. Surviving fragments printed in *Xu Xiake youji* (Shanghai: Shanghai Guji Chubanshe, 1980), vol. 2, pp. 1138-45.
    Xu compiled this gazetteer of Yunnan's famous Buddhist monastic complex at the request of an abbot there. The surviving fragments were collected and edited by his nephew Li Mengliang 李夢良.

Q15. *Jizu shanzhi* 雞足山志
[Gazetteer of Jizu Mountain]
    10 *juan*, by Fan Chengxun 范承勳 (d. 1714).

1692, with later inserts. Beijing (2 copies), Harvard, LC (3 copies), Toyo.
Fan was serving as military commander in Yunnan in 1691. His authorship was probably nominal, an extension of his patronage of Jinding Monastery 金頂寺.

Q16. *Jizu shanzhi bu* 雞足山志補
[Emendations to the gazetteer of Jizu Mountain]
    4 *juan*, by Zhao Fan 趙藩 (1851-1927).
    1913. Harvard, LC, Shifan, Toyo.

R. Guizhou

Guiyang

R1. *Guiyang shanquan zhi* 貴陽山泉志
[Gazetteer of the mountains and springs of Guiyang]
    1 *juan*, by Shen Meng 愼蒙 .
    1646 Shuofu edition.

R2. *Qianling shanzhi* 黔靈山志
[Gazetteer of Qianling Mountain]
    12 *juan*, by He Suru 何素儒 .
    1705.
    1739 reprint with insert in *juan* 11. Toyo.
    The nominal authorship of this Buddhist monastic gazetteer
    is attributed to the monastery's founder, Daoling Chisong
    道嶺赤松 .

Anshun: Yongning zhou: Dingying si

R3. *Tieqiao zhishu* 鐵橋志書
[Gazetteer of Iron-Chain Bridge]
    2 *juan*, by Liang Yuxi 梁于溪 , ed. Zhu Chaoyuan 朱潮遠 .
    1665. Gest(m), LC, Taibei.
    Compiled 1643, with preface by Zhu dated 1657. The
    iron-chain suspension bridge was built by Lieuten-
    ant-Governor Zhu Jiamin (1569-1642) in 1628-30. Zhu
    Chaoyuan was the governor's son. The original bridge was
    replaced in 1943.

Index of Authors

Index of Titles

Taihu beikao, B47
Taihu beikao xubian, B48
Taihu quanzhi, B49
Taihu zhilüe, B46
Taihua xiaozhi, G12
Tailao shanzhi, N33
Tainan donglin zhi, M60
Taishan daoli ji, D9
Taishan shuji, D11
Taishan tuzhi, D13
Taishan xiaoshi, D10
Taishan zhi, D7, D13
Taiyang zhou Xiao hou
    miaozhi, I41
Tangquan zhi, C35
Tangyin jingzhong miaozhi,
    F19
Tanzhe shan xiuyun sizhi,
    A12
Tanzhe shanzhi, A11
Taohua yuan zhilüe, K10
Taohua yuanzhi, K11
Taoyuan dongzhi, K9
Tianhou shengmu shengji
    tuzhi, N13
Tianhou zhi, N13
Tianlong sizhi, L28
Tianmu shan mingsheng
    zhi, L100
Tianning situ, B38
Tianning sizhi, B96
Tiantai shan fangwai
    zhi, M65
Tiantai shan fangwai
    zhiyao, M66, M67
Tiantai shan quanzhi, M68
Tiantai shan youlan zhi,
    M70
Tiantai shanji jisheng, M69
Tiantai shengji, M64
Tiantai shengji lu, M64
Tiantong si xuzhi, M40

Tiantong sizhi, M38, M39
Tianxia lucheng, 5.1.6
Tianxia luchengtu, 1.1.2
Tianxia shuilu lucheng
    xinbian, 5.2.1
Tianzhu shanzhi (Anhui),
    C6
Tianzhu shanzhi (Zhejiang),
    L26
Tianzhu xuzhi beigao, L27
Tieqiao zhishu, R3
Tonghui hezhi, A3
Tongji yanzhi, M76
Tongjing dadao, 6.2.1
Tongren cilu, L80
Wanbao quanshu, 1.2.1,
    1.2.2, 1.2.4
Wancheng di xuzhi, J16
Wanchang dizhi, J15
Wang shi liangyuan tuyong,
    B41
Wang wang miao zhilüe, L30
Wangchuan zhi, G9
Wangjiang louzhi, H7
Wangwu shanzhi, E14
Wanhua caotang zhi, H4
Wanjin quanshu, 1.2.3
Wanjuan xingluo, 1.2.11
Wannian qiaozhi, I33
Wanshou gongzhi, J14
Wanshou ting chongjian
    jishi, B97
Wanshu yuanhai, 1.2.7
Wanyong zhengzong, 1.2.6
Wanyong zhengzong
    buqiuren quanbian, 1.2.10
Weimo sizhi, B86
Weiyu shan xuzhi, M63
Weiyu shanzhi, M62
Wenchang qiao zhilüe, I35
Wenchang qiaozhi, I34
Wenjin yuanzhi, J7

Index of Prefectures, Subprefectures, and Counties

Note: Citations are to the first entry listed under the county or subprefecture in Part II.